Gardening in the Coastal South

Marie Harrison

Pineapple Press, Inc.
Sarasota, Florida

Inquiries should be addressed to:

Pineapple Press, Inc.
P.O. Box 3889
Sarasota, Florida 34230
www.pineapplepress.com

Library of Congress Cataloging-in-Publication Data

Harrison, Marie
    Gardening in the coastal South / Marie Harrison.
        p. cm.
    Includes bibliographical references (p.   ) index.
        ISBN 1-56164-274-6 (pbk. : alk. paper)
        1. Plants, Ornamental—Southern States. 2. Plants, Ornamental—Gulf Coast (U.S.) 3. Plants, Ornamental—Atlantic Coast (U.S.) 4. Gardening—Southern States. 5. Gardening—Gulf Coast (U.S.) 6. Gardening—Atlantic Coast (U.S.) I. Title.
        SB408 .H375 2003
        635.9'0975—dc21

                                                                        2002014156

First Edition
10 9 8 7 6 5 4 3 2 1

Design by Shé Sicks
Printed in the United States of America

Table of Contents

Herbs

Shrubs and Small Trees

Vines

Coastal Considerations

Environmental Issues

Wildlife

Seasonal Musings

Spring

Summer

Fall

Winter

Gardening for the Love of It

Where is the Coastal South?

The coastal South includes the lower parts of Texas except for the extreme southern tip. It extends from the Rio Grande eastward, including San Antonio, Houston, and Beaumont, as well as the coastal areas of Corpus Christi and Galveston. In Louisiana it includes the expanse of land surrounding and including Lake Charles, Alexandria, Lafayette, Baton Rouge, Hammond, and New Orleans. Through Louisiana, Mississippi, Alabama, and much of Texas, Interstate 10 marks a line through the coastal South with roughly equal regions to the north and south of it. The Mississippi cities of Picayune, Gulfport, Biloxi, and Pascagoula are located solidly within the realm. In Alabama, Mobile, Atmore, and Brewton lie within its range.

Regions termed the coastal South also include the state of Florida down to and including Orlando. Coastal areas of Georgia and South Carolina further extend its range. Throughout its confines, gardeners will identify with the author's experiences. Gardeners living in other areas of the South will recognize many of their dependable landscape plants as well.

The coastal South is ruled by the Gulf of Mexico and the Atlantic Ocean. These two major bodies of water ensure short, mild winters and long, hot, humid summers. Winters at the northern end may reach 17 to 25 degrees while those in the southern end may drop to between 25 and 32 degrees. Brief periods of extreme weather may lower these temperature readings. However, subtropical plants such as oleander, Indian hawthorn, gingers, loquat, and holly fern flourish. Huge live oaks, Southern Indica azaleas, and St. Augustine lawns grow with abandon.

The coastal South includes USDA Hardiness Zones 8B and 9A.

Introduction

Confessions of a Hortimaniac

Oh, yes, I am one—an avid gardener. Some folks would even call me a floraholic, a hortimaniac! Furthermore, I have been this way ever since my mother held me in her arms and said, "See the pretty flower?" My heart was all atwitter and my senses attuned. I yearned to possess and take into the very heart of myself this beautiful object—to have and to hold, then and forever after. Its beauty seeped into my being, and I was forever filled with the desire to grow and have for my own as many beautiful plants as I could manage. And so my journey began.

I've come to this state of affairs quite honestly. It's a genetic thing. Daddy was a painter by necessity. He had to support all seven of his children, but he was a farmer at heart. Most of the food we ate came from the large garden that he tended on evenings and weekends. Granddaddy Seamon was a farmer, and Great-Granddaddy Richard, also. Great-great Granddaddy Charles Glen was killed in the Civil War, but he, too, was a farmer before the war claimed him. My forebears on my father's side have been farmers since before they crossed the ocean.

Mother's family represents a long line of educators. So here I am, an educator/gardener. This book is the culmination of generations of horticulturists and educators. I can't help it. It was predetermined; written in my genes and coursing through my veins. I'm a retired teacher who writes and gardens. Naturally. Honestly.

If the reader is looking for a comprehensive book about landscape plants, this is the wrong one. This book is about some favorite flowering plants that have grown successfully in my coastal garden. Some were handed down from generations of gardeners; others are recent introductions.

Whether a plant is native or introduced is of little consequence. Of greater importance is the plant's ability to withstand the rigors of southern winters and summers, the latter of which often prove to be the supreme test. I have no trick, either, with disease- and pest-ridden plants. Many have been banished from my garden because I was not willing to deal with the problems that accompany them.

This book also attempts to explain some of my feelings about gardening. On many occasions it has been my lifeline and conservator of my mental health. Environmental concerns are a major factor in my gardening strategies. Gardening for wildlife is a prime interest. Herbs spice up my garden and my meals. Seasonal opportunities and challenges of gardening in the coastal South are discussed.

From my garden in Valparaiso in Northwest Florida, I have experimented with the art of gardening. It is from here that I grow, observe, write, and teach. In this garden I continue my love affair with gardening in all of its dimensions. It is my hope that others will benefit from my experiences, learn from my mistakes, and develop an appreciation and love for the wonders of the garden.

What's in a Name?

Gardeners sometimes groan when faced with scientific names. Often they are hard to spell and pronounce. "What's the point?" we think. "Sweetgum" is so much easier than *Liquidambar styraciflua*. But then we travel and realize that the "mountain laurel" of the East, a pink-flowered shrub related to azaleas and rhododendrons, is totally different from the "mountain laurel" of central Texas—a blue-flowered shrub related to peas and beans. Two different plant species may have the same common name, and many species have more than one common name. I use common, scientific and horticultural names in this book. I'll try to explain them as painlessly as possible.

Let's start with family. Scientific plant family names always end in "-aceae," which is added to the name of the first genus in the family. The Liliaceae is the name of the lily family. It includes lilies (members of the genus *Lilium*) as well as many others—hostas and hyacinths, for example. A few old plant family names didn't end in "-aceae" and some people still use them. The Fabaceae—the family of peas, beans and other legumes—used to be called the Leguminosae. And the family that includes asters and daisies is now called the Asteraceae rather than the Compositae. Much of the time we use the common name of the family, as the "rose family" for Rosaceae and the "heath family" for Ericaceae.

Genus (plural genera) comes next. *Lilium* is a genus, as are *Aster* and *Liquidambar*. Often we identify a plant only by its genus name. *Lilium* sp. means "a species of *Lilium*" and "spp." means more than one species.

Species comes after genus. When we identify a species, both genus and specific names are used, though sometimes the genus name is abbreviated as the first letter. Easter lily is *Lilium longiflorum*, and tiger lily is *L. lancifolium*. The specific name is usually descriptive, never capitalized and never used alone. For example, *longiflorum* means long-flowered and *lancifolium* means lance-shaped leaves.

Further subcategories used by botanists include subspecies (subsp.) and variety (var.). Usually one or the other is used, not both, and the abbreviation of the category is used as well. Examples are *Magnolia macrophylla* subsp. *ashei*, Ashe magnolia, and *Lupinus westianus* var. *aridorum*, scrub lupine.

Many plants used by gardeners are hybrids between two species or two genera. The names of hybrid plants are preceded by an "x." Thus, a hybrid genus is designated as x *Guzvriesea*, for example, and a hybrid species by *Gloriosa x greenii*.

Scientific names are always italicized because they are treated as Latin words. Sometimes the scientific and common names are the same, as in Iris and Caladium. When this is true, I do not italicize the name.

Next, we'll consider horticultural names. Horticulturists have been busy cultivating special varieties of plants for centuries. The "cultivars" as we call them, are usually named with English words so they are not italicized, but the first letter of each word is capitalized and they are enclosed in single quotation marks. *Asclepias tuberosa* 'Hello Yellow' is the name of a bright yellow cultivar of our native butterfly weed, which is orange. When the cultivars are of hybrid or unknown origin, the cultivar name may follow the genus name, as in *Juniperus* 'Gray Owl'.

Finally, we come to common names. "The easiest ones," you are thinking. Think again. They are easier to spell, and there are no special rules, but there are four different plants in three different genera that are known by the name dusty miller! And that's just in English— no doubt the Italians, Germans, and Brazilians all have their own names for these plants. Now you know why we have to use all three kinds of names.

—Dr. Gail S. Baker,
friend and horticultural
advisor for this book

Acknowledgments

Many people made valuable contributions to this book. To my good friends Teresa Arlund and Vivian Justice, thanks for proofing my work and helping correct my grammatical blunders. To friends Leona Venettozzi and Gail Baker, thanks for helping me with some horticultural and scientific intricacies that much increased the accuracy of information contained herein. Your input corrected many glitches that befuddled me, and my book is better because of your help.

To many friends and readers who encouraged me along the way, I also owe a debt of gratitude. It was you who first allowed me to believe that I had something to say that other people might like to read.

And to Amiable Spouse, I fervently say, "Thanks, honey! My dreams took flight when I married you!"

Illustrated by:
    John W. Harrison, Jr. (Amiable Spouse)
    Joseph Jay Harrison (Amiable Spouse's Talented Son)
    Marie Harrison (Amiable Spouse's Lucky Wife)
    Joe Stoy (Friend)
    Christina Livingston (drew "the Floraholic," Her Mother, Myself)

Photo References

Numbers in brackets in the text refer to color photographs in the section between pages 130 and 131. In the color section, page numbers at the end of captions refer to text where the pictured plant is discussed.

Perennials

Perennials have been my greatest passion through the years. Forming major portions of my borders, many of them are mainstays that can be depended on for year after year of carefree beauty.

In this section I have included many of my favorites. It is not intended, however, to be a list of all perennials that grow well in the coastal South. Rather, it highlights some that have given me particular pleasure. At the end of the chapter is a more comprehensive—though still far from complete—list of perennials that can be expected to succeed in our unique area of the world.

Butterfly Weed, Milkweed (Asclepias tuberosa) [3]

Our beautiful native butterfly weed has an iron constitution. It withstands the heat and drought of July, the wind and saltwater blown in by storms, and repeated defoliation by monarch butterfly caterpillars.

In spite of all that nature can dish out, it blooms orange, yellow, or red blossoms during the hottest part of the summer. Hardy in Zones 4 to 9 and tolerant of most native soils, it can be grown almost anywhere in the United States. Clumps grow 18 to 36 inches tall. Full sun suits it best, and good drainage is an absolute necessity. Butterfly weed should be planted where it will stay. A long taproot makes it difficult to move. Never, ever, should it be removed from the wild. Usually it is available in containers from nurseries in the spring, or it can be started from seed.

Sometimes called pleurisy root, milkweed was widely used in the nineteenth century as an expectorant. American Indians sometimes treated bronchitis, pneumonia, and dysentery with chewed roots or a tea made from them.

Slender seed pods develop following the blooms. When they are mature, the pods split open and the seeds fly away on their own downy parachutes. Observant collectors may gather the seeds just before they disperse. They may be planted immediately, as dry seeds are more difficult to germinate. Alternatively, they may be stored in an airtight container in the lower part of the refrigerator until spring. Seeds stored in this manner may germinate more readily after a type of pretreatment called stratification (see next page).

Red aphids sometimes cover the growing tips and new flowers of butterfly weed. They can be washed off with a strong jet of water. These aphids do not move to other plants, since they are milkweed aphids. Insecticides should be avoided for the sake of the monarchs and other butterflies who feast on the nectar-rich flowers. Furthermore, hummingbirds rely on aphids for necessary protein in their diet, so they can be enlisted to help in the battle.

The bright colors of butterfly weed are an integral part of my favorite color combination. Our native butterfly weed is bright orange. The cultivar 'Hello Yellow' is bright yellow, and 'Gay Butterflies' has yellow, red, and orange blossoms. Nothing is more striking in the garden than these bright colors combined with blue or purple. I know that some gardeners with refined tastes will turn up their delicate noses, but they are the losers if such a vibrant mix of colors upsets their tender sensibilities. *Asclepias curassivica*, also known as Mexican oleander or bloodflower, may be better suited to some gardens. A fibrous root system makes it easier to transplant than our native, and its ever-blooming clumps are easily divided. In wet areas, swamp milkweed (*Asclepias incarnata*) is a good choice. The cultivar 'Ice Ballet' has showy umbrella-shaped flower heads that are vanilla scented. All of the *Asclepias* species are very rich in nectar and useful to many beneficial insects and butterflies. Several other native milkweeds may be found in nature, but they are not usually available at retail outlets.

Unbeatable combinations result from intermingling butterfly weed with mealy blue sages such as *Salvia* 'Indigo Spires' or the beautiful princess flower (*Tibouchina urvilleana*). Folks who can't quite take all that color can tone it down a bit with white lantana or pentas. Green is a natural blender, and God made plenty of that with almost every plant. That's all it really needs.

Stratification

Butterfly weed seeds may be stratified by placing them in moist sand and chilling at 36°F to 40°F for six to eight weeks. You may do this in a jar or plastic bag in your refrigerator. Seeds may then be sown shallowly in a seed-starting mix and kept moist. They should germinate in three to four weeks if kept at about 70°F. Six to eight weeks after germinating, they may be hardened off by placing them outside for increasingly longer times. When the plants are acclimated to outdoor growing conditions, they may be transplanted to permanent sites in the landscape.

Mexican Heather, Cigar Plant, Bat Face [2]
(*Cuphea* spp.)

Some time ago I was visiting a friend's garden. I noticed a beautiful little plant about two feet high loaded with tiny tubular flowers. Leaves were small, elliptical, and bright green.

"What is that pretty thing?" I asked. My friend Kay had no idea. She had purchased it at a local nursery. Naturally, I took home a clipping.

Later when we were at my house, she saw my cigar plant (*Cuphea ignea*). "I think maybe that's what my little flower is!" she speculated. "Sure, it's a different type, but it looks similar."

Well, Kay was right. Her little flower was indeed a *Cuphea*. My clipping rooted readily and now closely resembles hers in size and beauty.

For a long time I have admired cigar plant in my landscape. Blooms emerge in spring almost as soon as it arises from the ground. Pretty, tubular, red-orange flowers continue until frost. Before the growing season is over, it has attained a height of about four feet.

Mexican heather (*Cuphea hyssopifolia*) is familiar to most Southern gardeners. A pretty, one-foot-tall plant with tiny, lance-shaped leaves, it is justifiably popular as a front-of-the-border subject. Small lavender, pink, or white flowers cover the plants all summer.

'Georgia Scarlet' is another captivating member of the clan. Tiny purple and red flowers look somewhat like a bat's face. The "face" is purple and the "ears" are red. It blooms beside my mailbox from early spring until the frost cuts it down. [2]

Recently I have become aware that these plants are not all there is to the *Cuphea* genus. At a Master Gardeners' conference in Gainesville, I saw *Cuphea varia* and *Cuphea* 'Purple Passion'. Both were plants I'd never seen.

To learn more about this group of plants, I looked it up on the web. I learned, interestingly, that *Cuphea* is a prospective crop for farmers. Oils contained in the seeds are used in the production of solvents, detergents, and emulsifiers. Now the imported coconut and palm kernel oils are the only commercially available sources of these medium-chain fatty acids.

All the *Cuphea* varieties are important to gardens, not only for the beauty of their flowers, but also for their value to pollinators. Bees and butterflies of various kinds are attracted to the nectar-rich blossoms. Operation Ruby Throat at www.rubythroat.com lists the cigar plant as one of the best plants to attract hummingbirds. Mexican heather is a sure-fire winner in butterfly gardens.

The *Cuphea* species are native to Mexico and Guatemala. In most of Zone 8, they may be killed to the ground by frost, but they will usually return the following spring. North of Zone 8 they may or may not return from roots following a cold winter. In areas where there is little frost, they are evergreen. Throughout the coastal South they are dependable landscape plants.

Research revealed several different species and many cultivars of each species. Some species mentioned were *Cuphea ignea, C. micropetala, C. purpurea, C. platycentra, C. llavea miniata, C. lanceolata, C. viscosissima,* and *C. cyanea.* Interesting cultivars were 'Candy Corn', 'Georgia Scarlet', 'Allyson Purple', 'Batface', 'David Verity', 'Firefly', and many others.

This suggests to me that many *Cupheas* are out there just waiting to be found. I will be on the lookout for these desirable plants wherever I go. A space for them can surely be found in my garden.

Purple Coneflower (*Echinacea* spp.)

Purple coneflower is native to the central and eastern United States. It keeps my garden alive with butterflies, birds, and beneficial insects. Sometimes called Indian root or scurvy root, it was once used to treat snakebite, scurvy, and other illnesses. Today the dried root is sold to combat colds, flu, and other infections, and it is highly touted for being able to boost the immune system.

Echinacea is a Greek word for "hedgehog," which refers to the bristly feel of the central cone of the flower. It grows best in full sun and average, moist, well-drained garden soil. Most gardeners purchase plants from garden centers, but they are easily started from seed. Purple coneflowers are endangered in the wild, so they should not be dug and removed from native stands. Hardy from USDA Zones 3 to 8, their colorful lavender blossoms decorate gardens throughout much of the country.

Several cultivars are available. Some are 'Bright Star', 'Magnus', 'Robert Bloom',

'White Swan', and 'Kim's Knee High'. These tough plants are tolerant of heat, sun, cold, and pests. No staking is needed because stiff stems hold the flowers upright. Division is probably not required. In fact, some experts claim that flowering diminishes after division, so they should be planted in drifts one and a half to two feet apart and left alone. Other growers recommend division every three or four years.

Purple coneflowers start easily from seed. It took me a while, however, to learn this lesson. I had tried planting seeds before with little luck. One summer I learned quite by accident why I was having so little success. A large pot of them sat in a bare garden spot, bloomed, and set seed. The following summer, I found several seedlings growing near the pot. The trick, I realized, is that the seeds need to fall on bare ground, and they need light to germinate. Well, of course! My coneflowers are in a heavily mulched area, and any time I tried planting seeds, I covered them well with soil. No wonder! Now I sprinkle them over bare soil and pat lightly to insure contact with the soil. My success rate has multiplied.

Purple coneflowers are unsurpassed as cut flowers. Even after the color has faded and the petals have dropped, the substantial cones add interest to dried arrangements. Left in the garden, they are a favorite food for the goldfinches who visit during the winter.

Gaura, Whirling Butterflies (Gaura lindeheimeri) [6]

Gaura is one of my most dependable perennials. I use it at midborder where its rather sparse base is covered with plants of more solid substance. Behind these solid plants, gaura provides a gauzy, light-hearted rendition of dancing ballerinas. Bumblebees love it, and in early morning when they are at work the plants are a study in motion. The heavy bumblebees light on the tall flower spikes that dip and wave in the early morning sunlight as the bees go about their business.

Gaura thrives in sandy, well-drained soils. Carrotlike tap roots can reach deep into the earth for moisture. Native to Texas and Louisiana, it is a popular perennial throughout the Southeast. Indeed, it seems to thrive on neglect. Plant it and water well until it becomes established, and then leave it alone. New plants spring up readily around the mother plant where seeds fall. Propagation is also easy from cuttings taken when the plants are blooming. Take a cutting, remove the blossoms, and stick it in a moist medium until it strikes roots.

Gaura provides a continuous parade of airy flowers that open from pink buds and drop off cleanly when spent. Flowers open from the bottom of the stalk and progress to the top. Individual flowers may shrivel by noon in the hot summer sun, but new flowers emerge the next morning to replace them. As a cut flower, the blooms continue to open, and its grace adds enchantment to many a summer bouquet.

As summer progresses, gaura benefits from a substantial pruning. It grows back, however, for another show almost equal to the spring blooms. Aphids sometimes line up on the stems, and these may be washed off with a stream of water from the hose. When this happens in my garden, it's pruning time.

Gaura lindeheimeri 'Siskiyou Pink' is a cultivar whose flowers are reliably pink and attractive in early spring. I have found, however, that it is lower growing and more sprawling than the parent species, and that it burns out in summer's heat much more quickly. A variegated form, 'Corrie's Gold', is also available.

Whirling butterflies is the common name given to gaura, and it is highly descriptive. When a breeze is blowing, the flowers resemble butterflies whirling about in the air. So light and airy are the slender stems that a solid background is needed to show the delicate flowers most advantageously. A backing such as blue green *Juniperus* 'Gray Owl' makes it light up its space. With 'Gray Owl' behind and a dark-colored sun coleus in front, it puts on an unforgettable show. Or you might choose to place it in front of a dark-colored fence or wall. I particularly like it in front of a wax myrtle (*Myrica cerifera*) hedge that backs my perennial border. Where no background is present to highlight the white flowers, much is lost because its presence is so delicate that it is almost ethereal.

Gaura is widely available at garden centers. Although it appears delicate, don't let it fool you. It is as tough as nails and will provide years of carefree beauty. Give it plenty of sun, water during periods of drought, and give it a solid background against which to shine. Your efforts will be amply rewarded.

Firebush (*Hamelia patens*)

Firebush is one of the prettiest plants in the fall garden. After getting killed back to the ground in winter, it starts growing with the first warm days. Blooming begins when plants are quite small. First one stalk blooms, and then from the base of that flower two stems grow and bloom. Before these two stems wither, two more grow from the base of each, so then there are four. This process continues all summer. Before the growing season is over, firebush is a bushy shrub some four feet tall with hundreds of clusters of beautiful, reddish-orange, tubular blossoms.

Firebush is native to Mexico, South Florida, the West Indies, and Central and South America. In its native habitat it is an evergreen shrub with blossoms most of the year. In the tropics it grows to a mature height and spread of ten feet by six feet and is classed as a large shrub or small tree. In most of the coastal South, however, it gets killed to the ground by frost and must start over each year, so it never attains that stature. North of I-10 it is usually grown as an annual. Like other tropicals, in regions where winters are severe it can be treated as a container plant and placed in the greenhouse or other protected locations during the winter.

Hummingbirds and butterflies admire this garden workhorse. During most of the summer, these winged critters make the firebush a part of their regular rounds. Firebush is one of our heat-loving plants. Thriving in full sun, it is a long-season, low-maintenance perennial for the coastal and tropical South. Each spring I give it a bit of slow-release fertilizer or compost, mulch it well, and let it proceed to do its pretty thing. Extremely insect and disease tolerant, the bush remains a picture of robust health throughout the summer. Never has any pest control been necessary.

Although firebush is drought tolerant, I have noticed that it responds well to regular watering. I have one firebush in an area that is watered on schedule and one in a place that rarely receives any extra water. The regularly watered shrub is twice as big as the one that has had to subsist on the water that nature provides. Nevertheless, the small one blooms well and has not given up. As temperatures cool in the fall, leaves of firebush turn fiery red. All summer the large, lance-shaped, prominently veined leaves are attractive with their red stems and red central veins. They perfectly complement the showy blossoms.

In its native habitat, firebush is esteemed as a herb (see below). The small black fruit is acidic and edible and has been made into a syrup to control dysentery. Leaves and stems have been used for tanning leather. Sometimes leaves are crushed and applied to cuts and bruises. Washes and lotions have been concocted and used to relieve swelling of the legs and to deodorize them.

Firebush was listed by the Florida Nursery Growers Association as a "Plant of the Year" for 1998. I got my first specimen at the University of Florida trial gardens in Milton. I brought the tiny plant home and planted it in a sunny place in the backyard. It grew there and delighted me, so I later decided to move it to the perennial border in the front yard where it would be in a more prominent position. It made the move just fine, and where I dug it out of the backyard I evidently left a root, because it regrew. Now I have two fine specimens, and I'm doubly delighted.

A very proper Herb

In this book I have chosen to adhere to the British practice of pronouncing the *h* in herb. Therefore, the designation is "a herb" instead of "an herb."

Louisiana Phlox *(Phlox divaricata laphamii* 'Louisiana Purple')

If someone asked me to suggest a ground cover for a sunny to partially sunny area or a good facer plant for a border, I would have to mention Louisiana phlox. It's always there—a pretty, green, slowly spreading presence at the foreground of my perennial bed. Sometimes when I think of ground covers, my heart palpitates and my breath rushes out in short gasps. I envision fast-spreading, rampantly running plants that somehow manage to encroach on every square inch of available space in a short time. Indeed, I have spent my fair share of time removing those space-grabbing monstrosities. They are great, of course, if the gardener wishes to fill an area bounded on all sides by a substantial barrier of concrete or something equally impenetrable. They are all right, too, if what they gobble up is of no concern. However, if well-mannered plants for the foreground of a bed are needed, something a bit more mannerly may be required.

Why not give Louisiana phlox a try? Through the worst of summer's unrelenting heat and humidity and winter's longest cold spell, it's in my garden, lending its presence to the more flamboyant plants that parade behind it. It adds constancy and unity to an ever-changing show put on by its compatriots.

Then comes spring. Lo and behold—glory is upon us! A solid carpet of royal purple or pale blue erupts upon the scene. For about a month, neighbors and passersby stop to see what I've planted at the edge of the border. They suddenly want to know what it is and where I got it. They beg a start. It's glorious, and one of the first things to bloom in early spring. The showy blossoms are held well above the foliage. A dense mass of fine-textured, opposite, linear leaves gives the plants a mosslike appearance.

Before it began to bloom, friends never mentioned it, nor did they even notice it. Nevertheless, they did mention how attractive the flower bed looked. Without being aware, they knew that everything was tied together and that the eye traveled around the green border easily. It provided a smooth transition between the driveway and the tall plants behind it. The fine green edging added a certain richness to the overall composition. It's one of those things that you really don't notice when it's there, but you would really miss if it were removed.

10

When bloom is finished, I cut off the faded blossoms, lightly fertilize with a complete fertilizer, and forget it. There it stays along the edge of my border, a pretty four-to-six-inch green groundcover that unites the varied plantings behind it. Native to the eastern U.S. and from Florida to East Texas, it grows best in a fairly sunny exposure but needs some protection from hot afternoon sun. Well-drained soil enriched with organic materials such as peat or compost is favored. Regular watering and a mulched bed help it to thrive.

Some confusion exists about this plant's scientific name. *Phlox divaricata*, or woodland or blue phlox, is the name of the species. Many varieties and hybrids exist. Thomas Fischer in the February 1998 issue of *Horticulture* gives a comprehensive discussion of all the parents and cousins this plant may have, and it is all very interesting reading. I believe the one that graces my border is *Phlox divaricata laphamii* 'Louisiana Purple'. This confusion does not in the least interfere with my enjoyment of the plant.

Louisiana phlox grows slowly. About ten years ago I purchased one plant from the nursery. Slowly but surely it increased in size. I've had enough to share with my gardening buddies and to border a small perennial bed, but I have not worried about invasiveness. It's controlled—a lady—a dream of orderliness in a sometimes disorderly garden; a dependable, disease and insect free, low maintenance, dream-of-a-plant. Try it. You'll love it!

Summer Phlox (*Phlox paniculata*) [1]

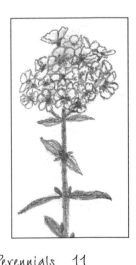

Nothing excites a dedicated gardener as much as finding a new plant. We can always talk ourselves into it. Such details as where we're going to plant it often do not enter the picture. Uncharted territory and the thrill of a new acquisition are far more important. With it comes the prospect of beauty not yet experienced and visions of loveliness not yet seen. Sometimes our experiments come to naught, but occasionally we find a real winner. Furthermore, we gardeners sometimes have short memories. In the middle of winter, it is easy to forget that the summer border was filled to overflowing. After all, in mid-January many perennials are frozen to the ground, and we long to fill the vacant spaces.

Such was the case with my summer phlox. Garden catalogs had arrived, and like many other flower-starved gardeners in January, I pored over the pages with serious intent. After much indecision, I selected a few plants. Summer phlox was one of them. An interesting cultivar named 'David' promised mildew resistance, fragrance, large clusters of pure white flowers, and a long period of bloom.

About six years ago I ordered a collection of pink flowers from Spring Hill Nurseries. The group had several perennials and assured years of carefree beauty. I don't remember what all the flowers were, but I still have two of them. One was a soapwort that I have enjoyed, and the other was *Phlox paniculata* 'Bright Eyes'.

'David' grows about three feet tall in my sunny border. 'Bright Eyes' is clear pink with darker eyes. It tops out at 24 to 30 inches and has exceptional fragrance. Both have been star performers.

Growing summer phlox has been a challenging experience for many Southern gardeners. Some varieties are plagued with powdery mildew that causes unsightly foliage and gradual decline. Selecting mildew-resistant varieties and following a few good cultural practices increase chances of success. Spacing that allows for adequate air circulation between plants discourages the development of fungal spores. Siting plants so that early morning sun dries the foliage also helps to keep powdery mildew at bay.

Several cultivars have been mildew resistant in trials at the Chicago Botanic Garden. Though I have not grown them, I would not hesitate to purchase *Phlox paniculata* 'Katherine', which is lavender with a white eye, or *P. paniculata* 'Franz Schubert', which is pink with darker pink eyes. Richard Bir, an extension specialist for North Carolina State University, adds 'Eva Cullum', 'Fairest One', 'Natascha', 'Orange Perfection', 'Robert Poore', 'Rosalinde', and 'Starfire' to the list. I might also try some of these. Experts caution, however, that good performance in one part of the country does not guarantee the same in all areas.

Summer phlox grows best in full sun in rich, well-drained soil. Organic material should be incorporated into the bed and slow-release fertilizer used once or twice during the growing season. Deep watering at least once a week will keep the soil evenly moist. Division every third or fourth year is recommended.

Quite accidentally I learned that phlox grows well from root cuttings. After I dug and moved 'David' last fall, new plants grew from the roots left in the ground to replace the old ones. I had several new plants to share with friends.

I heartily recommend 'David' and 'Bright Eyes' and other mildew-resistant varieties for gardeners in the coastal South. Native to the United States, they are hardy from Zones 4 to 9. Fall is the best time to add these beauties to the border. Failing that, order them in the winter as I did, and plant them in the spring.

Blue Plumbago (*Plumbago auriculata*)

Folks who garden know that one of life's greatest joys comes from sharing a special flower with a friend. That's how I got my start of blue plumbago. It happened when I went with my daughter to Pensacola to visit Inez, her husband's grandmother.

After I admired the plant, Inez took a shovel and cut me out a start. Planted in a sunny area, it continued its show in my garden. It's one of those "pass-along plants," a term used by Felder Rushing and Steve Bender in their book by that name. I've had the plumbago now for about six years. It is one of my most reliable perennials, and Inez would be pleased to know that many of my friends and garden club members grow blue plumbago that came from her yard.

Plumbago auriculata should not be confused with *Ceratostigma plumbaginoides* that is also called blue plumbago. The latter is a low groundcover plant that bears little resemblance to *P. auriculata*.

Plumbago auriculata blooms from June until the frost blackens its foliage. The dog days of summer do not affect its performance, for it continues to bloom unabatedly. Drought tolerance and ability to perform in poor soil make it an ideal selection for the coastal South. Mine has been pest and disease free. The reason I like it so well, however, is its nonstop display of phloxlike flowers in a clear, sky blue color. Selections in white and varying shades of blue are available. It's a sure-fire winner for gardeners of all levels of expertise.

Partially shaded or full sun exposure works well for plumbago. Mature height is usually three to four feet with an equal spread, though it may grow taller in areas where it is not cut down by frost. Suckers may spread around the plant, but this characteristic does not make it invasive. Keeping my planting in bounds has been a pleasurable way to increase my stock and to share some of these captivating plants with friends. When frost blackens its foliage, I cut it back to the ground. Well-established plants will come back reliably year after year in the coastal South, but it is treated as an annual north of Zone 8. In frost-free regions, plumbago is evergreen and may flower throughout the year. Since it withstands light salt drift from the ocean, it is an excellent choice for gardens near bodies of salt water.

Use plumbago in the landscape in several ways. Effective as a tall plant at the back or middle of a mixed or perennial border, it also makes an attractive mass planting by itself. Gracefully arching branches and soft, unobtrusive color make it an ideal mixer in the garden. Since its pastel flowers stand out in the evening hours, it would be a welcome addition to a moon garden. Blue plumbago fronted with a planting of white vinca is as cool and refreshing as a trip to the shopping mall in August.

Plumbago can be obtained from nurseries, or you might get a start from a friend who is willing to share. New plants often volunteer around old, established plantings. Additional plants may also be started from cuttings or by division. Plant plumbago in a partially shady to sunny exposure, water it during periods of extreme drought, and sit back and enjoy its nonstop show.

Black-eyed Susan (*Rudbeckia* spp.) [4]

Who can pass a bed of black-eyed Susans without smiling? Certainly not I, for they are as cheery a sight as any I know. They recall bygone days in rural Mississippi when as a young child I went into the woods to pick a bouquet for the house. The pleasure they provided then is no less than the joy I feel now when I see them blooming in the wild or in gardens throughout the South.

Black-eyed Susans are some of our most dependable bloomers. Many species and varieties exist; some are annual, some biennial, and some perennial. Whichever one you choose is sure to be a pleaser. Bold, bright, daisy flowers enliven any planting, and the show lasts for months.

Black-eyed Susans are very easy to grow. All they require is a sunny place in well-drained soil. Most are fairly drought resistant, and I never spray mine, although mildew sometimes mars the foliage in late summer. Annual types reseed every year with no help from me. Sometimes I pull out surplus plants and put them in other locations or give them to friends.

An improved strain, Gloriosa daisy (*Rudbeckia hirta* var. *gloriosa*), is also a dependable bloomer. 'Goldilocks' is a semidouble gloriosa daisy, and the 'Rustic Colors' mix provides flowers strikingly suffused with dark orange and rich mahogany colors. 'Irish Eyes' has green eyes and yellow to pale orange petals. Though often touted as perennial, gloriosa daisies diminish in vigor after the first year, so I plant new seeds each year.

The black-eyed Susan that I'm most excited about, however, is *Rudbeckia* 'Goldsturm', the Perennial Plant Association's pick for the 1999 Perennial Plant of the Year. Here's a black-eyed Susan with a pedigree. Bred by the Germans, its name means "storm of gold."

Available in most garden centers, it is an easy addition to the border. Cloaked with golden yellow flowers beginning in midsummer, it continues to bloom until frost. This hardy perennial spreads by underground runners to provide a substantial clump, but it is never invasive. It can be divided every three or four years. Performance of these hybrids is best in good soil improved with organic matter. They appreciate full sun and adequate moisture, though they are adaptable to less than ideal circumstances.

Plant black-eyed Susans in masses or drifts to provide large areas of color. Planted here and there in the landscape, they give an unsettling, polka-dot effect. One of the most attractive groupings I've ever seen used black-eyed Susans in front the spiky blue flowers of Salvia 'Indigo Spires'.

Many varieties of black-eyed Susan exist, and surely one can be found that is suitable for almost any purpose. Anyone can grow these highly adaptable flowers. They'll lighten your cares and bring a smile to your face!

Salvia, Sage (*Salvia* spp.) [5, 7, 8, 44]

Wouldn't you love to add some flowers to your garden that will attract scads of butterflies, hummingbirds, and bees? Wouldn't it be nice, too, if they would bloom all summer and provide color throughout the garden? Want tall plants? No problem. Small plants? Right on! Plants for the herb garden? You've got it! There is a salvia that will fit the bill. Enough diversity is offered by this group of plants to

satisfy almost any gardening need. In my own garden, I grow at least 15 different kinds, and that is a tiny sampling of the 700 to 900 recognized species.

Salvias are members of the mint family as suggested by their square stems. All have pungently aromatic foliage. Since noses differ in their assessment of scents, some that are objectionable to some people may not be to others. Someone on the Gardener's Forum on the Internet remarked that she had discarded all of her Salvia 'May Night' because it smelled like cat urine and she could not abide it. I grow 'May Night' in my perennial border and have never been offended by its scent. This low-growing plant sends up spikes of purple flowers throughout the summer and is perfect at the front of the border.

The sage that I grow in the herb garden

is *Salvia officinalis*. This is the aromatic herb that is often used to spice up the turkey and dressing. It is available in the familiar, two-foot shrubby bush of dull gray color, but cultivars such as 'Tricolor', 'Icterina', and 'Purpurea' with gold or purple leaves spice up the herb garden and the turkey.

Mealy-cup sage (*Salvia farinacea*) is high on my list of favorites. 'Victoria' [44] grows about 12 inches tall and sends up scads of spiky blue flowers all summer. 'Porcelain' is similar in habit, buts its flowers are silvery white. Planted in drifts or masses near the front of a perennial border, they provide dependable color all summer. *Salvia* 'Indigo Spires'(reported to be a cross between *S. farinacea* and *S. longispicata*) [7] tops out at four to six feet, so it is better suited to the back of the border. Its purple spires rise behind daylilies, black-eyed Susans, and purple coneflowers to color my summer garden.

Autumn sage (*Salvia greggii*) [5] is a welcome addition to my borders. It grows to about two and a half feet tall and has flowers of many different colors. Some recent cultivars are rather refined in nature. They literally sparkle in front of dark green shrubs or large, coarse-leaved flowers such as *Tibouchina* or sun coleus. Cut autumn sage in early morning or late afternoon after the sun has gone down and condition the stems in cool water for excellent floral design material. Cutting stimulates new growth and blooms. I have yet to figure out why it is called autumn sage, since it blooms dependably from early summer on.

Another favorite is the aromatic pineapple sage (*Salvia elegans*). Its foliage has the delightful scent of pineapple and grows to a bush three or more feet tall and wide. In fall it produces lovely, bright red, tubular flowers much favored by hummingbirds.

Russian sage (*S. perovskia*) is not long lived in my garden. It was the Perennial Plant Association's choice for the "Plant of the Year" in 1995. The most finely textured of all the sages, it is beloved for its silvery foliage and steely blue spikes of flowers that bloom from summer through fall. Perhaps the heat and humidity of the coastal South are a bit much for this beauty.

Mexican bush sage (*S. leucantha*) has a rounded, bushy habit and violet and white flower spikes from summer through fall. Its three-foot-tall and -wide bushy habit makes it suitable for the middle or back of the border.

A latecomer to my garden is forsythia sage (*S. madrensis*) [8]. It is the largest and most coarsely textured of any of my sages. I saw it at the garden center this summer, and true to my floraholic nature, I could not resist it. Scott Ogden, in the 1993 September/October issue of *Fine Gardening*, described it as "a subtropical delight with long spikes of medium yellow blooms that appear on robust, four-foot-tall stems." I had to have it!

Salvias have bold spikes of flowers that range in color from white through blue, purple, red, and yellow. Leaves may be gray and fuzzy or green and shiny, or they may be variegated and sport multiple colors. Height may vary from six inches to six feet. All of the salvias discussed so far are perennials, but *Salvia splendens* is a very popular annual bedding plant.

Most sages are drought tolerant and pest resistant. People who are trying to cut down on water consumption would do well to select from this group. Most prefer sunny locations and well-drained soil. Overhead irrigation is not recommended, although most of mine are watered by the sprinkler system, and they have done well. They tend to sprawl in rich soil, and fertilizer needs are very low.

Some perennial salvias are hardy as far north as USDA Hardiness Zone 4. Others are tender perennials unable to survive north of Zone 8. However, even these tender salvias can be grown in the North as annuals. Cuttings may be taken and overwintered indoors. In most of Florida and the coastal South, many types are perfectly winter hardy.

Propagation is easy from cuttings. I have had success taking cuttings during the growing season and pushing them into the ground in some out-of-the-way place. Later, I am surprised to find them growing and ready for planting in the perennial border. Rooted cuttings are quick to go at plant sales.

With so much variety, it is surprising that salvia is not in every garden. Butterflies, hummingbirds, and bees by the dozens are attracted by the spikes of tubular flowers. Some can hold their own at the back of the border mingled with other flowers or shrubs, while others can be used in front of the border as edging plants. They can even be grown in containers, and they are useful as cut flowers.

I think I just talked myself into another trip to the nursery. Surely a few varieties of this wonderful flower can be found that I don't have. I will check it out!

Goldmoss, Stonecrop (*Sedum acre*)

One of the more than 500 distinct species of stonecrops, goldmoss produces a bed of golden yellow flowers that glow for about three weeks in spring. It is a traffic stopper beside *Verbena* 'Homestead Purple', and it positively shines in front of evergreen shrubs such as the blue green *Juniperus* 'Grey Owl'. Goldmoss is a tough, hardy, groundcover succulent that likes hot weather, full sun, and poor soil. Almost no diseases or insects ever attack goldmoss. Some may show rot if placed in an area with poor drainage. The remedy is, of course, to improve drainage or move the plant to a better-drained site.

Propagation is as easy as inserting a stem where you want it to grow. A large area can be covered by tilling the soil and then spreading pieces where it is wanted. Cover the sprigs with soil and water generously. It spreads effortlessly, but has shallow, fibrous roots that dig out easily where it's not wanted.

This diminutive, two- to three-inch-tall, evergreen, chartreuse-colored plant seems to light up everything around it year-round. It's a perfect front-of-the-border companion for tall, spiky plants and is a wonderful color contrast with dark foliage or brightly colored flowers. Also extremely cold hardy, its presence in winter is especially welcome. Use it in containers or window boxes where it spills over the edges, or combine it in beds with annuals and perennials for a profusion of color. Since goldmoss requires very little soil to survive, it is a popular choice for rock gardens.

Goldmoss is hardy in Zones 3 to 8. It is dependably green in all parts of the South, but in colder parts of the country, it is semievergreen. Gardeners in the South can depend upon it for its continuous presence and year-round beauty in their yards.

Princess Flower (*Tibouchina urvilleana*)

One late-summer morning, I was out early surveying my domain before the heat became intolerable. As I walked around, someone I didn't know stopped and asked me the name of the purple flower blooming around the neighborhood. Well, several pretty purple flowers were blooming, so I couldn't say for sure. It might have been Mexican petunia, Philippine violet, or any number of things. Also, it might have been the beautiful princess flower. Since early spring, its lance-shaped, distinctly veined, fuzzy leaves have been a source of delight. Finally, in midsummer, it has unfurled its passionately purple flowers. Five-petaled, two-inch blossoms exhibit curly, protruding stamens that look like they have been curled with an eyelash curler.

Surely this deep, almost iridescent purple is the color of some rare jewel. If I were a rich lady, I would ask Amiable Spouse to fill my birthdays and Christmases with jewelry made from stones of this rich, royal color. I am sure that it would bedeck my fingers and ears and give me a royal appearance closely akin to the noble presence that this beautiful flower adds to my flower border.

Tibouchina urvilleana is an evergreen shrub or small tree in its tropical homes of Mexico, South America, and the West Indies. Although hardy in Zones 8 to 12, in Zone 8 it is a perennial that gets killed to the ground by winter's freezing temperatures. Each spring it returns reliably from roots. In southern parts of Florida it is evergreen. North of Zone 8 it must be grown as an annual or in a container that can be brought in during the winter.

I particularly enjoy princess flower's habits in my Zone 8b garden. Usually it begins growing in late March or early April. It masterfully illustrates the succession of blooms that makes a beautiful garden possible in all seasons. When the irises bloomed, princess flower was just emerging from its winter dormancy. How accommodating the princess is to be short in spring and tall in summer! The iris blossoms are revealed in their fullest measure of beauty, but later their unattractive, dying foliage is hidden from view. Such tricks of the trade often mean the difference between a beautiful border and one that has unsightly, empty spots during part of the year.

The princess flowers are in their glory from midsummer through fall. They open in succession from a cluster of buds at the ends of each stem. Each cluster produces flowers for a couple of weeks. A flush of bloom is followed by a growth flush so that the plant continues to grow and bloom all season. By summer's end, the shrub may be seven or eight feet tall. It can, however, be cut back after a bloom cycle to keep it smaller.

Princess flower does best in full morning sun, but like most plants in our part of the world, it appreciates some protection from the hot afternoon sun. Full all-day sun tends to yellow the foliage and shorten the life of the flowers. It thrives in well-drained, enriched soil and needs a steady supply of moisture during the growing season. Propagation is by softwood cuttings in late spring or semiripe cuttings in summer. Regrettably, princess flower is not salt tolerant.

So, here was my response to the inquisitive passerby. Look at the leaf of the plant. If it is a soft and velvety, lance-shaped leaf with prominent veins that extend from the bottom of the leaf to the tip in one continuous line, and if the flowers closely resemble my description, I believe that venturing a guess would be safe. The flower in question is most likely tibouchina or princess flower. It is a completely worthy addition to gardens from Zone 8 and southward.

Verbena (Verbena 'Homestead Purple')

One that could not miss my list of favorites is the perennial Verbena 'Homestead Purple'. In early spring it puts on a spectacular show. It's a ground-hugging mat that quickly fills large areas if allowed to grow unchecked. It can, however, be kept within bounds easily. I sometimes use a strong pair of scissors to trim all around the edges in order to keep it where I want it. According to Allan Armitage of the University of Georgia, it blooms all summer in Zones 3 to 7a. In Zones 7b and farther south, a hard cutting back in summer will stimulate more blooms.

In early spring, however, the sight of the bright purple blooms alongside the gold of *Sedum acre* is an unforgettable sight. Evergreen foliage holds its place in the border and makes it worthwhile even when it is not in bloom in our coastal South gardens.

Other Reliable Perennials

Name	Exposure *	Moisture * Requirement
Alstroemeria (*Alstroemeria psittacina* formerly *A. pulchella*)	PS	Moderate
Texas Blue Star (*Amsonia tabernaemontana*)	S	DT
Cast Iron Plant (*Aspidistra elatior*)	Sh	DT
Philippine violet (*Barleria cristata*)	S, PSh	Wide range
Shasta Daisy (*Chrysanthemum x superbum*)	S	Moist
Coreopsis (*Coreopsis lanceolata*)	S/PSh	DT
Chrysanthemum (*Chrysanthemum grandiflora*)	S	Moderate
Blanket Flower (*Gaillardia grandiflora*)	S	DT
Gerbera Daisy (*Gerbera jamesonii*)	S/PSh	Moderate

* See key on page 25

for the Coastal South

Blossom Color	Height	Comments
Reddish orange	2'–3'	Good cut flower can be invasive
Lt. blue	2'	Native
Foliage	2'–3'	Good cut greenery
Purple, white	4'	
White	1'–3'	Divide each fall
Yellow	1'–3'	Native, salt tolerant
Varies	1'–2'	Avoid night lights
Orange, yellow	1'–2'	Salt tolerant, some are annuals
Varies	1'–2'	Salt tolerant

continued on next page

Name	Exposure	Moisture Requirement
Daylily (Hemerocallis)	S/PSh	Moderate
Shrimp Plant (Justicia brandegeana)	S/PSh	DT
Lantana (Lantana camara)	S	DT
Blazing Star (Liatris elegans) (L. spicata)	S	DT
Firespike (Odontonema strictum)	PS/Sh	Moderate
Golden Shrimp Plant (Pachystachys lutea)	PSh	Wide range
Lavender Cotton (Santolina chamaecyparissus)	S	DT
Purple Heart (Setcreasea pallida)	S/PSh	DT
Stokesia (Stokesia laevis)	S	Moderate

Blossom Color	Height	Comments
Varies		Somewhat salt tolerant
Reddish bracts	4'–5'	Hummingbirds, butterflies
Varies	2'–4'	Salt tolerant, many new cultivars
Lavender, white	1'–2'	Native, butterflies, good cut flower
Red	5'–6'	Hummingbirds, butterflies
Yellow	3'–4'	
Gray/green foliage	1'	Well-drained soil
Purple foliage	1'	Groundcover
Lavender	1'	Native, salt tolerant

S - Sun
Sh - Shade
P - Part
DT - Drought Tolerant

Bulbs, Corms, Rhizomes, and Tubers

For too long, Southerners have tried to grow tulips, hyacinths, and other bulbs suited to the Netherlands and northern gardens. Dismal failure is often the result. We refrigerate them for weeks and then plant them out in winter for a short show in spring. Then they're dug and discarded, for that is the extent of their usefulness in our gardens. Mail-order sources tempt us with tantalizing pictures of beautiful German irises that start diminishing in vigor from the moment we set them out. We are now learning to make wiser choices. If we choose the right plants from this group, they are some of the most reliable and long-lived plants in our gardens

Used loosely, the term bulb refers to plants with enlarged leaf bases or stems that store food and water. These plant tissues may be rhizomes, bulbs, tubers, tuberous roots, or corms. The three big bulb families are lily, iris, and amaryllis (Liliaceae, Iridacea, Amaryllidaceae). Some that we call bulbs, however, are only distantly related to the big three.

All share storage mechanisms that allow them to be shipped for long distances without damage and survive for a long time on store shelves. The storage capability allows them to compete in cold or semiarid regions more ably than plants without such devices. They are easily passed on from gardener to gardener, and bulbs of one kind or another bloom throughout the year. Many bulbs are well suited to the coastal South. They bloom year after year and increase in beauty with the passage of time. It is these to which we need to pay attention. Many of them are part of our horticultural legacy that links us with gardens and gardeners long gone.

Hardy Orchid, Chinese Ground Orchid (Bletilla striata) [15]

Each winter when the gardening catalogs come in the mail, we gardeners pore over the offerings trying to find some horticultural treasure not yet tried. Such is the story of my Chinese ground orchid. The catalog pictured an orchid that was hardy in Zones 5 to 9 with white or lavender flowers of exceeding loveliness. Being tempted beyond my power to resist, I chose three of the lavender ones, and off the order went. When the bulbs arrived, they were planted in the shifting shade of tall pines.

They have far outstripped my expectations. Every spring I am delighted with their two-inch lavender blooms that resemble Cattleya orchids. Each plant bears seven or eight of these striking flowers that have the typical orchid shape: furrowed lower lips, two petals, and three sepals. After bloom, the green, strappy, almost pleated foliage remains in the garden all summer. Even if these plants did not produce such delightful flowers, I might plant them in my garden for the foliage alone. Growing to about 12 inches tall, they are a carefree delight, a striking accent, and a pleasing textural contrast to more rounded leaves and flowers nearby.

Ground orchids should be divided every few years. Before digging the bulbs, prepare a new bed. Enrich the bed if needed by digging in an inch or so of peat moss, manure, or other organic material. After a good soaking, the bed is ready for its new transplants. Dig the crowded bulbs, separate them carefully, and plant them in the new bed about six inches apart. Mulch with pine needles or other mulching material, water thoroughly to settle them in their new bed and remove air pockets, and expect a few more years of carefree growth.

Chinese ground orchids are hardy perennials with which any gardener in the coastal South can experience success. They are almost foolishly easy to grow. All that is needed is some shade in the hottest part of the summer and occasional division when the bed becomes crowded. In spring when growth begins, a bit of slow-release fertilizer can be added.

Some new hardy orchids are listed in one of my catalogs as *Calanthe* 'Kozu'. The catalog description is so tempting! "Hardy, hard-to-find orchids in an unparalleled variety of colors, clove-scented, eight- to ten-inch flower spikes are borne in middle to late spring in shades of white, pink, red, purple, brown, orange, and bicolors," it states. Hardiness is rated Zones 7 to 9. The price is only $54.95 each, or if you really want to save money, buy two for $100. I'm tempted—but this time, it is not beyond my power to resist. My pocketbook is just too limited!

If you hanker for Chinese ground orchids, they can be obtained from many mail-order sources. Besides white and lavender, these hardy orchids are available in yellow and pink. However you obtain these jewels, do add them to your garden. They will provide many years of beauty with minimum effort.

Caladium (*Caladium* spp.)

Most Southerners recognize caladiums. They flourish in our warm, humid summers. Dramatic displays of brilliantly colored leaves make them plants of choice for shady areas in the summer garden. Native to tropical America, they do well throughout the United States as long as temperatures are above 70°F. Two main types of caladiums are fancy-leafed (*Caladium x hortulanum*) and lance-leafed (derived from *C. albanense* crossed among the larger hybrids). The fancy-leafed caladiums have large leaves that can reach 12 inches or more in length and width on plants that grow 18 to 24 inches tall. The smaller lance-leafed caladiums have a decorative, frilly border and grow on plants 12 inches tall with three- to five-inch-wide leaves.

One of my favorite ways to grow caladiums is in pots or containers of various sizes. They are handy for moving about the landscape and filling in spaces as the summer progresses. Sometimes my caladiums get dressed up in fancy pots and sent to the middle school where I spent many years teaching children to read and write. There they decorate the stage for special programs. Their colorful foliage enlivens the ferns and other green plants. Sometimes they get whisked off to weddings to adorn a sanctuary or reception hall. After the festivities they return home to beautify my yard.

Under trees and other shady places, caladiums are striking with impatiens, hostas, ferns, and other shade lovers. In front of my house, a group of dark red ones absolutely glows behind a bed of gray dusty miller. In other places I use them to draw attention to focal areas and as a pleasing contrast to such plants as giant liriope, ginger, and aspidistra. Caladiums also do well in considerable sun if the soil is kept consistently moist.

Many people prefer caladiums planted in masses of a single color. They make a dramatic show when used in this way and positively glisten in the summer landscape. I think they are effective in mixtures, too, because most of the colors blend pleasingly. One of the most attractive displays I have ever seen was a large planting of 'Candidum', whose snow-white leaves with dark green veins were stunning near a shaded entrance. Caladiums should be planted in soil enriched with generous amounts of peat moss or organic matter after the soil has warmed and all danger of frost is past. They need well-drained, constantly moist, acid soil. Space tubers about 12 to 18 inches apart and bury them about two inches deep. Sprinkle slow-release fertilizer on top of the soil and cover with a light mulch such as pine needles to help keep the soil evenly moist. Using slow-release pelletized fertilizer simplifies matters because one application is usually enough to last throughout the season if the soil was well prepared before planting. However, balanced fertilizers such as 6-6-6 may also be used every month or so during the summer.

All my life I have heard that the odd, papery blooms that resemble calla lilies should be removed so that all the plant's energy can be used to produce the showy leaves. However, Carol Bishop Hipps, in her book *In a Southern Garden*, says that the leaves actually last longer if the flowers are left uncut. That suits me just fine. Sometimes I use the unusual flowers in floral designs. The leaves, too, are long lasting in a bouquet. Beth Wilson, one of my flower arranger buddies, sprays the back of the leaves with hair spray. She says that they hold their form better after this treatment.

After the leaves die down in fall, dig the tubers and store them over winter in a frost-free place. I simply dig mine, let them dry until most of the dirt falls off, and arrange them in a single layer in plastic flats. Then I place them on a storage shelf in the garage until it is time to replant them the following spring. Never have I lost a tuber, and never have I found it necessary to poison or dust them with fungicide as some references suggest.

If treated in this manner, the tubers will grow larger each year. When I first purchased my tubers, they were about one to one and a half inches in diameter. Now they are four to six inches in diameter and still growing. They could be cut apart like potatoes with one or two eyes per piece, but I rather like my giant tubers. The leaves that they produce are evidence of the fact that big tubers make big leaves. A visitor to my garden remarked that she had never seen caladium leaves as large as mine. Some gardeners use a sharp knife to remove the larger growing points from the tubers. This stimulates side branching and develops a lusher, leafier appearance.

Friends tell me that they have caladiums that return each year even if they are not dug. I have found that some do return because I occasionally miss one when I dig them. However, they tend to diminish in size and vigor. One year I didn't get around to digging my tubers in the fall. The next year some of them came up, but at least half of them failed to reappear. Gardeners in the southernmost parts of Florida and Texas (tropical South) can get away with this practice, but those of us in the coastal South do best to dig our tubers each fall.

Most local garden shops carry caladium tubers in the spring. Also, they may be purchased already started in containers. However, for the greatest choices in variety, order from mail-order sources. Whichever source you choose, be sure to add some of these beauties to your landscape for years of vibrant color.

Crinum Lily, Crinum (*Crinum* spp.) [9, 10, 11]

When the crinum lilies bloom, I think of Miss Willie, who grew them in her cottage garden in rural Mississippi. Every year they bloomed along with hundreds of daylilies and other perennials and reseeding annuals. I admired them from the school bus every morning and afternoon when it passed her house. Often she was in her garden lovingly tending her flowers. Here is proof positive that beautiful gardens are not the province of only the rich. Miss Willie was as poor as any of the rest of us just pulling out of the Great Depression, but her flowers remain a bright spot in my childhood memories.

Take a drive anywhere in the South almost anytime during the summer and you are sure to see crinum lilies blooming. Most are native to warm, temperate regions. Extremely long-lived, they are often found in old city gardens or abandoned home sites where they have bloomed for years. Many are passed down from generation to generation and have become treasured heirlooms.

Crinums are hardy members of the amaryllis family. Foliage is often two to three feet long or more and several inches wide. It grows in tall, radial clusters and is present throughout the growing season. After being killed to the ground in severe winters, it bounds back with spring's first warm days.

Flowers are white, pink, or red trumpet-shaped blossoms held well above the foliage on stout flower stalks or scapes. Some crinums produce from 6 to 20 or more buds per scape. The blooms make outstanding cut flowers, and their fragrance is hard to beat. A flower stalk will last for a couple of weeks, and some varieties send up new ones repeatedly for several months in spring and summer. Often they are called milk and wine lilies [11] because some have a stripe of pink down the center of each white petal.

Crinums have several uses in the landscape. Coarse, strappy foliage lends a tropical feel to the garden. Interest and drama are created when crinums are placed near fine-textured plants. The sculptural, irregular form lends itself to use as a specimen plant. Bold flowers add a vertical exclamation point to the flower border when they bloom. Since scent is most pervasive in the evening, they are naturals for a moon garden or placement near a deck or gazebo frequented during the late afternoon or evening. They are, of course, perennial bulbs that will return year after year and grow better with the passing years.

Place crinums in fertile, moist, well-drained soil in sun to partial shade. Like most plants in our area, they will benefit from the addition of organic matter to the soil and generous use of mulch. Try to locate them where they will stay for a long time because they may fail to flower unless left in place for several years. The older the clumps are and the more restricted they become, the better they flower. If division becomes necessary, divide and replant in late autumn. Fertilize bulbs in early spring with bonemeal or an all-purpose fertilizer.

Literally hundreds of varieties and cultivars are available. Many have been hybridized for outstanding foliage or flower features. *Crinum americanum* (Southern swamp crinum) is native to the South and grows in wet areas. It may be found in ditches or along creeks and riverbanks. A similar species from South America, *C. erubescens*, grows well in ordinary garden soil. Site it with the foreknowledge that roots quickly run about the garden if soil is to its liking.

C. asiaticum [9] produces large clusters of 15 or more white to pink flowers on tall scapes. The largest of the crinums is *C. augustum*. Considered the showiest, with tall flower scapes held high above the foliage, is *C. variable*. Two pink flowering cultivars that are very popular are 'Ellen Bosanquet' and 'Louis Bosanquet' [10].

Crinums have been hybridized for years, and a thorough discussion of all varieties may be next to impossible. Whichever variety you choose, add a few of these dependable lilies to your yard, for they will increase in beauty each year and provide a lifetime of pleasure. What more could one ask?

Glory Lily, Gloriosa Lily, Flame Lily
(Gloriosa rothschildiana)

Most gardeners have had the experience of seeing a picture of a flower and being smitten on the spot. That's the way it was with my glory lilies. In Lowe's one spring, I found them in a mesh bag in the bulb bin. A picture was stapled to it. Boy howdy, I thought to myself. What if that beautiful thing would grow and bloom in my garden? That was many years ago. It was a purchase that has given me years of pleasure.

The glory lily is one of our showiest floral treasures. Flowers remind one of flames with their undulating petals splayed outward and upward from the center of the downward-facing blooms. Support for their floppy stems is provided by tendrils on the ends of the leaves that grasp any support and pull the three- to six-foot stems up toward the sun.

These members of the lily family may be called climbing lilies, flame lilies, gloriosa lilies, or glory lilies. Odd L- or V-shaped tubers travel slowly underground. They should be dug and divided if needed at the end of the season after bloom when plants are fully mature. Since new tubers are formed each year, digging before the leaves are mature will result in immature specimens. Also, don't expect to find the tubers exactly where they were planted. As new ones are formed,

the old ones die. Over a period of a few years they may move several inches. Large pods with reddish, marblelike seeds are produced on glory lilies. Plant the seeds in spring, but don't give them up for dead after a month or so. At least four months are required for them to sprout. Young plants may be planted and expected to bloom in about three years.

The glory lily is dependably hardy only in the tropical South, but it can be grown in warmer areas of Zone 8, where it is killed to the ground by freezes. In my garden it has come back dependably every spring. I have it in a well-mulched area that offers some protection from the cold. A dramatic display blooms each year on a chain-link fence in a neighbor's yard.

Plant glory lily tubers in well-drained, organic, moisture-retentive soil in a location that receives light to medium shade. In areas where they are not hardy, dig in fall and store in a frost-free location. Alternatively, they may be grown in containers that may be dried out and moved inside until spring. One of the most interesting ways to grow glory lily is at the base of another plant. Any green shrub can provide support. It is surprising to see gloriosa lilies blooming on my banana shrub.

Different varieties and cultivars of glory lilies are available. *G. simplex* has orange and yellow blossoms with a light greenish tinge and reaches about three feet in length. *G. superba* varies in color, but the cultivar 'Lutea' is lemony yellow with slender petals. *G. carsoni*, *G. rothschildiana* var. *citrina*, and *G.* x *greenii* 'Wilhelmina Green' may sometimes be found in specialty catalogs or garden centers.

Gardeners in the coastal South grow glory lilies for their fantastically exotic flowers. Look for tubers in local garden centers or mail-order catalogs. Choose a few to add a different look to the garden and to fascinate you and your friends with captivating blossoms for many years.

Amaryllis (*Hippeastrum* spp.)

The stately amaryllis was the flower of my childhood. Daddy faithfully tended his amaryllis plants all the years I was growing up. Naturally, when I moved away, I took some of his favorites with me. At each residence throughout my adulthood, I've planted these hardy bulbs. I appreciate them as much as Daddy did.

Throughout most of the country, amaryllis bulbs are used for forcing at Christmas. For us in the coastal South, however, they are reliable, hardy perennials. Besides the usual reds, pinks, salmons, and whites, modern hybrid strains include unique picotees and flamboyant doubles. I recently saw a yellow one advertised in one of my catalogs, and butterfly amaryllis (*Hippeastrum papillio*) is available from several mail-order sources.

If putting on a spectacular show for two or three weeks in spring were all they did, I wouldn't be so smitten with amaryllis. Adding to their allure, however, is their substantial, strappy foliage that remains attractive throughout the summer. Later blooming flowers are provided a green partition of spiky foliage that weaves and blends everything together in the garden setting. Lining my front walkway as they do, they are a good example of repetition as an important design element. They unite the diverse plant materials behind them and are attractive without blooms. Leaves are killed by the first frost and may be removed at that time.

Amaryllis bulbs should be divided every four or five years. Bulblets need to be separated from the original bulb and transplanted where they have more room to grow. Fall is probably the most ideal time, but I have successfully divided them at almost any season. Balanced fertilizer immediately following bloom promotes growth and stores energy for next year's blooms. Although full sun is recommended, I find that protection from the blistering afternoon sun is beneficial.

Amaryllis plants are easily grown from seed. The fruit forms at the base of the spent flower, and after a couple of months, it dries out and splits. Then the flat black seeds may be collected and planted in sterile potting soil. Protect young seedlings from frost during their first winter, and transplant them in an out-of-the-way nursery bed the following spring. In two to five years, you will have many blooming-sized bulbs that may be placed in permanent places in the landscape. Be sure to plant so that the tops of the bulbs are slightly above the soil line. Bulbs planted too deeply will not bloom. Performance is best in well-drained, moist, fertile soil.

Imagine my surprise when I saw a magazine article recently about the Saint Joseph lily (*Hippeastrum* x *johnsonii*). "A rare flowering bulb," it was called. How common they were in the garden of my

youth! Mother mistakenly called them Easter lilies. They were planted all around the edges of the fence that surrounded our farmhouse.
Brilliant red, five-inch, funnel-shaped flowers with white-striped
petals bloomed each spring on 20-inch stalks. Each stalk had four to
six flowers, and as many as four stalks were produced per bulb.

Daddy thought his big hybrids, which descended from various
South American species, were more beautiful than Mother's "Easter"
lilies. I wish he could see some of the flatter-faced Dutch hybrids that
I have added to my collection. These are the ones that are commonly available in today's market. Most varieties send up at least two
four-flowered scapes under optimal conditions.

Plant some amaryllises in your yard. You'll be in for a treat—one
of those heart-gladdening, oh-my-goodness-I-can't-believe-my-eyes
thrills when you see the dewy loveliness of a newly opened blossom.

Iris (*Iris* spp.) [13,16]

How many times have I heard the question, "Why won't my irises
bloom?" Maybe the hopeful gardener brought some favorites from
the old home place in the northern reaches of our coastal South
states or points even farther north. There the irises bloomed beautifully year after year, but here they have not bloomed at all.

Such is my own story. Daddy in his Zone 8a garden grew tall purple bearded irises as big as dinner plates. He called them "flags," and
in spring they lit up the landscape for about two weeks. Henry
Mitchell, longtime garden writer for the *Washington Post*, believed
that these flags, or German irises, as they are often called, were the
most beautiful of all flowers.

Naturally, I wanted some of Daddy's flags for my Florida garden.
With great hopes and expectations, I dug a clump and brought it
home. I found a suitable spot and planted them just the way Daddy
instructed. Year after year they grew. The foliage was quite dependable, but never did the beautiful irises bloom. I believe they were the
old purple flag named *Iris germanica* 'Nepalensis'. They bloom
dependably in gardens not far north of mine.

A few years back I was seduced unmercifully by a colorful catalog that claimed its bearded irises would bloom in Zone 8. I sent off for the whole group: five variously colored, beautiful irises that would be the beginning of years of beauty in my yard. It was not to be, of course. They all bloomed the first year. After that I saw a bloom on one of the varieties for two years in a row, but since then, they have not bloomed at all. I finally discarded them and put in some irises that I knew would do well for me.

It is tempting to say that the tall bearded irises do not bloom in the coastal South. And yet, as soon as I have made this statement, some gardener will state emphatically that they most certainly do, and furthermore, they can be seen in his or her garden. So I am led to believe that some varieties are reliable. I can honestly say, however, that most of them have not done well for me.

Some types of irises, however, excel in my garden. One of my favorites is African iris (*Dietes vegeta* formerly *Moraea iriodes*, and *Dietes bicolor*). Well suited to our heat, humidity, and sandy soils, these irises bloom most prolifically in spring. Bloom continues sporadically throughout summer and fall. Though not nearly as spectacular as the bearded irises, they provide an element in the landscape that is difficult to achieve with any other plant. Cold hardy to 25°F, African iris is usually evergreen in my yard. If an occasional freeze does manage to cut it back to the ground, it springs back readily with the warming days of spring.

Spiky foliage grows about three feet tall and offers material for many of my cut floral designs. It provides a visual exclamation point among low, spreading plants that have contrasting textures. Flowers are white or yellow, and full sun is preferred, although mine have done well in partial shade. Unfortunately, they are not salt tolerant.

Other irises that do well for me are sometimes called "cemetery whites [16]." Often they are found growing wild and may be found at abandoned home sites or cemeteries where they have thrived for years without help of any kind. According to William C. Welch, in his book *Perennial Garden Color for Texas and the South*, they are a natural sterile hybrid properly identified as *Iris x albicans*. Sometimes these old, bearded irises are considered natives because they have become such a part of our landscapes. 'Early Purple' irises are also found in great quantities and are believed to be a different color form of the same iris. This is the one bearded iris that has done well for me.

I found my cemetery whites at an old abandoned cemetery in Alabama near where Amiable Spouse used to hunt. They had escaped the cemetery and spread down the adjoining hill. Of course, I had permission from the owner to remove a few specimens. Still, I have had a great deal of ribbing about my cemetery flowers. I like them, though, and consider myself lucky to have them in my garden.

I also grow Louisiana irises [13] in selected places in the landscape. Best suited to boggy or wet sites, they sulk in my regular garden soil during the summer. I place them where their unattractive summer foliage is hidden by other plants that emerge as soon as the irises finish blooming. These native irises, of which there are several species, may be had in a range of colors, including the most vivid reds seen among *Iris*.

The Virginia iris (*I. virginica*) grows along the riverbanks in Walton County where Amiable Spouse and I go fishing. I am content to enjoy it as we ride along in the boat. Southern gardeners may also try the Spanish, Italian, Japanese, and Dutch irises, the spurias, and many others. Instead of lamenting the failure of some of the tall bearded irises, we would do well to seek out those that thrive in the humid South.

Easter Lily (*Lilium longiflorum*)

About the end of May, the Easter lilies start blooming. In my flower bed is a collection of these lilies that Amiable Spouse has given me over the years at Easter. They are forced into bloom by the floral industry, and thousands are sold each year. For many years I did not realize that they were hardy perennials. Then I began to notice some in neighbors' yards, so I planted mine the following year. Sure enough, they came up and bloomed the next year and have continued to do so for many years.

Easter lilies respond dramatically to good cultural practices. Mine were doing pretty well, I thought, topping out at about three feet. They were getting pretty crowded, however, so I decided to divide them. First I prepared a new bed by digging the area and carefully removing all competing roots. Then I dug in generous amounts of peat moss and cow manure and sprinkled the entire bed with slow-release fertilizer. Into this newly prepared bed went my Easter lilies. The following year they grew to an amazing six feet tall and had masses of white trumpets all up and down their stems. They were a sight to behold until a strong wind laid them down on their pretty faces. There's a lesson to be learned here. Stake your tall lilies if you want them upright.

I thought I had learned that lesson well, or maybe I just hoped that the following spring wouldn't bring such a strong wind. At any rate, spring came and with it the lilies. Every time I passed them I was reminded that they needed to be staked, but somehow the right time never came, or I was busy with other tasks. In any event, they didn't get staked. The winds never came, but some of the towering spikes met another kind of misfortune.

Neighborhood cats have discovered that they can lurk among the shrubbery near my bird feeders and occasionally catch an unsuspecting bird. My dogs have learned where these wily creatures hang out, and when they are allowed in the front yard they sniff them out and chase them from their hiding places. Well, wouldn't you know that about the time the Easter lilies were ready to put on their show, the dogs found a cat under a nearby azalea. Out the cat ran with the dogs in hot pursuit—right through the middle of my lilies and into the woods beyond. Now, I couldn't really punish the dogs. They were doing their duty. The fault was mine! I never did get around to staking the lilies. Ah, well, win some, lose some. Maybe next time.

Few plants so richly reward good treatment. Down the street some Easter lilies grow in a bed where they have been for many years. Obviously the soil was not amended when the lilies were planted, nor are they fertilized regularly. These lilies grow about 12 inches tall and produce maybe one or two small trumpets at the tip of each stalk. No need to stake these lilies!

L. longiflorum is native in subtropical brushlands of Japan and Taiwan. Often bulbs grow in shallow pockets of soil just above the high tide line where spray from the waves splashes on the foliage. In the South they are an excellent choice for planting near the Gulf or Atlantic seacoast, for they are very salt tolerant. The fragrant lilies die down in the heat of summer. At this time the stalks may be removed. Fertilize at the first sign of growth next spring, and as Amiable Spouse sometimes says, echoing a famous ball player, "It's déjà vu all over again!"

Oriental Lily (*Lilium*, Oriental Hybrids) [17]

Several years ago I visited a friend's garden. We were walking around looking at her garden and remarking about this flower and that as gardeners often do. I was impressed as I always am when I visit a much-loved garden. When we walked into the back yard, however, I was conscious of a fragrance that pervaded the whole area. We continued to walk, and I tried to sniff it out.

Finally I had to ask, "What is that perfume?"

My friend replied offhandedly, "Oh, that's the 'Stargazer' lily."

At that moment, I knew that I would have one of these lilies. I had to have it! There was no choice. Life became a studied exercise in the pursuit of this elusive wonder. My first question at every nursery pertained to the object of my quest. I couldn't find it, and I was becoming desperate.

Finally the friendly mail carrier came to the rescue when he delivered a catalog from Wayside Gardens. There, inside the colorful pages, I found it. Listed with the Oriental lilies, the caption promised unsurpassed heavenly fragrance, vibrant pink color, and elegant form. Well, the rest is history. Have it I did, and several more just like it. In addition to 'Stargazer', other Oriental lilies struck my fancy, such as 'Casa Blanca'. Its enormous pure white flowers accented by rusty anthers beckoned to me from the glossy pages. I filled out the order form and off it went. Today both 'Stargazer' and 'Casa Blanca' [17] lend their considerable charm to my summer garden. They are some of my most loved garden treasures.

Oriental lilies prefer a slightly acidic soil enriched with compost or other organic matter. Full morning sun is preferred, but flowers last longer if they have some protection from hot, afternoon sun. Well-drained soil is necessary, but an inch or so of water per week will keep them growing well. Mulch will conserve moisture and block out weeds. Slow-release fertilizer added at the start of the growing season will last until bloom is over. A second application after flowers are gone will help them store up energy for next year's flowers.

'Casa Blanca' and 'Stargazer' are only two of the selections available. Still on my wish list is a beautiful selection that is white with a golden band running down the center of each petal. According to the catalogs, it bears the largest, most fragrant flowers of all. *Lilium auratum* var. *platyphyllum* 'Kimona Strain', it's called. That's a mouthful, to say the least, but the cumbersome name makes it no less beautiful.

There's a 'Golden Stardust' and an Oriental Lily Mix that has several different colors. Other named varieties include red pink 'Acapulco', 'Imperial Gold', 'Soft Moonbeam', 'Trance', 'Olivia', and many others.

Some references suggest that Oriental lilies may be short lived in gardens of the coastal South. 'Casa Blanca' and 'Stargazer' have flourished for me about six years. Both have increased in size and now form large clumps. I wouldn't care, however, if they were annuals. I'd still have them, for nothing else quite measures up when it's a beautiful Oriental lily you're a-hankering for.

Tiger Lily (Lilium lancifolium)

"Tiger Alley!" the grandchildren shout as they speed down the path that leads to the great tiger lilies. Down past Zebra Grass Meadow they run, and on past Monkey Grass Veldt. Eventually they dash by Spider Lily Savannah and Elephant Ear Jungle. Screaming like banshees, they tear down the path. "Bet'cha they can't catch me!" they shriek. One never knows what might be lurking in Mimi's garden!

The tiger lilies are about five feet tall this year, though frequently their stature is less imposing. Transplanted into improved soil last fall, they sprang forth with renewed vigor and energy. These hardy garden lilies have been grown for centuries in Japan, and they thrive in the acid soils of the South. Since they are sterile hybrids (probably a cross between *L. leichtlinii* and *L.* x *maculatum*), tiger lilies carry extra chromosomes (a triploid set), which results in increased stamina and resistance to viruses that affect other lilies. Consequently, gardeners are cautioned to keep tiger lilies away from other members of the tribe. They carry the virus that may kill other lilies, but the vigorous tiger lily remains unaffected.

Tiger lilies bear many pendulous, orange flowers spotted with black. Bulbils formed in the axils of the leaves provide an easy means of propagation. These black bulbils may be left to fall on the ground, or they can be planted in containers where they will sprout the following year. Grown in this way, they offer irresistible potted specimens for plant sales or to increase one's own stock. I had a few potted in this manner that I intended to donate for a fund-raiser at our garden club's district meeting. They did not make it to the sale. My garden club buddies snatched them up on sight. I will start some more this year. They will be handy to pass out in a couple of years when visitors to my garden take a fancy to them. Meanwhile, they will stay in their pots under the grapevine where they will take care of themselves until they are adopted. Perish the thought that one of my tiger lilies should expire when so little is required to assure its perpetuity!

My tiger lilies came from a friend and fellow gardener, Virginia Wilkes. While visiting her one day, I admired them growing in her garden. She picked off a handful of bulbils, and I carried them home and planted them in a container until they were large enough to plant in the garden. That was several years ago. Still, Virginia and I visit each other's gardens every year or so. Always I come home with some horticultural treasure. Virginia and her memory are a part of my garden for as long as I am able to remember. (Recently I have begun to wonder just how much longer this may be!)

Although orange is most commonly seen, other colors are available. At one time I had one that was very pale yellow, and it was quite lovely, though it lacked the stature and presence of the ordinary orange variety. Finally, one year, it just didn't come back. Burpee offers a collection that includes pink, red, white, and orange. Floraholic that I am, they tempt me unmercifully.

I like my tiger lilies in a bed mostly to themselves. They need a strong background against which to show to best advantage. My great fig tree serves such a purpose. Equally suitable would be a tall fence or green hedge of holly or wax myrtle. Tiger lilies need something in front of them, too; something that will tie the tall spikes of flowers to the ground and give them a foundation. Imagine them behind a planting of Agastache 'Honey Bee Blue', or even behind a low-growing hedge.

However they are grown, they will perform well if offered modestly prepared soil and protection from hot afternoon sun. Tiger lilies are favorite perennials for a good reason. They're unbeatable!

Society Garlic (*Tulbaghia violacea*) [18]

For many years I have enjoyed growing society garlic. The lavender, star-shaped blossoms arise in clusters on erect stalks to about two feet. Held well above the grassy clump of foliage, these delightful flowers are a constant presence in my garden from spring until the frost cuts them down in late fall.

Society garlic is a multipurpose plant. It excels as a long-blooming perennial, and it is edible. Hardly a salad graces my table that does not have a few of the tasty flowers and garlicky leaves sprinkled on it. The leaves can be used in the same way as garlic or onion chives.

Society garlic excels in full sun and well-drained, light, sandy soil. Its bulbs can be divided every four or five years, but I have not found this necessary. Whenever I want some in new beds, I divide existing clumps and reset them. The clumps grow slowly larger. Never, however, has it shown any tendency toward invasiveness. As a landscape plant it is unsurpassed. At the front of one of my beds, its delicate flowers are a lacy counterpoint against the solid hedge behind it. In the herb garden, its continuous bloom adds color to a group of plants where bloom is the exception rather than the rule. Its easy-care nature has made it a favorite for landscaping areas where low maintenance is important.

No pest has ever been persistent enough on this plant to require my attention. It performs well in front of one of my rental houses where it receives no supplemental irrigation. The city of Fort Walton Beach, Florida, uses it in the median of Highway 98, where it puts on a good show for the automobiles whizzing past 24 hours a day. What a stouthearted little soldier!

Rain Lily, Fairy Lily (*Zephyranthes* spp.) [48]

In spring the native rain lilies bloom. Often called fairy lilies, zephyr lilies, or atamasco lilies, they are small members of the amaryllis family. Most frequently they are sold as *Zephyranthes robusta*, but they may also be found in catalogs and nurseries under the names *Z. rosea*, *Z. grandiflora*, *Habranthus robustus*, or *H. tubispathus*. No matter which name is used, they are a delightful addition to the garden. After the first major rain of summer, expect these small lilies to erupt upon the scene. Spikes of rosy or white trumpets rise about nine inches above grassy foliage. Following the first big rain, the show is magnificent. Afterwards they bloom sporadically through-out the summer. They bestow one of nature's delightful little surprises.

Rain lilies thrive in full sun to partial shade. They appreciate frequent watering and fertile, moisture-retentive soil to which organic matter has been added. Though best performance results from these conditions, they are highly adaptable and will grow well in less favorable circumstances.

According to Scott Ogden in his book *Garden Bulbs for the*

South, the rain lily most frequently met in cultivation is probably *Z. grandiflora*. Its origins are obscure, but it is surely a native of tropical America. Although it is sterile and refuses to seed, it has been spread around by generations of gardeners and is naturalized in our area.

Ogden further asserts that what the nursery trade calls *Zephyranthes robusta* is actually *Habranthus robustus* [48]. I suspect that it is this flower that blooms so reliably in my yard. It sets seed prolifically, and seeds should be planted when they ripen because their viability is very short. Propagation is also easy by division of established clumps. Bulbs may be planted anytime, but fall is ideal.

If you are unsure whether your rain lilies are *Zephyranthes* or *Habranthus*, two clues may reveal their identity. *Habranthus* holds its flowers sideways like the amaryllis, but *Zephyranthes* holds its blossom straight up with no bend between the stem and the flower. *Habranthus* sets seeds, and *Zephyranthes* does not.

Rain lilies are useful in the landscape in several ways. Their short, grassy foliage and low stature make them ideal border plants. They may be massed in the landscape or planted in beds with other bulbs. One way that I enjoy them is scattered throughout the landscape where their intermittent flowering habit provides charming surprises throughout the growing season.

A naturally occurring species of rain lily is *Z. citrina*, the most common yellow rain lily in cultivation. It is sometimes sold as *Z. sulfurea*, and bears golden yellow blooms from midsummer through fall. *Z. candida*, the white rain lily, is sometimes called autumn crocus because its flowers appear in late summer and continue well into fall.

Z. atamasco is the species that Amiable Spouse observes in the spring woods during turkey hunting season. He encounters these beautiful Southeastern natives in woodsy, poorly drained areas. Sometimes they bloom in masses at the bottom of a hill, or they may fill a damp hammock with large, funnel-shaped white blooms. Rapidly spreading clumps of grassy foliage green up the winter landscape, and they become dormant with the arrival of summer.

Hybridizers have created many cultivars of these tiny amaryllids. 'Ruth Page' is a deep rose color. 'Ellen Korsakoff' sports peach-colored blossoms, and 'Capricorn' is burnt orange. 'Grandjax' is a vigorous pale pink, and 'Aquarius' shines in the landscape with creamy yellow flowers. 'Prairie Sunset' is an ever-blooming orange blend. These hybrids are only rarely available from hobbyists and specialty bulb dealers.

Some people enjoy growing rain lilies in pots. One grower in Fairview, Tennessee, fills the saucers under her containerized lilies with water whenever they get slightly dry. She feeds them every two weeks with a liquid fertilizer that is low in nitrogen but high in phosphorus. This strategy keeps them in continuous bloom.

Zephyranthes literally means "flowers of the west wind." They are beautiful, tough garden plants. Don't pass them by if you have a friend who is willing to share or can obtain bulbs from other sources. Add them to your garden for years of dependable beauty.

Ginger (*Zingiberaceae*) [12, 14, 19, 20, 21]

When most Southerners think of gingers, they think of tropical oddities that can be seen only in southern Florida or such places as Hawaii. They may be acquainted with the delightfully fragrant white butterfly ginger, but many will be surprised to learn that it is only one of many gingers that grow well in Southern gardens. Most gingers have rhizomes, fleshy horizontal underground stems, which can survive freezing temperatures and resprout in spring if the ground does not freeze. A good mulch of bark, pine needles, or other coarse organic material will help to prevent damage.

The butterfly gingers (*Hedychium* spp.) [12, 14, 20] are well suited to the coastal South. Most grow quite large—from three to eight feet. This makes them an excellent choice for the back of the border. Available colors include orange, pink, gold, salmon, and bicolor. Flowers continue to bloom after they are cut, so they are long lasting in a vase.

Pinecone ginger (*Zingiber zerumbet*) [21] is also easy to grow. Tropical looking 18-inch leaves fan out from stems six feet tall. While the plant itself looks much like butterfly ginger, the flowers are completely different. Clublike structures resembling pine cones arise from the rhizomes on stalks of their own. The actual flowers are small, yellowish blossoms that appear between the "scales" of the "pine cone." The "pine cone" gradually turns from green to red and is a favorite of floral designers.

Dancing lady gingers (*Globba* spp.) are easy perennials. Plants range from one to three feet in height, which makes them more manageable in the flower border than their tall-growing cousins. Delicate white, yellow, or lavender flowers hang from the tips of each shoot. New plantlets formed at the end of each flower cluster fall to the ground and root, enabling them to spread quickly.

One of my favorites is the beautiful Hawaiian, or hidden ginger (*Curcuma* spp.) [19]. The flowers come up from the ground like the pinecone ginger, but they are covered with fluted petals of various colors. In some varieties flowers are hidden by the foliage, hence the name. Some, however, shoot up from the ground before the foliage comes up or are held above the foliage. These plants have leaves that resemble those of bananas, and height varies from ten inches to seven feet. My beautiful 'Giant Plume' [19] thrills me each May with its large inflorescence of electric mauve.

Another group of gingers hardy to our area is the peacock ginger (*Kaempferia* spp.). Leaves of this diminutive ginger hug the ground and look like a jeweled prayer plant. Leaf markings may be lavender or purple, white or silver, and texture may be pleated or smooth. Rarely exceeding eight to ten inches tall, this ginger promises to be a beautiful ground cover for shady areas. Lavender to purple four-petaled flowers bloom all summer.

Some spiral gingers (*Costus* spp.) are hardy in the coastal South. The varieties with green leaves seem hardier than those with variegated leaves. In my garden, the beautiful spiral ginger with variegated leaves did not return from the roots after its first winter. I should have cut some of the stems and placed them horizontally in soil. They, unlike any of the other gingers, would have rooted at each joint. If I had kept them in the greenhouse, I would still have these beauties. Live and learn.

I do not expect shell ginger (*Alpinia* spp.) to bloom in my garden. According to Dr. Rick Schoellhorn, horticultural researcher from the University of Florida, if the shell gingers are killed to the ground during the winter, it takes a year or more for them to grow back to flowering size. Blooms may be seen if these gingers are overwintered in a greenhouse or other protected location and not allowed to die down.

By and large, the gingers are mostly pest free and easy to grow. They do best in moist soil and need some protection from the hot afternoon sun. Flower heads may be cut off when they are finished. Fertilizer needs can be met by broadcasting commercial 6-6-6 or 10-10-10 fertilizer with minor elements around the plants once a month or so during the growing season. With just a little care, gardens throughout the coastal South can have some of these lovely plants to embellish their gardens.

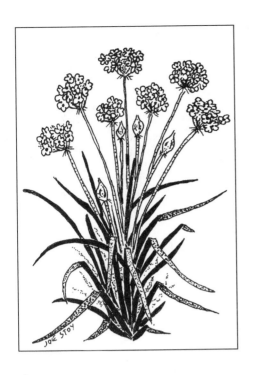

Herbs

Of all the parts of my garden, perhaps none brings as much pleasure as the herb garden. I find reasons to visit it frequently. Sometimes I just like to walk among the plants and run my hands over the various herbs to feel their diverse textures and smell their sumptuous scents. Sometimes I collect a few snippets for a salad or for seasoning a special dish. Visitors are usually treated to a sniff of this and a whiff of that. It is a sensory experience, perhaps more than any other kind of gardening.

Growing herbs is a year-round pleasurable experience. Though I have a formal herb garden divided into four quadrants with pathways between and a birdbath in the middle, my herbs are not restricted to this specialty garden. Some are in containers, and some serve as ground covers and edgings for various areas. Some of my favorite perennials, in fact, are herbs. Come to think of it, there are very few landscape needs that one herb or another cannot adequately fill.

A bit of learning must take place, however, if herbs are to be grown successfully in the coastal South. I remember my first experiences. To begin with I didn't know which herbs were annual and which were perennial. I didn't know which ones were winter hardy and which ones were best planted in spring. Learning was a slow process. One thing that helped me more than anything else, I think, was a book entitled *Southern Herb Growing* by Madalene Hill and Gwen Barclay. This book continues to be my favorite reference, and I highly recommend it to aspiring herb gardeners.

Basil (*Ocimum basilicum*)

Basil is perennial in frost-free climates, but in our neck of the woods it is an annual that bites the dust at the first hint of frost. It is an excellent addition to the herb garden or the flower border. *Ocimum*, the genus name of sweet basil, is from a Greek verb that means "to be fragrant." The species name, *basilicum*, comes from a Greek word meaning "king or prince." It is often called the "king of herbs." That comes as no surprise, for it is one of the most popular of all herbs.

Four basic types of garden basils are sweet green basil, dwarf green basil, purple-leaved basil, and scented-leaf basil. The most widely grown is *O. basilicum*, or sweet basil. It grows to about two feet tall, and its large, two- to three-inch-long leaves complement many kinds of dishes and combine with other herbs for pleasing taste effects.

Dwarf basil (*O. basilicum minimum*) reaches a compact 10 to 12 inches high. 'Spicy Globe' and 'Green Bouquet' are two popular dwarf cultivars. 'Spicy Globe' has leaves about half an inch long and grows naturally into rounded, globe shapes. Perhaps most ornamental are the purple-leaved basils. Three popular cultivars are 'Dark Opal', 'Purple Ruffles', and 'Red Rubin'. Leaves on these basils tend to be ruffled, frilled, or deeply cut. Flowers are pink to lavender purple.

Scented-leafed basils offer different aromas to the species. Lemon basil has a very definite lemon flavor, especially in 'Sweet Dani', which has been an All-America Selections winner. Grayish green leaves and white flowers make the plant ornamental. Cinnamon basil and anise basil round out the potpourri of scents.

Basils are easy to start by sowing seeds directly into the ground. Select a sunny spot and sow seeds about half an inch deep in good garden soil after all danger of frost is past. Keep moist until seeds germinate. Thin according to package directions. Pinch out growing tips when seedlings are three to four inches tall to encourage bushiness. Basils are also easily started from cuttings that root quickly in damp soil.

In sandy or infertile soil basil should be fertilized lightly but regularly for continuous growth. If soil was amended before planting, fertilizer may not be necessary. Flowers should be cut off to insure continuous leaf production in a culinary garden. Water enough to insure about an inch of water a week for best growth.

Basil plants are readily available at garden centers or nurseries. Choose young, compact plants. If they tend toward legginess, cut them back after they have been planted. Plant on a cloudy, calm day or late in the afternoon. Water thoroughly to settle soil around the plants.

Basil is a natural in the kitchen. Many cooks chop fresh basil and sprinkle it on tomatoes with a dash of premium olive oil. Freshly harvested leaves add pizzazz to lettuce salads and are the perfect addition to classic pesto sauce. Basil butter adds a surprise to the palate when served on hot biscuits or slathered over a fresh ear of boiled corn-on-the-cob. Make by creaming together one stick of unsalted butter and one to three tablespoons of dried, crushed basil or two to six tablespoons of fresh, minced basil. Refrigerate for at least an hour before serving. Basil vinegar can be made by heating vinegar in an enamel pan, pouring it into a bottle, and adding several sprigs of basil. Use this concoction after it has aged a couple of weeks to spice up a salad dressing.

Basil fits well in many areas of the garden. Plant it in the flower border if you wish. Blossoms attract many beneficial insects. The purple-leafed varieties are beautiful in any part of the garden. If nothing else, plant one in a container and set it near the kitchen door so that it will be handy for seasoning or just for pinching and sniffing. It's a pleasure I allow myself with my favorite herbs. I need no other reason to grow this delightful plant.

Bay *(Laurus nobilis)*

Finally I've decided I'd better move the bay to a more protected location. After all this time, I'd hate to lose it. Started from a wee rooted snippet ordered from a mail-order nursery several years ago, it now stands about four feet tall. All these years it has lived in a pot. Its first home was a small, six-inch container. Gradually it grew to fill its present 14-inch clay pot.

All summer the bay lived at the back side of a flower bed. There it received water when it rained or when I thought to drag the hose that way. At the beginning of the growing season I sprinkled a bit of slow-release, pelleted fertilizer in the pot, and from that time, it was left alone. Now, however, a frost threatens, and I must protect it from freezing.

Bay has a long and colorful history. Apollo, the Greek god of the sun, was madly in love with the beautiful Daphne. No matter how relentlessly he tried, he could never win her favor. Poor Apollo was doomed to failure in this love affair, for Cupid had shot Daphne with an arrow that made her hate him. Daphne's father, to help her escape Apollo's determined pursuit, changed her into a laurel tree. Apollo fell upon his knees before this tree and declared it eternally sacred.

The laurel tree later became a sign of

glory, honor, and greatness. Men and women of Greece and Rome wove wreaths of bay to crown the heads of their scholars, poets, rulers, triumphant warriors, and athletic victors. Champions of the first Olympics in 776 B.C. were presented laurel garlands.

In my kitchen, a bay leaf is always added to the water when cooking dried beans. For a nourishing meal of Southern soul food, wash and sort a bag of great northerns, white limas, red beans, or other dried beans of your choice. Place them in a crock pot with plenty of water. Throw in a ham bone or ham hock and add a bit of salt and a bay leaf. Cook all day. Serve with sliced onions and crispy cornbread. To make the meal truly memorable, serve fresh cabbage slaw seasoned with salt, pepper, and mayonnaise dressing.

Many cooks put a bay leaf in nearly every soup or stew. They're added to Spanish, Creole, and French soups, stews, marinades, and sauces. Add them to shrimp and crab boils, or toss a couple of bay leaves into the cavity of chicken and turkey before baking. Amiable Spouse must have a bay leaf when he cooks up his special recipe of barbecued beans.

When I moved the bay to the shelter of my covered patio, I noticed that a few small branches had died. I removed them but did not throw away the leaves. They were a beautiful tan color, still in good shape, and perfect for using in the junior gardeners' potpourri bowls. With a sprig of lavender, a bit of eucalyptus, a sprig of rosemary, a few juniper berries, and assorted small cones, they had a fine introduction to fragrant herbs.

Bay is a multitalented plant. Leaves may be boiled in water, steeped for a bit, and the liquid added to bath water to sooth the skin. A friend pushes bay leaves under the shelf paper in her cabinets and in little hidden nooks and crannies all around her kitchen. She maintains that they repel insects. Maybe so. I remember that Grandmother kept bay leaves in her flour barrel.

Do not confuse this bay with Carolina bay or redbay (*Persea borbonia*). While the leaves of Carolina bay have long been used either fresh or dried to flavor soups, stews, and seafood, they are quite different from *Laurus nobilis*, which is native to the Mediterranean and marginally hardy in the coastal South. Carolina bay is a completely hardy native that is frequent in swamps and wet woods from Florida along the coastal plain to Virginia and Texas. It grows 20 to 30 feet tall and appears to be quite salt tolerant.

My bay (*Laurus nobilis*) is in a pot because I'm afraid I'll lose it in freezing weather. Supposedly, mature plants are hardy to about 15°F. I never really expect to see such a temperature in my garden, but I hesitate. I do not trust those weather gods with my bay. Maybe one day I'll get brave and plant it out, but until that time it seems content in its pot. Better yet, perhaps I'll get a new one to start in a little pot and plant my large specimen out. That way I'll never be without it.

Maybe I'll keep one beside my front door. According to Culpeper, the British herbalist, a man standing near a bay tree cannot be hurt by witches, the devil, thunder, or lightning. A little bit of insurance couldn't hurt.

Borage (*Borago officinalis*)

Looking for something pretty for the herb garden? Something that will bloom and embellish the garden and stimulate flagging appetites at the table? A plant that will delight the eye and the palate? One that will cheer the heart and lift the spirits? A bit of borage will surely do the trick. Since Elizabethan times a few borage flowers have been floated in wine, and it has been reported that this practice

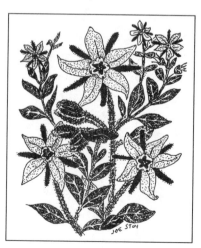

"maketh men merrie." That sounds reasonable to me, because a bit of wine maketh me merry, and the beauty of the blossoms lifts my spirits as well.

According to the ancients, drinking borage tea gave instant courage. Wives and sweethearts offered their men cups of borage tea before the battle, and they rode off to war full of courage. Modern research has revealed that the plant stimulates the adrenal glands. Maybe the ancients knew what they were doing.

Borage is a favorite herb for embellishing salads and summer dishes. Creative cooks find many uses for the cucumber-flavored herb. Sprinkle a few of the sky-blue, star-shaped flowers atop a salad for a special zing. Scatter a few on deviled eggs for extra pizzazz. Freeze a few flowers in ice cubes to sparkle in cold beverages. Candy the dainty petals to make delicious decorations for cakes and other desserts. Float a few blossoms in chilled vegetable soups.

For a taste-tempting treat, cream together an eight-ounce package of softened cream cheese, a sprinkling of garlic salt, and a tablespoon of milk. Then stir in a quarter cup of chopped bell pepper and a couple of tablespoons of shredded carrots or cucumbers. Spread this mixture over toasted miniature bagels and top them with young borage leaves and flowers. Yum!

Borage leaves should be eaten when they are young. Older leaves develop prickly hairs that can irritate the skin. The hairy sepals should be removed from flowers before they are used. Young leaves can be eaten raw or lightly steamed, boiled, or sautéed. Stems can be peeled and used like celery. The flavor complements cheese, fish, poultry, vegetables, green salads, and dressings.

Borage is easily started from seed planted in spring. It grows best in full sun and fertile, moist soil. Sow seeds of this annual herb shallowly and thin so that plants are 12 to 18 inches apart. Although borage does not transplant very successfully, it reseeds reliably. New plants spring up around a mature plant. I often pull up the old plant and let the new ones take over.

Even gardeners who eschew eating flowers may wish to plant borage near their vegetable gardens or orchards for pollination purposes. Bees are attracted by the flowers, and it helps them make delicious honey. Butterflies, too, come in for their share of the nectar.

In addition to all the uses for borage that I have described above, I have uncovered evidence that it was once used to treat lunacy. Hmm. I wonder if it works.

Chives (*Allium schoenoprasum*)

A restaurant, I used to think, was the only place I could get a baked potato sprinkled with fresh chives. Imagine my delight when a gardener friend sprinkled chives over giblet gravy and served it from a beautiful gravy boat! Then picture me, if you can, when I learned that I could grow my own supply of chives to use whenever I wanted!

Almost nothing in the herb garden is as easy to use as chives. Simply cut the slender leaves from the plant with sharp scissors. Rinse under cold water and pat dry. Snip the leaves finely. Then sprinkle them liberally over egg and cheese dishes, starchy vegetables, meats, sauces, soups, or any other dish enhanced by a delicate onion flavor. Be sure, however, not to heat or cook chives. Cooking destroys the flavor, aroma, vitamin C content, and beneficial digestive properties. The rule is to add minced leaves after everything is cooked.

Extra chives may be frozen. Kept this way, they retain more flavor than dried. To freeze, cut fresh chives into small pieces and place them in an ice cube tray filled with water. After cubes are frozen, they may be emptied into plastic bags. To use, put a cube of the frozen chives in a strainer until the ice melts and drains away.

For a flavorful herb butter, add one tablespoon of finely chopped chives and one tablespoon of minced parsley to one-half pound of butter or margarine. Serve over baked or steamed potatoes, hot breads, or steamed vegetables.

Chives have many uses besides the obvious culinary ones. They are high in vitamin C, folic acid, and potassium. Research shows that chives also stimulate the body's digestion of fat. Eaten regularly, they may help lower blood cholesterol levels. Because of high concentrations of sulfur compounds, the herb may also help the body fight bacteria that can cause disease.

Chives are almost foolishly easy to

grow. They like light, rich, moist soil and plenty of sun. Cut them back frequently to promote thick growth. Do not worry about cutting an entire plant to within an inch or so of the ground. Established plants rebound quickly. New growth is evident the next day!

When started from seed, the new sprouts look like fine, hairlike leaves. These seedlings usually take about a year to reach maturity. If you wish to harvest chives in less than a year, select plants from the garden center and set them out in the garden. When they are established, harvest can begin.

Established plantings should be divided every three or four years. A freeze will nip the tender leaves to the ground, but they return reliably from roots. After they have died down, a protective mulch of pine needles or other light mulch will be beneficial. Grow a clump in a container on a sunny windowsill for a continuous supply.

Low-growing chives make attractive and useful border plants. Pretty lavender, globelike flowers bloom in spring and are delicious shredded into salads or floated in soups. After flowers fade, but before seeds are set, cut the entire plant down nearly to the ground with sharp scissors. Within a week or so, they will have grown enough to begin harvesting the flavorful leaves as garnishes for summer dishes.

Don't, like me, use ignorance as a reason for not having fresh chives whenever they are wanted. Now you know. No excuses!

Cilantro/Coriander (*Coriandrum sativum*)

In the middle of winter, cilantro/coriander grows vigorously. Used in cooking since ancient times, it is a member of the parsley (Apiaceae formerly Umbelliferae) family, which includes parsley, carrots, fennel, and dill. Lower leaves of the plant, commonly called cilantro or Chinese parsley, are round with scalloped edges. These bright green, lacy leaves are reason enough to grow this herb, and it is perfectly winter hardy in our area.

As spring and warmer weather approach, the plants shoot up, and secondary foliage much different from the plant's lower leaves develops. Lacy umbels of pale mauve, pink, or white flowers attract bees and other beneficial insects, including lacewings, ladybugs, hoverflies, and parasitic wasps. The flowers will form fruits whose seeds are harvested for the spice we know as coriander.

Cilantro may be planted as soon as winter's approach brings cool weather. Directly sown into a prepared bed, it soon sprouts and begins to produce its prettily scalloped leaves. These leaves are a staple ingredient in many Indian, Asian, and Mexican dishes. Fresh chopped leaves are a flavorful addition to guacamole, bean dishes, fried rice, salsa, and stir fried foods. Leaves should be added late in cooking as the flavor cooks out at high temperatures. Leaves are best used fresh. Much of the flavor and aroma is lost when they are dried. However, some aficionados blend the leaves in salad oil and freeze the mixture with good results.

Seeds should be harvested when flowers turn about two-thirds brown. Cut the flower heads and tie them in bundles. Hang them upside down with a paper sack tied over them to catch the seeds as they dry. Coriander seeds are aromatic and have slight hints of citrus. Do not, however, form your opinion of these seeds until they are thoroughly dry. The green seeds have a "stink bug" odor, but develop a warm, nutty flavor when dried. The older they are, the nuttier and more flavorful they become. Dried seeds should be stored in the refrigerator since they are prone to have weevils. Crushed or whole ripe coriander seeds may be used to season soups, sauces, salad, fish, meat, fowl, and game dishes. In potpourri these seeds impart a pleasant, lemony scent.

Like many herbs, coriander has medicinal uses besides its culinary applications. Three teaspoons of freshly crushed coriander seed steeped 10 to 15 minutes in boiling water makes a tea said to soothe an upset stomach or promote good digestion. Poultices made from crushed seeds reportedly relieve pains associated with rheumatism. In modern medicine, coriander is sometimes used as a flavoring agent that masks the taste of other compounds and calms the irritating effects on the stomach that certain medicines produce.

If I had no herb garden and no yard, I surely would have cilantro/coriander in a container. Then all I would need would be a sunny spot and a bit of soil. The old poem that says "And all I need is a tall ship and a star to steer her by" might be reworded to read, "And all I need is a small pot and some soil to grow it in."

Dill (Anethum graveolens)

As fall approached one year I decided that if I wanted dill in my fall garden I'd better get busy. I had seeds saved from last year's harvest. Fellow gardeners know the doubt associated with saved seeds. Would they sprout? Since I believed that the seeds might not still be viable, I scattered them thickly into my garden plot. Lo and behold, I think every one of them sprouted! Every visitor to my garden was given dill plants, and I potted up several to share with garden club members and junior gardeners. Several were planted in the garden club's butterfly garden. Still, I had more dill than I knew what to do with.

Dill is also a member of the parsley family. It is valued for its flavorful foliage and pungent seeds. The name comes from an old Norse word, "dilla," which means "to lull." Frequently in times past, it was prescribed as a tea to treat insomnia and digestive problems. Today its essential oil is used in pharmaceuticals, cosmetics, and liqueurs.

Dill is a delightful herb with many culinary uses. Fresh or dried, it adds a distinctive flavor to salads, fish, vegetable casseroles, and soups. Dill seeds add zest to breads, cheeses, and salad dressings. Of course, it is best known as a pickling herb for cucumbers, and it is also a popular seasoning for green beans, carrots, and beets.

In much of the country dill is a summer herb. For us, though, barring an unusually harsh winter, it is best grown in the winter garden. Common garden dill will grow up to four feet tall in good garden soil in full sun. Dwarf versions grow from 24 to 36 inches tall, making them a better candidate for containers. Dill will grow all winter and bloom in the first warm days of spring and then set seed. For a continuous supply of dill through the summer, a new crop can be planted every few weeks. In the heat, dill will flower rapidly, but young plants can be harvested before they go to seed.

In the South, dill and cucumbers often do not mature simultaneously. However, the herb is easily harvested and kept until needed. Flower heads, leaves, and stalks may be harvested, cut into pieces, and preserved in plastic or glass containers. White vinegar should be poured over the dill and stored tightly covered in a cool dark place. When the cucumbers are ripe, drain the dill and pack the pieces with the cukes. Use some of the vinegar. Replace any unused dill and cover again with white vinegar. Preserved in this way, it will keep for years. It can also be preserved by layering with pickling salt in a covered jar in the refrigerator. Simply wash the leaves when you are ready to use them.

Dill may be dried and stored in a tightly sealed jar. It can be dried in the microwave or food dehydrator, or bunches of stems can be hung upside down in a dark, dry, airy place until they are crumbly. Dill can also be frozen by cutting the leaves and long stems into sections short enough to fit into plastic bags. They will keep in the freezer for up to six months.

Be sure to leave some dill in the garden long enough for seed heads to form. Collect seed heads when most of the seeds have formed, usually about two to three weeks after blossoming starts. Some of the flowers may still be blooming. Hang the seed heads upside down by their stems in a paper bag. Seeds will fall to the bottom of the bag where they can be easily collected.

Dill is a beneficial plant for the garden even if none of it is eaten. Combined with flowers in the flower bed or border, its foliage provides a soft background for other sun-loving annuals. Its yellow umbrella-like flowers are great additions to bouquets. Beneficial insects, including bees, parasitic wasps, and tachinid flies, are attracted to dill. In orchards it attracts insects that control codling moths and tent caterpillars. Wherever it blooms, it contributes to the welfare of neighboring plants.

I include dill in the butterfly garden where it attracts the Eastern black swallowtail butterfly. Its larva, the beautiful parsley worm, feeds on dill and other members of the parsley family. I always plant enough for the butterflies and me.

Fennel (*Foeniculum vulgare*)

Fennel has long been recognized as a desirable plant for the herb garden. Lately, however, folks are planting it in the flower garden where its beauty holds its own with other ornamentals. Bronze-foliaged types of fennel rise from the back of the border with wispy gracefulness. Green varieties are also good mixers with equally fine, ferny foliage.

Planted at the back of the flower bed, bronze fennel provides an airy backdrop for flowers of almost any color. I particularly enjoy it in combination with plants that have bright, chartreuse-colored leaves. 'Margarita' sweet potato (*Ipomoea batatas* 'Margarita') offers a striking contrast in color and texture during the summer. In the winter garden, fennel is striking with ornamental kales and cabbages, pansies, snapdragons, or any other flower with which it is paired. In spring it is stunning with yellow and orange nasturtiums or with pink and purple sweet peas. In fact, I can think of no flower color that would not work with this pretty mixer.

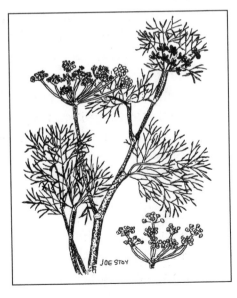

JOE STOY

Fennel is a hardy plant for the coastal South. It will grow all winter. In spring tall spikes of flowers that resemble a yellow version of Queen Anne's lace add to the show. Allow these flowers to set seed. Cut off the flower heads when they are mature and drop them into a paper bag and hang in an airy place until dry. Seeds may be stored for cooking, or they may be planted for a new crop of fennel.

The visual attractiveness of fennel in the garden is not its only allure. Its fresh, aniselike fragrance makes just passing by it a pleasant experience. Even weeding becomes an agreeable exercise when fennel is near. Not the least of its assets is its appeal to Eastern black swallowtail butterflies. Other plants from the Parsley family, such as dill, parsley, and carrot, are also irresistible to the swallowtails. The female lays her eggs on these plants so that the larvae hatch out to their favorite meal. I don't mind this process. By the time the larvae hatch out, the fennel needs cutting back anyway. It recovers quickly. The yellow flowers are hosts to many beneficial insects and pollinators, such as bees and parasitic wasps.

All parts of the fennel plant are edible. Minced leaves add a delightful flavor to salads, eggs, and fish dishes. For something different, sprinkle leaves in a bread pan before dough is added. An unforgettable flavor and aroma will be infused into the finished loaf. The flowers add their flavorful and colorful accompaniment to salads. Seeds may be used in rice or fish dishes.

Various medicinal properties have been attributed to fennel. It is reputed to ease digestive complaints, upper respiratory distress, and colic, to name a few.

Several types of fennel are available. Florence fennel forms a bulblike base considered a delicacy by some. German, Russian, Romanian, and several others may be chosen. Whichever kind you decide to plant will add beauty and interest to your garden. Buy a packet of seed and sow according to package directions, or buy plants ready for the bed at local garden centers. Plant fennel in full sun in loose, well-drained soil amended with organic matter. Give it plenty of room to spread its delicate, finely cut stems, and stand back. It will grow to about five or six feet tall. Walk by often for a sniff, a pinch for the kitchen, or the sight of a caterpillar in the process of transforming itself into a beautiful butterfly.

As always, enjoy! This is, after all, the reason most of us garden.

Garlic Chives (*Allium tuberosum*)

Garlic chives are multitalented plants in the garden. They can be used effectively as blooming perennials where their straplike, blue green leaves contrast nicely with broader leaves of nearby plants even when they are not in bloom. They are a favorite of many floral designers who have discovered that the freshly cut white flowers are long-lasting and pleasantly scented in floral designs. Or they may be used as herbs for flavoring various dishes. I frequently cut the flat leaves and use them in salads, potatoes, and other dishes where more common onion chives might be used. Egg or cheese dishes, starchy vegetables, meats—anything that might benefit from the taste of garlic—is enhanced by the addition of garlic chives.

The flowers, too, may be sprinkled on salads or used as garnishes. Though small, these clusters of pure white, star-shaped flowers have a delicate scent of violets. Flower spikes may be cut and used in dried floral designs as well. Pick them after the seed has set, but before they have completely dried. Hang them upside down inside a paper bag to dry. They can then be spray painted if desired and used like any other flower.

Recently a friend asked me how I prevented garlic chives from taking over my garden. She knew that they reseed prolifically. If blossoms are cut before seeds are formed, gardeners will not be bothered by unwanted plants. Clumps spread slowly, and division is easily accomplished by digging the plants and separating the bulbs into several clumps. These clumps are easy to pot up for friends or plant sales.

Garlic chives grow to two feet tall in almost any soil and are hardy throughout the South. They bloom during the dog days and into the fall, which makes them especially welcome in borders that may be flagging from heat. Garlic chives bloom their hearts out and never miss a beat right through summer's hottest days.

I remember wanting garlic chives a long time before I was able to find plants. I was especially pleased when a friend shared a start of hers with me. They have been one of my all-time garden favorites. During mild winters they are evergreen, but a hard frost nips them back to the ground. However, they recover quickly with spring's warm days. I treasure their perky presence in my garden.

Lavender (*Lavandula* spp.)

I've got the guest room all ready. Amiable Spouse and I are expecting company. Clean sheets and freshly dusted and polished furniture await her. She has fresh towels in the bathroom, sufficient tissue, and lotions, soaps, and potions. Last, but not least, she has a vase of freshly picked lavender on the dresser and in the bathroom. It adds just the right touch of welcome.

After the bouquet has wilted in the vase, I let it dry. Leaves and flowers are stripped from the stems and placed in pretty little bowls to set around the house. They retain their scent for years. When too many bowls of lavender are scattered about, I sew up a few sachet bags and stuff them with a few pinches of lavender. They make my sheets smell good when placed in the closet where they are kept. Tucked in and around the drawer where my table napkins are stored, they add a clean, sweet, but never overpowering fragrance to the linens.

Another of my favorite uses for lavender is making bath bags. They can be fancy and given as gifts, but just for everyday use I tie a bit of lavender in the toe of an old stocking. Sometimes I add a few sprigs of chamomile, lemon balm, mint, or other herbs. The addition of oatmeal or powdered milk adds skin-soothing properties. Tossed into the tub under warm, running water, they make the bath particularly welcome and relaxing.

Only the leaves and flowers of lavender are used in bath bags or sachets. Woody stems can be burned individually as incense sticks or tied in bundles and placed in a basket by the fireplace. Their fragrance can be enjoyed the next time the fire is lit.

For centuries lavender has been a popular garden plant. The scented leaves and flowers are used for making soaps, perfumes, oils, room fresheners, and smelling salts. They are also used for cooking and for teas and flavored drinks. Lavender has several medicinal applications, including its use as a relaxant, antispasmodic, circulatory stimulant, and carminative. Antibacterial and antiseptic attributes make it useful as a germ-killing cleaning agent in and around the house and for cleaning and treating wounds.

What's more, some lavenders grow well in the coastal South. Most of the English lavenders (*Lavandula angustifolia*) are very short lived in our warm, humid climate and are treated as annuals. More success may be had with Spanish lavender (*Lavandula stoechas*) or French lavender (*Lavandula dentata*). French lavender is very tender and must be wintered in a protected place. Spanish lavender is a bit hardier and thrives in the heat and high humidity of our Southern summers.

All lavenders require full sun and very well drained soil. They are happiest in alkaline soil. A bit of lime can be added if soil is too acid. Add a few of these plants to your garden and enjoy the many pleasures they offer. Amiable Spouse likes to keep a plentiful supply on hand because he has learned that it can be used for calming women who are much given to hysteria. He wants to help every way he can.

Lemongrass (*Cymbopogon citratus*)

A large clump of lemongrass has grown at the base of my tall pink crape myrtle for several years. It began with a four-inch pot purchased from a nursery in spring. From there it grew all summer and into the next year. Subsequent divisions have increased my planting significantly and provided many starts for friends and plant sales.

Lemongrass is a large, tropical grass that is marginally hardy in my Zone 8b garden. Frost cuts it back significantly, and I have at times lost major portions of the planting. However, some always sur-

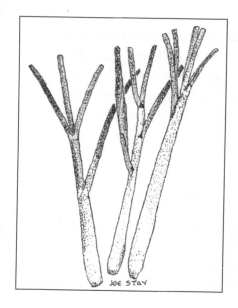
JOE STAY

vives and grows back vigorously the next spring. In areas farther north, it can be cut to the ground in late fall and covered with a thick mulch. In areas where the ground freezes, it can be grown in the summer garden and overwintered in a pot.

All summer lemongrass grows and lends its dark green, grassy gracefulness to my garden. Frost turns it brown, but it continues to hold its place and rustle in the winter wind. In late winter or early spring just before new growth begins, I get out the hedge trimmers and cut the lemongrass back to within a few inches of the ground. It bounds back with vigor to resume its place in the land-scape. Lemongrass grows best in full sun and is drought tolerant once it is established. Propagation is easy by division of the crown. Dig up part of a plant and divide it into chunks four to six inches in diameter. Then plant the divisions in prepared soil and water thoroughly.

Lemongrass is native to southern India and Ceylon, and its rich-ly aromatic leaves are used to season Vietnamese, Thai, and other Asian cuisine. In these regions it is popular in folk medicine and is called fever grass. It is said not only to reduce fever and headache, but also to calm upset stomach and cure athlete's foot and ringworm.

Lemongrass can be used either fresh or dried. Cooks generally use the tender base of the leaf when it is fresh. Slice or chop the bot-tom four to six inches of the leaf and add it to curried sauces, rice and noodle dishes, vegetable stir fries, and casseroles made with chicken or seafood. Fresh leftovers can be placed in plastic bags and frozen.

To dry, lay the leaves in an airy, shady spot until they are com-pletely dry. Chop and store in an airtight container in a cool place. Use the dried leaves for tea by pouring a cup of boiling water over a teaspoon of dried lemongrass. Cover and steep for 10 to 15 minutes, strain, and drink. For a double whammy of its calming effect, take your tea to the tub. Tie chopped leaves in a cotton bag or the toe of an old pair of hose and toss into the tub under running hot water.

Step in, lay your head back, and soak away the troubles of the day as you relax in the lemon-scented water and sip the refreshing tea.

Although lemongrass is considered safe, allergic reactions have been reported after topical use. As always, consult a qualified health professional for treatment of any serious medical conditions or symptoms.

Mexican Mint Marigold (*Tagetes lucida*)

In the herb garden I always pinch a leaf off the Mexican mint marigold and take a sniff. I pass it around when visitors come. They're always enchanted with the licorice scent of the leaves. In spring, and more prolifically in fall, yellow marigold flowers bloom, making it an even more handsome addition to the garden.

This herb is one that I have grown for many years. Sometimes it is labeled Mexican or Spanish tarragon. Other common names include Texas tarragon, pericon, and sweet mace. It is perennial and reliable in Zones 8 to 11. In severe winters it may be killed to the ground, but it bounds back in spring. North of Zone 8 it is grown as an annual or in containers and brought indoors for the winter. In the southern tips of Florida and Texas, it never dies down.

One of my Master Gardener friends once remarked that Mexican mint marigold spreads all over the place. I did not understand her statement at the time. I had always pruned mine after it flowered to keep it compact. Little did I realize that stems lying on the ground would root, or that every seed that fell to the ground would germinate. One particularly busy year, I didn't get around to this task. The next year I understood perfectly what my friend was talking about. Seeds are formed in small, open-ended capsules much like French marigolds. They are easily collected. Just pick off a seed cap-

JOE STOY

sule and turn it upside down. They fall out readily. It is also easily propagated from stem cuttings, or it can be divided.

Mexican mint marigold is the South's answer to French tarragon (*Artemisia dracunculus*). True tarragon does not grow well in our heat and humidity. But never mind. Mexican mint marigold may be used instead. It is a little stronger than French tarragon and has more of an anise flavor. The pretty yellow flowers are a tasty addition to fresh green salads. A few leaves flavor a pot of chicken soup nicely. The flavor is an important element in remoulade, tartar and bearnaise sauces, and in French salad dressing. A soothing, aromatic herbal tea may be made from the leaves, and it is useful in herbal vinegars.

Mexican mint marigold is an attractive landscape ornamental. In the perennial border its shiny leaves and little golden flowers make a mannerly statement. The half-hardy, semiwoody subshrub grows 18 to 30 inches tall. Plant in well-drained soil in sun or partial sun. Once established it is fairly drought tolerant.

The Signet marigolds (*T. tenuifolia*) are closely related. They include the citrus-scented 'Lemon Gem' and 'Orange Gem' cultivars. They have delicate, fragrant leaves and small yellow or orange flowers.

Nigella, Love-in-a-Mist (*Nigella damascena*)

Some of the most outstanding flowers in coastal gardens are started in the fall. These hardy, fall-planted annuals are often overlooked as a source for spring color. Sometimes thinking about spring during the fall when everything is preparing for winter is difficult for the gardener. Such planning ahead is necessary, however, if we are to enjoy some of spring's most delightful flowers.

One such plant is nigella, or love-in-a-mist. My first introduction to this lovely flower came from a Master Gardener friend. She brought me a bouquet of the delicate blue flowers from her garden one spring. I had never seen it before except in catalogs, and I had no idea that it would grow in the coastal South. I was fascinated. She saved some seeds for me, and thus began my love affair with this beautiful flower.

That October I prepared a planting bed by digging in a bit of peat moss and cow manure. Then I leveled the bed and broadcast the tiny seeds over the area. Cold weather came, and the seeds began to sprout. As winter progressed, they continued to grow. In March, they really shot up, and in April and May they bloomed to beat the band.

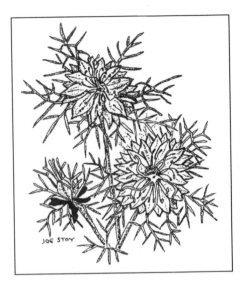

Nigella grows into a branching plant one to two feet tall. Leaves are finely cut and almost threadlike. Even the flowers are surrounded by these frilly leaves, giving them a lacy appearance. Blue, white, or rose flowers a little more than one inch across adorn the ends of each branch. Following the flowers, curious papery-textured, horned seed capsules, much treasured by floral designers, are formed.

'Miss Jekyll' is a cultivar that has semidouble blue blossoms, and 'Persian Jewels' is available in mixed colors. Nigella appreciates full sun or partial shade and regular water. They will dry up in summer's heat. I know, however, that I will have them again next spring because they self sow freely. I will collect the ornamental seed pods to use in my crafts, and I will save some seed just in case I need some more and so that I can share with friends.

Nigella (*N. sativa*) seeds are the "black fitches" of the Bible. Sometimes called black cumin or black caraway, the seeds have long been used in light breads. Seeds are used in India and the Middle East as a spice and condiment. In Europe they are sometimes used as both a pepper substitute and a spice. Seeds have been used since antiquity by Asian herbalists and pharmacists. Many medicinal benefits have been attributed to these black seeds. Sometimes they are used like moth balls because they are known to repel certain insects. Black seed oil is used in face and body soaps, shampoos, and skin care products.

Nigella seeds are available from friends who are usually willing to share, and they may be purchased from seed racks in local stores. Also, they may be ordered from seed catalogs. Plant them in the herb garden or flower border in the fall. Come spring you will be amply rewarded for your efforts.

Parsley (*Petroselinum crispum*)

No discussion of herbs suitable for gardens in the coastal South would be complete without the inclusion of parsley. It is one of our most easily grown and most useful herbs. In the kitchen it has an impressive array of uses, and in the garden it is beautiful enough to be a star in the flower border or in the herb garden.

There are at least three kinds of parsley. One is the curly-leafed French parsley that is used ornamentally in the garden and for garnishing dishes at the table. The flat-leafed Italian parsley is reputed to have superior flavor and is often chosen by discerning cooks. The Hamburg variety is cultivated as a root crop.

In the coastal South parsley is best planted in the fall. Germination is usually slow, but may be hastened by soaking the seeds in warm water for several hours before planting. Another trick is to freeze seeds in ice cubes—two or three seeds per cube—and then to plant the cubes. It comes up in a few days and grows all winter. With the coming of warm weather the following summer, it often blooms and then dies. Sometimes removing the bloom stalk as it emerges from the crown of the plant will allow parsley to stay a bit longer in the garden.

Expect the beautiful Eastern black swallowtail to visit the parsley patch and to deposit her eggs on it. Plant enough for the larvae and for your own needs. I remind myself that shortly after the butterfly emerges from the chrysalis, the parsley blooms and then dies. Such is the life of the biennial.

Parsley has a very high chlorophyll content that gives it its beautiful green color and makes it useful as a breath freshener. It is no accident that a sprig of parsley is used to garnish many garlicky dishes. The chlorophyll content also cleanses the palate and allows each taste to come through and yet serves as a blending agent, thereby acting as a sort of culinary liaison.

Parsley is the principal ingredient in most *bouquets garnis*. A couple of sprigs of parsley and a couple of other herbs add versatile and appealing flavors to many dishes. Tie together two or three sprigs of parsley, a bay leaf, and a sprig of rosemary to use with lamb, game, and baked or grilled fish. Try sage, bay, and parsley with pork, goose, and veal dishes. For a pleasing addition to the stock pot, use thyme, parsley, and bay. Parsley is a great facilitator that smoothes the strong-flavored herbs and reinforces the milder ones.

Parsley can be kept fresh in the refrigerator for several days by wrapping it in a damp paper towel and placing it in a plastic bag. It can be frozen and used as needed. Add parsley to complement potatoes, fish, poultry, pasta, and vegetables. Or use it just because it's beautiful! Don't forget to eat it, though, for it is very high in vitamins A, B, and C and is a rich source of iron.

Try making up a batch of green butter. Mix one stick of softened butter or margarine and one bunch or about half a cup of fresh parsley, snipped fine. Add one tablespoon of fresh lemon juice. Mix and refrigerate. Use to season hot carrots, potatoes, or other vegetable dishes. Spread on hot biscuits or cornbread. Yummy!

Pineapple Sage (Salvia elegans)

During the fall, pineapple sage begins to sport its bright red flowers. Hummingbirds and butterflies do not fail to notice, and they visit regularly to sip the sweet nectar.

All summer the pineapple sage grows. Each time the gardener passes by, a leaf is apt to be pinched off and its fragrance enjoyed. In fall it is in its glory, and everybody notices the bright addition to the garden. Children, particularly, are enchanted with scented herbs like pineapple sage. They not only enjoy the flowers, but when they can also taste, feel, and smell the garden's offerings, they develop a much longer lasting appreciation and memory of the subject.

JOE STOY

Pineapple sage is particularly obliging in this respect. Observers immediately notice the bright red flowers. One sniff of the leaves reveals a delightful, pineapple scent. Touch introduces soft, downy hairs that cover the leaves and young stems. Offer kids an ice cream cone garnished with the red flowers, or toss the blossoms on top of puddings or salads to complete the total experience. They will not soon forget pineapple sage.

Vivid scarlet blossoms are inch-long, slender tubes arranged in whorls on long, terminal spikes. While the flowers are not scented, when they are dried the color is retained for a long time. The colorful dried blossoms make an attractive addition to the potpourri bowl, or they may be pressed and used in dried flower crafts.

In the coastal South, this Mexican native is a tender perennial that returns reliably from roots. Farther north it must be treated as an annual or protected during the winter. In frost-free areas, the leaves are evergreen. Flowering is initiated by short day length, so expect blossoms in the fall as the days begin to shorten.

A site with full or partial sun suits it well, but some protection from hot afternoon sun will be beneficial. Rich, fertile, moist soil is preferred, and a steady source of nutrients will encourage optimal growth. Cuttings root easily in late fall as the weather turns cooler and frost threatens. These cuttings are insurance against a particularly hard winter. They may be potted up and shared with friends or used to increase your stock of this desirable herb. After frost kills the plants to the ground, cut them off at ground level and cover with a blanket of pine needles or other loose, protective mulch.

When growth begins in spring from established plantings, the new growth can be very dense. Close inspection will reveal that many stems have rooted where they emerge from the ground. Many new plants may be potted up or moved to other areas. If they are all left, the plant will not grow as vigorously.

If aphids, spider mites, whiteflies, or other pests become bothersome, mix a tablespoon of liquid dishwashing soap and an equal amount of salad oil in a half gallon of water and spray the leaves until they drip. Repeat once or twice at weekly intervals when the temperature is below 85°F.

Use the fragrant leaves when they are fresh. Much of their fragrance and flavor is lost when they are dried. Young leaves may be tossed into salads. A handful of crushed leaves steeped in a pitcher of iced water makes a great summer refresher. Fresh leaves beautifully garnish a fruit cup or drink. Try snipping a few into a favorite cream cheese recipe for a different flavor sensation. Don't forget to toss in a few of the flowers for a dash of color.

Pineapple sage is usually available from area garden centers in spring and early summer. Since it is so fast growing, a plant in a four-inch pot can grow into a three- to four-foot specimen by fall. Look for it next spring and include it as a satisfying addition to your garden.

Rosemary (*Rosmarinus officinalis*)

Rosemary is planted at the back of my perennial border beside the path that separates my property from Agreeable Neighbor's. I put it there on purpose so that I can brush against it or trail my fingers over it each time I pass. The volatile oils rub off and the piney fragrance suffuses the air and perfumes my fingertips. Granddaughter Emily is enchanted with the aromatic plant as well. She copies everything that "Mimi" does, so she has been touching the rosemary and then smelling her hands since she could walk.

Why, one might ask, would rose-

JOE STOY

mary be planted in the perennial border? My answer to that question is simply to point to the border. At the back, its grayish green, dense form is mounded, but in a spiky sort of way. Individual branches ascend skyward, up and away from the mound, forming an irregular and interesting outline much like the skyline of a city. The fine, needlelike texture contrasts nicely with large, coarser leaves nearby. Subtle color variations between the grayish leaves of the rosemary and assorted tints and shades of green in other plants add additional interest.

Rosemary has always grown in my garden. In the coastal South, it is dependable and long lived. Propagation is easy from cuttings or by layering. Because transplanting is risky, always try to place rosemary where you want it to stay for many years. A sunny site is best, and if your soil is acidic, apply lime, wood ashes, crushed eggshells, or another soil sweetener every two or three years. Most soils are rich enough for rosemary, but very poor soil might need to have a little fertilizer added occasionally. Well-drained soil is an absolute must.

The word "officinalis" suggests that rosemary has medicinal uses. Herbal physicians have prescribed an infusion of the leaves as a tonic, astringent, and for treatment of depression, headaches, and muscle spasms. As recently as World War II, a mixture of rosemary leaves and juniper berries was burned in hospitals to kill germs. Amiable Spouse declares that rubbing his shoulder with a concoction of rosemary leaves steeped in water, strained, and mixed with olive oil helps his almost constant pain. I suspect that he just likes me to rub it, but who knows?

Rosemary is an authoritative herb in recipes. Its flavor harmonizes with poultry, fish, lamb, beef, veal, pork, and game. It also enhances tomatoes, spinach, peas, mushrooms, squash, cheese, eggs, and many other foods. Also, it is useful as a scented addition to soaps, creams, lotions, perfumes, and other toiletries. One of my favorite ways to use rosemary is to tie a few sprigs in a cheesecloth bag and toss it into my bath water. After a hard day's work in the garden, it stimulates and refreshes my weary body. Amiable Spouse likes to tie a few sprigs together and use them as a barbecue brush when cooking pork or chicken on the grill.

Many varieties of rosemary may be chosen for the garden. Some are upright, and some prostrate. Flower colors may be pink, blue, or white. Some varieties are hardier than others, and leaf size and color vary with each variety or cultivar.

It's good to know, too, that a herb that I esteem so much protects me against evil spirits and improves my memory. At least some of that must be true, because I haven't seen any evil spirits lately. I have noticed, however, that my memory keeps slipping in spite of all the rosemary can do. Maybe it's not all it's trumped up to be.

Sage (Salvia officinalis)

Hog-killing day in Mississippi during the days of my childhood was a memorable occasion. On the first cold day of winter, Daddy invited Granny and Papa to come and help. The hogs were killed, and we spent all day processing the meat and getting it ready for the smokehouse or pork barrel. We made new cracklings and sausages. The iron wash pots were used to render the fat that was our only source of lard. Huge hams and slabs of bacon were hung in the smokehouse where they were smoked for days with hickory limbs gathered from the woods.

I remember, too, that sage was a necessary part of this process. Mother didn't grow sage in the garden, but it grew naturally on a sunny hillside near the house. I don't know if at some time she planted it there, but she always knew where it was. This sage was harvested during hog killing time. It was used to season the fresh sausage and the hogshead cheese that she and Granny made. Though I don't still process my own pork, I usually have sage in the herb garden. Gotta have it, you know, for the Thanksgiving and Christmas turkeys! Amiable Spouse and I are fond of it

in the pheasant and quail that he brings home from his hunts.

Garden sage is grown and used almost worldwide. We use it for seasoning a variety of foods including pork sausage and poultry. The Russians use it when baking the goose, and the English are fond of it in cheese. In Yugoslavia, it is an important export. Fields of it are planted and harvested like hay three times a year. The Chinese value it for tea and its curative properties. Colonists often used sage to help cure meats, for it has antibacterial properties. More recently, distilled sage extracts have been used to increase the shelf life of foods. The stability of soy oil and potato chips has been improved by using tasteless and odorless antioxidants prepared from sage and rosemary.

The Ancients believed that sage increased mental capacity and longevity. It has been used to treat snakebite, to cure warts and epilepsy, and for insomnia, measles, seasickness, and worms. In more recent history, antiseptic properties have made it useful in treating a range of irritations from sore throats to cuts and bruises. Research shows that it lowers blood sugar in diabetics.

Though sage is perennial in most of the country and hardy in Zones 4 to 8, the summer heat and humidity of the coastal South often contribute to its demise. New plants set out in fall grow and remain evergreen during the winter and last through much of the summer. From these, enough leaves can be harvested and dried to have a constant supply for the kitchen. I guess that's not too bad a record. Growers in other parts of the country recommend replacing sage every third or fourth year, anyway. It becomes woody and less vigorous as it ages.

Common sage is an attractive plant in the garden. Silver green leaves provide a pleasant color contrast for darker green plants. Other varieties are available, however, for different color effects in the garden. 'Aurea', or golden sage, has leaves edged in chartreuse and cream. 'Purpurea' has purple foliage, and 'Tricolor' has purple and white streaks in its green leaves. All are equally well suited for the kitchen.

Writing about sage conjures up several treasured memories: of Mother and Daddy during their young adult years, of my brothers and sisters and me as children, of grandparents during their middle age, and of breakfasts on the farm. We could depend on a big pan of Mother's buttermilk biscuits. She fried fresh eggs that we had gathered from the laying hens. Always on the table was a bottle of cane syrup that we made ourselves and stored in the barn in gallon buckets. We poured this syrup on our plates beside the egg, put some fresh cream on top of it and used the biscuits to sop it up. On the side we had smoked ham, bacon, cracklings, or sausage. We were extraordinarily well fed!

It was a good life, but I don't believe I'd go back there even if I could. I'll just buy most of my food from the grocery. Sage, however, I will continue to grow, for I enjoy its aroma, its flavor in my food, and its beauty in the garden.

Scented Geraniums (*Pelargonium* spp.)

Few plants in the garden have given me as much pleasure as scented geraniums. I should have known when I first discovered this fragrant group of plants that one would not be enough. With more than 75 species and hybrids of these South African natives available, finding a few to suit my fancy was not difficult.

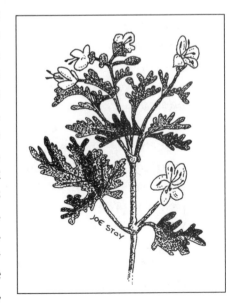

Scented geraniums are not grown for their flowers. Although they bloom during the spring and their delicate flowers are lovely, that is not the reason for their popularity. Foliage of the scenteds, as they are frequently called, is their main drawing card. Generally the fragrance can be grouped into rose, peppermint, lemon, spice, or pungent scents. Within these groups, fragrances include variations on mint, apricot, apple, strawberry, lavender, lemon, rose, nutmeg, and coconut. Sizes and textures of the leaves vary widely. Some are large and may be shiny, velvety, smooth, or crinkly. Others are small and delicate. Shape ranges from deeply cut to gently lobed. Some are plain green while others have white or cream variegation.

Do not confuse the scenteds with the brightly colored geraniums grown for their blooms (*Pelargonium* x *hortorum*). Those with brightly colored flowers are not very pleasantly scented. They grow best when night temperatures range between 60°F and 65°F and day temperatures do not exceed 85°F. Preference for these conditions severely limits their use in the coastal South. Neither should they be confused with the native *Geranium* genus commonly known as cranesbills or wild geraniums. For optimum growth, plant scenteds in good soil that is well drained. Lightly feed with a balanced fertilizer. Prune throughout the growing season to keep plants compact and give plenty of material for rooted cuttings or other uses.

Many growers in the coastal South prefer to grow their scenteds in containers that can be brought in during the winter. Generally they tolerate temperatures in the upper 30s without severe damage. Although I plant mine in the garden, I always take cuttings of my favorites. Hardy in Zones 10 and 11, these tender perennials are usually treated as annuals or protected during the winter in most of the coastal South.

Foliage of the scenteds has many uses around the house. Usually the flavor matches their fragrance, and they are used in ice cream, herbal butter, jelly, and iced tea. Rose geranium pound cake is a classic dessert. Lemon-scented varieties are popular in finger bowls. Any extra leaves are simply tossed into the potpourri bowl where they retain their fragrance for a long time.

Propagation is easy from cuttings. It took me a while to learn that the cut end needs to cure in the open air for six to eight hours before they are placed in the rooting medium. Sometimes I take cuttings, lay them out on the potting bench, and let them stay until the next day. They look all wilted and hopeless, but I'm not fooled by their pouting pose. Stuck in moist, freely draining medium, they will perk up and root in three to four weeks.

I am constantly on the lookout for a scented geranium that I don't already have. I guess I've become addicted—again.

Sorrel (*Rumex acetosa*)

Amiable Spouse and I always enjoy the winter salad season. Time and time again I pluck tender lettuces, small green onions, dill, chives, and other tasty greens to toss into a salad. Sometimes they're garnished with colorful viola flowers; sometimes we eat them plain. But always, sorrel is a flavorful addition to our salads.

Sorrel imparts a sour "zing," and the dark green leaves perfectly complement the light-colored lettuces. The palate feels fresh and clean after a bite of the tangy, astringent leaf. Almost lemony in taste, it is not surprising that it is a good source of vitamin C. On tuna or tomato sandwiches it adds a tart freshness. Sorrel soup made with chicken broth and light cream is popular. The flavor stands up well to the heat of cooking, so it is a delicious accent to soups and casseroles.

I discovered this tasty herb only recently. My parents never grew it in their garden in Mississippi. I discovered it quite by accident at our neighborhood garden center one spring. I was buying all the herbs I could find for my newly installed herb garden. I didn't know anything about sorrel, but I bought it anyway. Never again will I do without it if I can help it. One or two plants supply all the leaves that Amiable Spouse and I can use. In the summer it gets a bit ragged looking, but with the cooling days of autumn it perks up. It needs a bit of protection from hot afternoon summer sun. In winter, sorrel is at its best.

Once a plant is established, propagation is easy. Small sections cut from the main root can be planted about a foot apart in a prepared garden bed. They quickly grow and fill their space. Seeds sown in spring will produce edible leaves by fall. Rusty red flowers should be removed so that the plant's energy is spent producing leaves instead of flowers and seed. Be persistent with the cutting. When the clump finally insists on going to seed, simply cut the plant to the ground. In a few weeks new growth will begin.

To harvest, simply pinch the tender leaves from the center of the plant. To keep the bed looking neat, remove the outer leaves as they yellow and add them to the compost bin. Sorrel is reliably hardy in the coastal South, and it is a long-lived cousin of our native dock. According to references, plants live about ten years. With division, I believe that it might last even longer.

Never has it been necessary to treat sorrel with insecticide. Sometimes I find a few chewed leaves, but I cannot see the aggressor. A few holes seem preferable to the poison that might be necessary to keep them at bay. Sorrel appreciates a fairly rich, moist soil. Regular applications of fish emulsion or manure tea will keep it growing vigorously. Add a couple of plants to your garden and experience for yourself the delightful addition that sorrel makes to your meals.

Thyme (*Thymus praecox*)

Two plants that have given me as much pleasure as any of the others are members of the thyme clan. Both grow in a sunny bed near the street at the outer edge of the sprinkler system's area of coverage.

Both are *Thymus praecox* cultivars and are tiny, creeping thymes.

One of them hugs the ground and grows about one or two inches tall. Looking back at my records, I find that it is *T. praecox* 'Coccineus', and it has been in my garden now for about five years. It started as a tiny plant ordered from Wayside Gardens. Gradually it has spread to fill an area about two feet square. I keep pulling up other plants nearby and encouraging it to spread and fill the area.

Another creeping variety grows in close proximity. Reaching three or four inches tall, it has been growing and sporting its tiny rose-colored blossoms for about ten years. Last year it got a bit shaggy looking, so I pruned it back nearly to the ground. It responded by sending out fresh new growth and becoming beautiful all over again.

These tiny thymes hug the ground in a dense mass. They are perfect at the front edge of the border where they form an evergreen groundcover of tiny leaves. I'm tempted to stoop down and pat them whenever I walk by, for their feel and texture is as interesting as their familiar aroma.

According to Madeline Hill and Gwen Barclay, herb growers in Texas, there are about 400 varieties of thyme. They cross pollinate readily, and new varieties spring up around established plantings. Thymes come in different scents, such as camphor, lemon, caraway, and nutmeg. Flower colors may be pink, lavender, crimson, and white, and size varies from 2 to 15 inches tall.

Thymes flourish in well-drained soil and plenty of sunshine. Upright varieties should be kept pruned lightly and regularly. Left unpruned, they become woody and split easily. Culinary varieties are usually replaced every two or three years because of their tendency to become woody and straggly. Propagation is from seed, division, or cuttings.

Thyme, like most other herbs, has a variety of uses other than beauty in the garden. Medicinally, it has been used to flavor cough medicines. It is particularly beneficial in quieting gastrointestinal complaints and ailments of the digestive system. A tea has been prescribed for congested lungs and other breathing difficulties. It has antispasmodic qualities and can be used as an antiseptic and fumigant.

In the kitchen, thyme (*T. vulgaris*) plays a leading role. The French use it as one of the *fines herbes*. Leaves and sprigs are used in clam chowder, *bouquet garnis*, and French, Creole, and Cajun cuisines. It works well with veal, lamb, beef, poultry, fish, sausages, stews—and on and on. The list is so long that I would venture a guess and say that thyme works with almost anything. One herbal rule of thumb for confused cooks is, "When in doubt, use thyme."

Insect-repelling properties make it useful in linen closets and among woolens to protect them from insects. Antiseptic and stimulating properties make it effective in lotions and baths. Thymol, its active ingredient, is used in making colognes, aftershave lotions, and other toiletries.

I, for one, will always have thyme somewhere in my garden if the Good Lord is willing and the creeks don't rise. I'll remember it, too, if I am ever plagued with nightmares or nervous disorders. I'll simply brew up a little thyme tea and be done with that.

Edible Flowers

Gardeners grow flowers for many reasons. Mainly we grow them for the beauty and diversity they add to the landscape. Many people, however, grow flowers for eating. I'm one of those weirdos! When company comes for a meal at my house, they're disappointed if no flowers garnish the salad or if some dishes are not decorated with flowers.

Many flowers are edible. Do not, however, run out right now and gather flowers for dinner. Certain rules should be observed before any flower is eaten. First, eat only those flowers you know are edible. Don't guess, but depend upon solid research and proven statistics for your information source. Just because a flower is pretty or smells good does

not mean that it is edible.

Remember that just because a flower is served with food doesn't mean it's edible. In my own home, I would not even consider garnishing or decorating a dish with a flower that is not edible, but I cannot speak for other people. I do know, however, that wedding cakes and such are sometimes decorated purely for beauty, and if the guests ate the flowers on the cake, the joyous occasion might turn into a disaster.

Flowers should be eaten only if they were grown organically.

Never eat flowers that have had poisons sprayed on them. If you suspect that there may be bugs inside the petals of flowers, they can be soaked in soapy water about five minutes and then rinsed well. That should take care of the nasty critters and keep unexpected scurryings from upsetting guests at the dinner table.

A few more words of caution are in order before flowers are included in your diet. People who suffer from bad allergies or asthma should not eat flowers. Flowers picked from the side of the road may be contaminated with car emissions. Those purchased at a florist, nursery, or garden center are likely to have been sprayed with all sorts of chemicals. Pistils and stamens are usually removed and only the petals are eaten. Flowers should be introduced into the diet slowly— one at a time and in small quantities. Remember that some flowers are extremely poisonous, so if you are unsure, do not eat the flowers!

Some flowers that I eat in season are nasturtium, pansy, calendula, rose, hibiscus, Johnny jump-up, garden pea, pineapple sage, society garlic, violet, and blossoms of all culinary herbs. This fall I will plant nasturtiums, pansies, and Johnny jump-ups. They will be stuffed, crystallized, tossed into salads, or sprinkled atop various dishes. During the summer, society garlic, daylilies, and various herb flowers spice up my salads and add a titillating visual punch to meals. Daylilies have been eaten for centuries. Large blossoms can be stuffed with chicken or tuna salad. The buds, both fresh and dried, make a tasty addition to soups, stir fries, and pastas. Buds two inches long or smaller are usually the best tasting.

A good book on the subject is *Edible Flowers from Garden to Palate* by Cathy Wilkinson Barash. Recipes are included as well as a list of toxic flowers.

So there you go. Flowers are beautiful not only in the garden, but on the table as well. Add life to your dishes from a beautiful array of edible petals. Enjoy yet another dimension from the wonderful world of flowers!

Herbs for the Flower Border

The longer I garden, the less distinct the lines become that separate herbs from other annuals and perennials. Many of my favorite plants have simply moved out of the herb garden into the annual and perennial border.

One of my favorites is silver licorice plant (*Helichrysum petiolatum*). Small, oval-shaped, one-inch leaves cover this ground-hugging, tender perennial. Licorice plant is a sensory pleasure. Soft, wooly leaves emit a licorice aroma. Creeping around and among other flowers in the border, it weaves together the various colors like the background of a tapestry. It is also very effective cascading down the sides of a hanging basket or combination container planting.

Licorice plant is also useful dried. Each summer I gather bunches and tie them together in small groups. Hung upside down to dry in my laundry room, air currents from the air-conditioning system dry them quickly. They are particularly pretty in dried herbal or floral wreaths. I don't mind cutting them as winter approaches because they will be killed by the first frost.

Another useful herb is Cuban oregano (*Plectranthus amboinicus*). Green and white variegated leaves blend easily with any color. I love this plant not only for its outstanding foliage, but also because it smells good and is tough as nails. Fleshy leaves have a flavor and aroma somewhere between that of thyme and oregano. Leaves can be chopped and used in sauces, soups, and various dishes. Place this succulent plant in full sun and a well-drained location. It is very drought tolerant, but not at all winter hardy. Cuttings can be taken which root easily and overwinter in the greenhouse or in a sunny window.

Lavender cotton (*Santolina chamaecyparissus*) is another herb that does full duty in my perennial border. Available in either green or gray, it grows about one foot tall and makes a well-mannered, mounded plant about two feet in diameter. Fragrance, drought tolerance, and rough, narrow leaves make it a pleasant addition to the garden. Dried branches are sometimes tied together and hung in closets, where the fresh, benzoin-like scent may repel moths. Site this plant in full sun in a high and dry location. Although lavender cotton is perennial, I have found it necessary to replace it after a few years because it has a tendency to spread out from the top and become unattractive as it ages.

Many plants from the herb garden are effective in the flower border. After a time it gets all mixed up. Pansies are in the herb garden and oregano is in the perennial border. Just because a plant is a herb does not negate its usefulness in other areas of the garden. Don't overlook this serviceable group of plants.

Common Name	Plant type
Aloe vera (*Aloe barbadensis*)	Tender perennial
Anise (*Pimpinella anisum*)	Annual
Artemisia (*Artemisia* spp.)	Perennial
Bergamot (*Monarda* spp.)	Perennial
Betony (*Stachys officinalis*)	Perennial
Bouncing Bet (*Saponaria officinalis*)	Perennial
Capsicum (*Capsicum* spp.)	Tropical perennial, grown as annual
Caraway (*Carum carvi*)	Biennial
Cardamom (*Elettaria cardamomum*)	Perennial rhizome
Catnip (*Nepeta cataria*)	Perennial
Chamomile (*Chamaemelum nobile*)	Annual in South
Comfrey (*Symphytum peregrinum* or *S. officinale*)	Perennial
Curry (*Helichrysum angustifolium*)	Perennial

Season to plant	Comments
Any	Protect from cold; best in container
Spring	Easy from seed
Any	Many kinds, some invasive; some grown as ornamentals
Any	Native, *M. fistulosa, M. punctata, M. citriodora*
Any	Historical use as wound dressing
Any	Roots produce lather; used as soap, pink flowers
Summer	Peppers, varying degrees of warmth
Fall	Best in winter garden
Any	Killed to ground in winter; resembles ginger cousins
Any	Attractive to cats
Fall	Reseeds, winter hardy
Any	4'–5' tall, grows year-round
Any	Full sun, dry area; may be short lived in South

continued on next page

Common Name	Plant type
Garlic (*Allium sativum*)	Perennial
Ginger (*Zingiber officinale*)	Perennial
Gotu Kola (*Centella asiatica*)	Perennial
Horehound (*Marrubium vulgare*)	Perennial
Horseradish (*Armoracia rusticana*)	Perennial
Lemon Balm (*Melissa officinalis*)	Perennial
Mint (*Mentha* spp.)	Perennial
Mullein (*Verbascum thapsus*)	Biennial
Mustard (*Brassica* spp.)	Annual
Nasturtium (*Tropaeolum majus*)	Annual
Oregano (*Origanum* spp.)	Perennial
Perilla (*Perilla frutescens*)	Annual
Poliomintha (*Poliomintha longiflora*)	Perennial
Pot Marigold (*Calendula officinalis*)	Annual
Purslane (*Portulaca oleracea*)	Annual

Season to plant	Comments
Fall	Elephant garlic (*Allium scorodoprasum*) also easy
Any	Rhizomes very aromatic
Any	Best in hanging basket may become invasive
Spring	Horehound candy helps relieve sore throat
Any	Does not make fat roots in sandy soil; spicy leaves
Any	Easy from seeds, cuttings, or division
Any	Tends to invasiveness; many types
Any	Native
Fall	Potherb; use seeds for prepared mustard
Fall	Flowers and leaves edible; does not like summer heat
Any	Many kinds
Spring	Purple leaves; self-sows
Any	Tubular flowers attractive to hummingbirds
Fall	Yellow, orange flowers in winter and spring
Spring	Potherb, edible flowers; weedily self-sows

continued on next page

Common Name	Plant type
Roquette (*Eruca versicaria* subsp. *sativa*)	Annual
Rue (*Ruta graveolens*)	Perennial
Santolina (*Santolina chamaecyparissus*)	Perennial
St. John's Wort (*Hypericum perforatum*)	Perennial
Stevia (*Stevia rebaudiana*)	Perennial
Violet (*Viola odorata*)	Perennial
Yarrow (*Achillea millefolium*)	Perennial

Season to plant	Comments
Fall	Salad herb, arugula, best in cool seasons
Any	May cause dermatitis in sensitive individuals
Any	Gray and green varieties; likes hot, dry situation
Any	Yellow flowers, showy
Any	Ten times sweeter than sugar
Any	Edible leaves and flowers; multiplies rapidly
Any	Prolific growth, creeping roots, can be invasive

Shrubs and Small Trees

Shrubs are a necessary part of every garden. They provide framework, color, texture, and fragrance. More than just necessary, however, some are beautiful enough to be stars in the border. Others are included because they are part of my Southern heritage, and any garden of mine is apt to have some of these plants scattered about.

Angel's Trumpet (*Brugmansia* and *Datura*)

My angel's trumpets delight me with wave after wave of spectacular blooms. I have a purple one, a peach-colored one, and a white one. Although *Daturas* and *Brugmansias* are both called angel's trumpets, there are some differences. *Brugmansia* is a large shrub or small tree with large, pendent, down-facing, fragrant flowers that may last several days. *Datura*, on the other hand, is a shrub or annual plant with

flowers that face upwards and last about a day. The flowers are not what I'd call fragrant. The seed pods are entirely different.

My purple angel's trumpet (*Datura*) blooms with double flowers that are purple on the outside and white on the inside. The double blossoms give the appearance of two flowers in one. One summer a plant volunteered beside the street. Of course it interfered with garbage collection. How could I place the garbage cans by the street when an angel's trumpet was growing where the trash belonged? I am sure that it delighted Valparaiso's trash collection crew! It certainly enthralled flower show judges who awarded it the Award of Horticultural Merit in the flower show that year.

The purple *Datura* usually behaves like a reseeding annual. Round, bristly seed pods about one inch in diameter form as the flowers fade. When these pods begin to split open or turn brown, they may be pulled from the plant and seeds contained inside it collected. Seeds may then be dried and packaged for friends or plant sales. Planted next spring, they will grace many gardens with their beauty. Each year I save seeds, but I rarely have to plant them because volunteers come up around last year's plants.

The white angel's trumpet (*Datura*) spreads along the ground and produces white blossoms that bloom mostly at night. Somehow one volunteered beside my driveway last year. Topping out at 12 to 18 inches, these angel's trumpets spread to cover several square feet. They last for some time during the day but usually close before noon. Once I planted white *Daturas* beneath the purple ones, and they created quite a show.

My peach-colored *Brugmansia* started as a rooted cutting given to me by a friend. During its first winter it survived in my greenhouse. When warm weather arrived, however, it began to grow quite rapidly. I transplanted it to a three-gallon container and later to a ten-gallon container. Keeping it watered in the containers was difficult, so I finally planted it in the ground. Today it has grown into a beautiful specimen about eight feet tall. Beautiful, pendulous, peach-colored blossoms grace my yard for much of the summer.

I am uncertain about its hardiness outdoors in the winter. Though mine has come back from the roots for several years, I still want a little insurance. I always take some cuttings before frost just to be sure that I have some for next year. Cuttings root well if they include a "heel," or a part of the stem that includes a joint. My research shows that *Brugmansia* plants can also be started from seed, but I have had little success with this method.

Only one seed pod has formed on my peach angel's trumpet. It was a long, pointed structure somewhat like an okra pod. The seeds inside, however, didn't look anything like okra seeds. They were angular, tightly packed chunks of brown matter that didn't look at all like seeds. I planted them, and one came up. However, cuttings root readily, so I have decided that cuttings are the easiest way to propagate this angel's trumpet.

Several colors of *Brugmansia* are available. *B. sanguinea* has red trumpets. Other species and hybrids have pink, yellow, or pale orange flowers. All grow into large shrubs or small trees that are evergreen in frost-free climates. For a spectacular show, try *Brugmansia* or *Datura* in your yard. Site them in a protected place, for the tender leaves are easily damaged by such things as falling pine needles. Be forewarned that they are very poisonous, so keep them away from children. Properly placed, however, they are so exquisite that they cause the floraholics among us to suck in our breath and gasp in awe-struck delight.

Beautyberry (*Callicarpa americana*)

My beautyberry turns purple in fall, and the mockingbird uses the top of it for her perching site. She's going to be there if an intruder

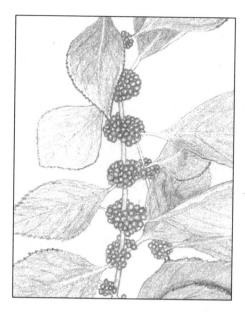

decides to get some berries. Not if I can help it! she's thinking. She swoops and dives. She scolds approaching people, dogs, and cats. Frequently she and the brown thrasher can be seen chasing each other about. Both relish the purple berries. Beautyberry is at its best during the fall season. Though inconspicuous most of the year, fall brings a startling but delightful change. Vibrant violet to magenta fruits surround the long stems in rounded clusters tightly pressed around the leaf bases. The name *Callicarpa* means "beautiful fruit" which is very appropriate.

In the United States, this shrub is native from Maryland south to Florida and west into Texas. It also grows in Mexico, Bermuda, the Bahamas, and Cuba. Commonly it inhabits open, well-drained woodlands and hammocks. Though sometimes called French mulberry, there is nothing French about it.

Beautyberry has played a part in my life from a very early age. When we were very young, my sister and I made playhouses during the summer. We'd turn some of Daddy's used paint cans upside down and place boards across them for our kitchen cabinets and ovens. Making mud pies was a favored playhouse activity, and one of our favorites was called purple berry pie. It was made of beautyberries. We'd pick them and mix in a generous quantity of soil and water and bake them in paint can lids in the sun. It was great fun. The pies made excellent targets to throw at Raymond (older brother) and John Dale (first cousin a quarter-mile down the road) when they tried to tear our playhouses down. For some reason, tormenting us in such ways was one of their favorite pastimes.

There are several species of beautyberries that range in size, hardiness, foliar quality, and refinement. Our native beautyberry is the largest and coarsest. Large, yellowish green leaves are borne on loose, open stems. The shrub can get quite massive and ungainly, but since it flowers on new growth, it can be pruned nearly to the ground each spring or late winter. Recently I ordered a white-fruited form called *Callicarpa americana* var. *lactea*. It promises to give a different look to my garden.

The Japanese beautyberry (*Callicarpa japonica*) is hardier and a bit more refined than our native, but it will still reach six to eight feet in height and spread. China's version (*Callicarpa bodinieri*) is moderately coarse in texture, about the same size as Japanese beautyberry, and has bluish fruits. It may not be tolerant of our hot, humid climate. *Callicarpa dichotoma* from China and Japan is the most refined and graceful beautyberry. Smaller than the others, its foliage is darker colored, smaller, and denser. Fruit is bright lilac and prolific. It may be a better plant for gardens of limited space.

As for me, however, I favor the old native that provided my sister and me ample material for mud pies when we were children. I want the one that grows in the woods and is suited to our climate and resistant to our pests. I enjoy the bold, lanky, outward pointing branches that gracefully curve with their load of berries. The familiar smell of them and the memories they conjure up are enough reason for their space in my garden. Maybe one day I'll show our granddaughter Emily how to make a purple berry pie.

Camellia (Camellia spp.) [23]

Without camellias, our winter landscapes would be lackluster. Flowers ranging from purest white to deepest red sparkle in area gardens. Early, middle, and late season varieties add color from September until late February or early March.

The genus *Camellia* contains more than 260 species. Embellishing our landscapes are *Camellia japonica*, *C. reticulata*, and *C. sasanqua*. Since the life span of these handsome, evergreen plants is reckoned in centuries, they are a long-lasting garden investment. Camellias should be planted in partial shade. In dense shade, flowering will be sparse, so they are best placed under shifting shade such as that found under tall pines. Protection from wind and scorching midday and afternoon sun is also advised.

Acidic, well-drained soil that is rich in organic matter is best for camellias. If necessary, incorporate composted manure, leaves, peat moss, or other organic material into the bed at planting time. Set plants at or slightly above the level at which they were positioned in their containers. Maintain a two- to four-inch layer of organic mulch such as pine needles, ground bark, partially rotted leaves, or other organic materials around the base of camellias. Mulch preserves moisture, inhibits weeds, moderates soil temperature, and supplies nutrients as it decomposes.

The American Camellia Society recommends applying fertilizer in early spring after the blooming season and danger of freezing weather has passed. It advises an application of 16-4-8 slow-release fertilizer with trace elements at the rate of one tablespoon per foot of height. Spread the fertilizer around the base of the plant half-way from the trunk and out to the drip line of the limbs. About four months after the first feeding, apply 5-10-15 with trace elements. In October, a small feeding of 0-20-10 should aid in bloom production. The society cautions that too little fertilizer is better than too much. Young plants should be fertilized regularly. However, older established plants may not require fertilizer at all. Decomposing organic matter often supplies all of the nutrients needed.

Tea scale and spider mites are the most frequently encountered camellia pests. Effective control can be achieved with a variety of insecticides that can be recommended by local nurseries or the county extension agency. Growers who do not wish to use poisons can effectively control these pests with a mixture of oil, detergent, and water. This mixture can be made by adding two tablespoons of liquid soap and two tablespoons of vegetable oil per gallon of water. Camellia diseases include die back, petal blight, occasional root rot, and algal leaf spot. Fungicide application helps to prevent some of them. Cultural practices, such as providing air space in and around shrubs and removing spent blossoms, help to prevent diseases.

Pruning should be done immediately after flowering and before new growth begins. Prune to shape and control size and to renew vigor in older plants. Clip off any dead or tangled branches, and thin to open the center and allow better air circulation. Always prune to an outward-facing bud, back to a larger branch, or to the main trunk.

Propagation of camellias can be done by grafting, layering, seed, or cuttings. Cuttings are best made in late spring after new growth has hardened. They can be cut and placed in a container or a damp, shady place in the landscape.

Many hobbyists grow camellias mainly to enter in flower shows. These growers have precise schedules and practices that they follow in order to produce the most spectacular blooms. Buds treated with gibberellic acid, a plant hormone, bloom quickly and make larger, showier specimens.

Visit local nurseries and gardens to see these fantastic plants in bloom. Choose some that strike your fancy. Nothing equals them in the midwinter when little else is blooming.

Grancy Gray-beard, Fringe Tree, Old Man's Beard
(Chionanthus virginicus) [27]

Grancy gray-beard is a large shrub or small tree that is native over much of the United States (Zones 3 to 9). In nature it may reach 25 to 30 feet with an equal spread, but in our yards it more commonly grows from 12 to 20 feet tall and wide.

In spring, white honey-scented flowers cover the plant and perfume the area for about three weeks. Each blossom has four very narrow petals about an inch long that dangle from threadlike stems in delicate, fleecy clusters six to eight inches long. Soft to the touch, these flowers quiver in the slightest breeze. Because it is highly visible in the woods, I can hardly drive down the highway and keep my eyes on the road when they are in bloom.

In the landscape grancy gray-beard is a beautiful specimen shrub or small tree. It is effective in groups, borders, or near large buildings. Pollution tolerance makes it an excellent choice for cities. Thomas Jefferson planted them at the edges of his fields in informal groups at Monticello. He delighted in their spring blossoms and in their brilliant yellow fall foliage.

Male trees put on a bigger show in spring because flowers have longer petals. However, the female bears fruit that is good wildlife food. Dark blue, egg-shaped fruits about a half-inch long ripen by late summer. Place male plants beside a patio or other area where falling fruit may be a problem, but choose a female for a mixed border and to provide food for songbirds.

Propagation of grancy gray-beard takes a bit of understanding because the seed has a double dormancy. Three to five months of warmth are required for the root to develop, but the stem remains dormant. Then low temperature of at least 41°F for one or more months is required for the stem to develop. Seeds sown outside in fall don't show stem growth until the second spring, and first year seedlings grow very little. However, if you have the patience and can find some seeds on a female plant before the birds make off with them, your efforts will pay off in a few years. Cuttings appear hard to root, but limited success may be possible from softwood cuttings taken in spring.

Young container plants can be planted in the landscape anytime but have the greatest chance to succeed if planted in late fall through winter. Though best in slightly acid, fairly rich soil in open sun, they tolerate a wide range of conditions and seem immune to diseases and pests. For gardens with humus-starved soil, mulching generously with leaves, pine needles, or other organic material will help.

Dwarf fringetree (*Chionanthus pygmaeus*) is a dwarf form sometimes spotted in sandy soils of the coastal South. It blooms just as beautifully as its larger cousin, but on a smaller framework. These dwarfs may reach three to four feet high and literally droop with large, fleecy, white clusters in spring. The Chinese version of this plant (*C. retusus*) is very showy, perhaps even more so than our native. It has excellent heat tolerance and retains its vibrant green color throughout the summer.

Why not choose a grancy gray-beard for your property—perhaps instead of the more disease-prone dogwood? After establishment it should provide years of beauty with only the care that nature chooses to provide.

Common Fig *(Ficus carica)*

My fig tree must be the mother of all figs. It is a source of never-ending pleasure. Folks in regions that have colder winters would give their eye teeth for such a tree! Sited at the back corner of my house, I see it every time I enter the Florida room where wraparound windows allow an unrestricted view of the outside. Amiable Spouse and I once took measurements of the tree. We actually used a measuring tape, because I wanted to be sure that I was not telling a fish tale. Its canopy measurement from one side to the other was 27 feet, and it was 18 feet tall and growing.

The thick, fuzzy leaves are bright dark green and deeply lobed. Some measure eight by ten inches, and they cover the tree from ground to crown. Nothing in my yard comes near it in beauty and stature. Even if it bore no fruit, I would want this highly ornamental tree in the yard. But bear fruit it does! For several weeks in July, I am busy gathering and canning the fruit. Family and friends share the bounty as well as the squirrels and birds who also relish the figs. I enjoy picking and eating them fresh from the tree.

The fig tree is about 34 years old. Amiable Spouse got it as a rooted specimen from friends and planted it that many years ago. It has survived drought, being jumped over and fallen into by several kids and dogs, repeated pruning, several hurricanes, and all manner of adversity during its lifetime. Maybe its struggle for survival during those early years gave it a strong constitution.

Today the great fig tree is "king of the hill." The ground underneath is mulched. Each year the leaves fall and remain in place. Oak leaves and pine needles are added as they become available. Decay of this natural mulch over the years has given it a rich, brown, crumbly soil in which to grow. It is well watered because it hogs most of the water from one of the sprinkler heads. Although it needs plenty of water, especially when fruit is forming, it must have well-drained soil. My fig is a 'Brown Turkey'. Its fruit is medium sized and rosy to purplish brown. Other varieties suited to the deep South include 'Celeste', 'Green Ischia', 'San Piero', and 'Magnolia'.

Many folks have fig trees that were started from mine. In early winter when the tree is dormant, I cut off a few twigs about a foot long and up to three quarters of an inch in diameter. Sometimes I place these cuttings in pots, but most of the time I just stick them in the soil underneath the tree. By the following spring they are rooted and ready to be potted up for plant sales or shared with friends. One winter I took cuttings about six inches long, bound them with a rubber band, and laid them horizontally in a box of dampened perlite. I was astonished when I examined the container in spring. Roots were growing everywhere! Potted up, they were a main attraction at the garden club's spring plant sale. Bare-root figs should be planted in winter when they are dormant. Container figs are best planted in early spring.

One fig tree is usually enough for an average-sized family. Be sure to plant it in an area where it receives full sun, and allow it plenty of room to grow. Since figs do not require cross pollination, only one tree is required. You can expect about 50 pounds of fruit a year from a mature tree. Figs are an organic gardener's delight. In all my years of growing figs, I have never had to spray for any pests. My primary pests are squirrels and birds, and I grow enough to share with them. Sometimes I get out early in the morning to harvest the figs before they have selected the best of the crop for themselves.

Most of my figs are preserved exactly the way my mother did them when I was a child. She taught me to wash them thoroughly and remove the stems. Then place them in a pot with slightly less than an equal amount of sugar. Cook over low heat until the sugar begins to melt and combines with the juice from the figs. Turn heat to high and bring mixture to a boil. Cook until figs are tender and liquid is syrupy. Pack and seal mixture in sterilized jars. Many mornings my mother served these fig preserves to her family of seven children along with hot buttermilk biscuits and milk. On other occasions she made what she called fig tarts. She would roll out a circular piece of biscuit dough about nine inches in diameter and put a dollop of fig preserves in the center. After folding and sealing the edges with her fingers, she fried them in a black skillet in hot grease. What a lady! She knew how to please a hungry bunch!

Confederate Rose (Hibiscus mutabilis) [22]

One spring during turkey-hunting season, Amiable Spouse came home with a plant for me. The people in Alabama where he hunts know that I am a flower fancier, so one of the ladies sent me a potted specimen of Confederate rose (*Hibiscus mutabilis*). I planted it out beside the garage. It grew all summer into a shrub about six to eight feet tall. In November it had exquisite flowers, and it continued to bloom until frost.

Mine is the double-flowered one that opens white one day, turns pink on the second day, and withers on the third day. At any one time the large shrub has flowers of white and all shades of pink. Others that you may see include a double flower that opens pink and turns white. There is also a single-flowered form that opens red and stays red, and a pink that gradually turns to a deeper pink.

Confederate rose blooms all winter in frost-free areas. In places that have light frosts, it drops its leaves in winter and sprouts again in spring. In zones with heavy frosts and prolonged cold periods, it gets killed to the ground each year but sprouts up again in spring. People up north where the ground freezes must treat it as an annual.

Rich, well-drained soil and full sun produce the best growth. However, it also grows and blooms in partial shade. In ideal circumstances, it grows 14 to 16 feet tall. When a freeze threatens the plants, cuttings should be taken. Place a handful of year-old stems in a bucket of water. By spring the ends will have callused over and roots may have formed. Plant them in the ground where they are to grow or put them in containers to share with friends.

Althea, Rose of Sharon (*Hibiscus syriacus*)

Granny was a gardener who made every drop of water count. No wonder. She drew water up from a well with a bucket attached to a pulley. Getting water was hard work. Her eight children were kept busy drawing enough water for cooking, bathing, and scrubbing floors. Plants and flowers got the leftovers.

Granny had no lawn. I remember sweeping her yard. She had a brush broom made of saplings tied with twine. Back then folks brushed the bare ground clean. If a weed or grass grew, it was pulled up. I remember sweeping all the way across the ground in broad, semicircular motions. I'd go all the way across and turn around and go all the way back. When I finished, the yard was a beautiful pattern of wavy lines. I'd fuss if anyone walked on it and messed up my wonderful design.

Granny and Papa had little money to buy fertilizers and poisons. Yet they grew a garden for a lifetime that fed all ten members of their household. Leaves and barnyard manure enriched the soil. Ducks, chickens, and guinea fowl kept the bug population under control.

Granny had beautiful flowers. Lately I've been thinking back and remembering what she grew in her flower garden that so impressed me as a child. Those flowers, I am quite sure, were extremely drought tolerant. Our recent scarcity of rain has set me thinking. One of the flowers that I remember from Granny's yard is althea. They were planted beside her doors and around the house where they bloomed most of the summer.

Now there's a plant that has been around for a long time. Rose of Sharon or althea belongs to the mallow family. It becomes a large shrub or small, multitrunked tree that blooms from June through August. Flowers may be lavender, pink, rose, red, or white. Some have a red splotch in the center. Granny had a white one with a red splotch, and a lavender one. They figure in my early childhood memories of pretty flowers. Double and semidouble flowers are also available.

Ants love the flowers. When examined closely, I can always find a few crawling up and down the branches. Seeds sprout around established bushes, and plants can be had at almost any plant sale or from friends who have rose of Sharon growing in their yards. They are easily rooted from cuttings taken in June and July, and seeds come up readily.

When I first moved into my house, a bush with solid white flowers grew in an untamed section of the landscape. Later, a lavender-flowered bush joined the border, and then one that is lavender with a red center splotch joined the group. I did not plant these shrubs in the border. Some wayward seed recognized a good place and put down roots.

Never have I fertilized these shrubs. They are in a part of the yard that does not get irrigated. Heavy pine needle and oak leaf mulch covers the ground, and they survive on whatever water the Good Lord sees fit to send their way. They continue to delight me as I look across the yard through my kitchen window and see a crop of pretty flowers day after day.

Low-maintenance shrubs like rose of Sharon definitely have a place in my garden. In this corner of the yard I have tried to establish a native garden of tough, easy-care plants. I cannot bring myself to take out these nonnatives, however. They are too well adapted—and too pretty. Anyway, they remind me of Granny. I've decided that I'm not a native plant purist. Any old adaptable, pretty thing will do. Rose of Sharon is here to stay.

Hydrangea (*Hydrangea macrophylla*) [28]

Bigleaf hydrangeas steal the show in May and June. The cultivars are divided into two different groups. Hortensias, informally called mopheads, have large, showy clusters of sterile blooms. Lacecaps have flat heads with tiny fertile flowers in the center surrounded by larger petaled, sterile flowers. Both are worthy landscape subjects.

Variegated lacecap hydrangea (*Hydrangea macrophylla*

'Variegata') [28] has mottled gray-green leaves with creamy white margins that stand out in the landscape. Jazzing up the performance are flat flower heads that last about six weeks. Although the flower show lasts a short time, the shrub is so spectacular that its space in the garden is well deserved. The leaves continue to sparkle throughout the summer. The light-colored leaves make it a perfect background for dark-colored groundcovers such as *Ajuga* 'Burgundy Glow', black sweet potato vine, or black mondo grass. Dark-colored coleus positively glows at its feet.

For landscaping purposes, site hydrangeas in a place where winter's dormancy will not leave a gaping hole. Culturally, they need dappled sun in the morning and protection from hot afternoon sun. Well-drained, moist soil that is rich in organic matter is best. Mulch is beneficial in summer to conserve moisture and in winter to protect canes from severe freezes. The north or east side of a building with cool, moist soils is normally a good environment. Pests are few, and usually no spraying or other measures are necessary to maintain good health. Pruning should be done immediately after flowering. Some old canes should be removed along with any dead branches. New shoots should not be pruned because they will bear next year's flowers.

Color of the blossoms may be almost any shade of blue, purple, or pink and is influenced by variety, amount of light, and chemistry of the soil. Generally, the higher the pH of the soil, the pinker the flowers, and the lower the pH, the bluer the flowers. Color manipulation is easy in the home garden, since the addition of lime will raise pH, and adding aluminum sulfate will lower pH. These changes should be done carefully over time. Remember, too, that nutrients become unavailable to plants grown in soil that is either too acid or too sweet, so moderation is the key. Hydrangeas are very salt tolerant, and according to my favorite expert, Michael Dirr, will tolerate seashore conditions and actually flourish near the shore.

Propagation can be accomplished by taking softwood cuttings in late May, June, or July. Semihardwood and hardwood cuttings will also root. Old established shrubs can also be divided. I once dug a very large specimen and cut it into five pieces with a chain saw. All five are now mature shrubs. Layering is another easy means of propagation.

Simply dig a trench near the plant and bend a section of limb down into the trench. Use a knife to injure the bark on the underside or remove a small ring of outer bark about one inch wide all the way around the limb. Then cover the injured section with soil. Be sure to leave 6 to 12 inches of the tip growth uncovered. Layering done during the summer should be ready for transplanting the following winter.

However you get your hydrangeas, do add them to your garden for a long season of spectacular blooms. Toward the end of the summer, cut hydrangea blossoms after the dew has dried. Simply stick them in a vase without water and let them dry. They'll make a beautiful bouquet that will last all winter.

Oakleaf Hydrangea (*Hydrangea quercifolia*) [25]

A few years ago members of the Valparaiso Garden Club decided to select one specific plant for each member to grow. This experiment was an attempt to win an award offered by the Florida Federation of Garden Clubs. They all had to grow the chosen plant for one year, keep records on its culture and growth, and send these records in at the end of the year along with the award application. They chose the beautiful oakleaf hydrangea for their experiment. Each member secured a rooted cutting and planted it. Today the results of their efforts are evident all around town.

The oakleaf hydrangea is a deciduous shrub that is native to Alabama, Georgia, Florida, and Mississippi. It grows to about eight feet tall and as wide or wider, as it suckers from the roots. Handsome, five-lobed leaves reminiscent of the red oak decorate the landscape in fall with their bronze or crimson colors. Elongated clusters of fertile and sterile white flowers bloom in early summer. Individual flower spikes are borne in 4- to 12-inch-long, erect clusters that taper to a point. They turn pinkish purple and then brown as they age.

Optimal growing requirements are moist, fertile, well-drained soil and partial shade. It flourishes in mulched areas with a cool, moist root environment. The species seems quite disease and insect resistant. If pruning is necessary, it should be accomplished immediately after flowering since flower buds are formed on the preceding year's growth. One thing that our members learned is that this shrub grows quite large. It should be located away from the house where its six- to eight-foot-tall form has plenty of room. Coarse-textured leaves and peeling bark make it interesting all year.

The blooms condition well and are beautiful in floral designs. One of the most exquisite mass designs that I ever saw featured blooms of oakleaf hydrangea and was displayed in a silver urn. It occupied the entrance to a district meeting of the Florida Federation of Garden Clubs. I was captivated by its loveliness.

Several cultivars are available, including 'Harmony', 'PeeWee', 'Snowflake', and 'Snow Queen'. Louisiana Nursery in Opelousas has introduced several cultivars that may be ordered from their catalog.

Propagation of this native is relatively easy. Seed can be sown and will germinate. Dried flower clusters can be collected anytime from November through January. Inside each flower cluster are hundreds of tiny, brown seeds about half the size of a grain of sand. These seeds can be sprinkled over a seed-starting mix. They should not be covered since light is necessary for germination. Seeds should sprout in about 18 days if the flat is kept in a warm, sunny spot and not allowed to dry out. When seedlings are about one inch tall, they should be transplanted to individual four-inch pots. Fertilize with a weak solution of fertilizer, and pinch out the top to encourage branching. When roots fill the pot they can be planted outside. Started in fall or winter, new seedlings should be ready to set out the following fall. Layers and divisions of the parent plant provide new starts, and firmwood cuttings can be taken during the summer. Potted specimens are available at many local nurseries.

I don't know whether the garden club won the award they were after, because this happened before I was associated with the club. They did, however, gain a masterpiece for their yards that continues to reward their efforts in a real and beautiful way.

Crape Myrtle (Lagerstroemia)

Perhaps no flowering tree or shrub is more familiar to folks in the South than crape myrtle. From the fence rows of the country to the medians of streets in almost every city, it blooms in profusion. Almost every rural and suburban yard features one or more of these glorious plants.

Why is it so popular? Perhaps the main reason is that it puts on a year-round show. During the summer, colorful clusters of hundreds of crepelike, crinkled flowers bloom on the tips of branches. Autumn brings a second show when the leaves turn brilliant colors of yellow, orange, or red. In winter the gnarled, sinuous trunks of mature specimens invite one to touch and enjoy the smooth, muscular texture. In many specimens the bark peels to reveal new bark in various colors.

Crape myrtles should be planted in an area that offers plenty of sun and good air circulation. In shade, they will produce fewer blooms, and powdery mildew is much more likely to cause problems. It is adaptable to a wide range of soil types, but good drainage is required. Though very drought tolerant, regular irrigation is required during the first year or until it becomes established. Lack of salt tolerance limits its use near the Gulf.

A plant of low fertility requirements, an established crape myrtle usually does not need fertilizer because its root system extends into the lawn where nutrients can be absorbed from lawn fertilizers. A light sprinkling of balanced fertilizer around young plants during the growing season will stimulate growth.

Pruning should be done only to improve plant form. It can be done during the winter before spring growth. Flowers are produced on new wood, so pruning while the plant is dormant will not interfere with flower production. Some people think that a crape myrtle should resemble a popsicle on a stick. Such drastic pruning destroys the natural shape of the plant and weakens limbs so that they break and fall off when laden with bloom or whipped about by sudden winds. The natural sinewy trunks of the crape myrtle make a beautiful statement in winter. Amputated and disfigured stubs where branches once were are a travesty of the beauty that should be.

One solution for trees butchered in this manner is to prune them back to ground level and let new trunks grow. Rapid growth will result because they will be growing from well-established root systems. Select three or four of the strongest and most well-placed shoots and remove all others. Suckers may have to be removed several times during the growing season, but be patient. With proper training the tree can be a beauty once again.

New breeding programs have produced cultivars that take the South's heat and humidity better than most of the old-fashioned types. They show increased tolerance to powdery mildew and are offered in many sizes and colors. The University of Florida is growing more than 70 cultivars and species of crape myrtles at various research facilities throughout the state. They are being evaluated and compared with older cultivars for pest susceptibility, flowering, growth, and overall adaptability.

During the summer, Master Gardeners from Florida attend a field day at these facilities to see and learn about the trials. All sizes and colors of crape myrtles are on display—some of which are not yet available commercially. New varieties range from 18 inches tall to more than 20 feet. Colors include almost any shade of red, pink, lavender, purple, and white. Forms are mounding, rounded, vase-shaped, or upright and spreading. Bark color ranges from nondescript tan to light or dark brown, beige, orange, cinnamon, gray, pinkish cream, or whitish beige. With all these choices, finding one to suit specific needs is easier than ever. One exists that will exactly fit almost any space and color scheme.

Removal of seed pods on the newer cultivars is not necessary because they are more free flowering, and the large seed pods add winter interest. New foliage colors are a trend to watch for in the future. A grower in Oklahoma has produced one that has dark burgundy new growth. One interesting cultivar is 'Dynamite', which grows to 20 feet and sports new foliage and twigs of bright ruby red tipped with clusters of round, red buds that open to reveal cherry red flowers. 'Red Rocket' (to 20 feet) has deep crimson buds and new leaves and large trusses of fiery red flowers. A fragrant selection is 'Whitcomb's Raspberry Sundae', which grows to 15 feet and has soft crimson flowers edged with white.

I personally fell in love with a cultivar named 'Apalachee'. It grows to about 20 feet tall or more. Pale lavender flowers are delightfully scented, and the bark is dark cinnamon. From the time I first laid eyes on this beautiful specimen, I became single-minded in its pursuit. How and where could I obtain one of these jewels?

Some were being given away at the field day. We all had numbered tickets. When drawing time came, tension mounted. Would I be one of the lucky ones? My number was finally called, but 'Apalachee' was all gone. I won a coral honeysuckle. Disappointed but not outdone, I hung my hopes on Tallahassee Nursery. We planned to stop there on the way home. Would Lady Luck smile on me this day? Would I find the object of my desire?

Well, Lady Luck was with me. I headed home with joy in my heart, visions of beauty in my head, and 'Apalachee' in the back of the van. What a glorious day it turned out to be!

Chinese Fringe, Fringe Flower, Loropetalum
(Loropetalum chinense) [29]

Early one spring morning my friend Normie came speeding up in her car. I was working in the front yard, and she was positively wide-eyed with excitement. "Get in!" she demanded. "There's something down the street you've just got to see!" I climbed in, and away we went, around the corner and about a block down the street. She stopped and pointed. "See?" she exclaimed. "Didn't I tell you?"

In front of us was a shrub about five feet tall. An impressive sight it was, too, with its mass of magenta, fringelike blossoms. Colorful, twisted, straplike petals three-quarters of an inch long hung in clusters from the ends of branches. "What is it?" Normie wanted to know.

"That, my friend," I replied, "is loropetalum."

"Well, where did it come from? Where can I get one?" Norma's questions echoed those of many observers who have seen loropetalum in bloom for the first time.

Chinese fringe or fringe flower (*Loropetalum chinense* var. *rubrum*) blooms in spring. Hailing from China, this evergreen shrub is pest and disease resistant. Site it in moist, acid, well-drained soil with lots of organic matter in full sun or light shade. Prune in late spring as soon as the flowers fade if necessary. However, much of the natural arching and tiered effect of the branches is lost if shrubs are pruned into

rounded, meatball shapes. Mulch to conserve moisture as performance will be poor in dry soil. Use azalea/camellia fertilizer to prevent
leaf yellowing and to promote the acid soil in which loropetalum
thrives. Propagation is by cuttings taken after new growth has hardened in midsummer.

Pay attention to where you place this saucy cousin of the witch
hazel. Not only can this floozy of a flower clash with other spring-
blooming shrubs, but it can grow from 10 to 15 feet high and wide in
about ten years. Loropetalum can be used successfully as a single
specimen plant, and it is good in corner and understory plantings,
screens, or mixed shrub borders. Older specimens may serve as small,
multitrunked trees if lower branches are removed.

Several cultivars are available. 'Burgundy' has electric, dark-pink
flowers and rich, reddish purple foliage that matures to purplish
green. 'Blush' has lighter, pink-tinged leaves and paler, rose-colored
flowers. 'Ruby' is the smallest variety. Other selections are 'Monraz'
and 'Zhuzou'. Because the plants have not been on the market for
long, names are sometimes confusing. Two different growers might
name the same plant two different names. For instance, 'Blush' and
'Razzleberri' are probably the same plant. 'Hines Purpleleaf' and
'Plum Delight' resemble each other greatly. Young leaves of most cultivars are burgundy, maturing to green, especially in the center of the
plant. Some cultivars stay redder than others, and some vary in
height. The creamy white-flowered variety has green leaves and has
been on the scene for many years.

Loropetalum chinense var. *rubrum* has been selected as one of the
Florida Plants of the Year by the Florida Nurserymen and Growers
Association. No doubt everyone will soon recognize this shrub,
because something so showy could not remain a stranger for long.

Saucer Magnolia (*Magnolia* x *soulangiana*) [26]

The saucer magnolia behind the greenhouse is resplendent.
Hundreds of large, goblet-shaped, rose purple blossoms seem lit
from within because the inside of the petals is white. What a sight! A
warm spell in mid-February brought about this magnificent scene.

Gardeners in our neck of the woods are prepared to have these blossoms turned to brown mush by a sudden freeze. We plant them anyway. Most years we get to see the blossoms and are rewarded with a spectacular show.

Native to China and Japan, these trees are deciduous. The blooms appear in spring before the leaves. All winter the upcoming show is evident. Pussy-willow–like buds hold the blossoms captive until just the right moment. When that time comes, a scene unfolds that dazzles passersby with its loveliness.

Saucer magnolias like full sun or very light shade and moist, fertile, well-drained soil. Shallow roots make them susceptible to extended drought, so they should be mulched well and watered during dry spells. Mulch should extend outward from the trunk at least two feet in all directions. This will prevent injury to the thin bark by lawn mowers and string trimmers. Saucer magnolias are generally long lived and trouble free. Mature specimens reach 20 to 30 feet in height with an equal spread. Growth rate is medium, and a newly planted specimen will grow from 10 to 15 feet over a ten-year period.

A cross between *M. denudata* and *M. liliiflora* spawned the original hybrid in a garden of Soulange-Brodin in France. The plant first flowered in 1826, and the cultivars have since become widespread in American gardens. Michael Dirr, in his book *Manual of Woody Landscape Plants*, lists 14 cultivars of this popular magnolia.

The beautiful saucer magnolia always reminds me of my dear friend and neighbor Fran McCoy. She died and was buried when the magnolias bloomed a few years ago. How I miss her! Isn't it amazing the way plants can remind us of people and events? I think of her, too, in the spring when I see the orchard orioles preparing their nest. She identified this bird long before I did. I remember when she rescued a baby bird and fed it with an eye dropper every couple of hours, night and day.

So for me, the bloom of the saucer magnolia is bittersweet. I marvel at its beauty, but at the same time I suffer a heartache. It's a melancholy sort of seeing and remembering. I believe Fran would appreciate the fact that such a beautiful flower stirs my memory of her. Here's to you, girl! It's spring, the season of the magnolia!

Turk's Cap (*Malvaviscus arboreus*)

We gardeners acquire our plants in a variety of ways. I'm almost ashamed to say how I got my start of giant Turk's cap. I will, however, just so readers will know how easy it is to get started.

While walking around my neighborhood one summer not so very long ago, I admired a Turk's cap blooming in a neighbor's yard. Not knowing these neighbors, and never seeing any of them outside, I left it alone. One day, however, I noticed that these neighbors had moved. The house was empty! I seized the opportunity and broke off a twig near the bottom of the plant where it would never be missed. I took it home, put it in a glass of water, and within a few weeks it had struck roots. Then I planted it in a container where it stayed for the winter. The following spring I planted it in its permanent place in the landscape.

Am I a flower thief? A guilty conscience has plagued me ever since I took that cutting. One day I will see someone outside the house and confess my plant-snatching atrocity. My feelings of shame, though, are somewhat assuaged when I see the Turk's cap in bloom. Maybe it was worth it. In late fall it is a traffic stopper. Two-and-a-half-inch-long, bright red, tubular flowers hang from the limbs in glorious profusion. The flowers resemble hibiscus buds that have not opened. Five petals twist like a pinwheel around a projecting column of stamens and pistils.

Sun or shade suits it well. Mine blooms profusely in partial shade. This amazing plant has been drought tolerant, pest and disease resistant, and a high performer in the fall garden. Though it is evergreen in its native Mexico, here it dies back to the ground in winter. During its first year my plant grew to about three feet tall. When frost cut it down, I pruned it back to the ground. The next year the plant surprised me by growing to about five or six feet tall and putting on a show that was even more spectacular.

I also have a variety of this plant (*Malvaviscus arboreus* var. *drummondii*) [24] that has smaller flowers. It is a native of tropical America and prevalent in Texas where it has escaped cultivation in some areas. It tends to get rather rangy in the landscape, so cutting back early in the season to force branching and compactness improves its looks. I got my start of this plant years ago from a friend's mother. It has come back reliably every year, and I have shared it with many people.

Both varieties of Turk's cap are attractive to butterflies and hummingbirds. Bumblebees like them too, but they do not have long tongues like the butterflies and hummers. They shred the flowers to get to the nectar inside.

Do, please, purchase your plant. Keep your eyes open. Maybe a generous friend will give you a cutting. Don't be, like me, forever tormented with a guilty conscience.

Banana Shrub (*Michela figo*)

The scents of spring are so tantalizing! Gardeners who are admirers of fragrant plants go to great extremes to find specimens to add to their collection. It is possible to have plants that smell good in the garden year-round. We humans are content simply to enjoy the fragrance of plants. Sometimes we forget that it serves an important biological function. Scent is believed to be even more important than color in attracting pollinating bees, birds, moths, flies, beetles, and bats. Night and evening bloomers such as four o'clock (*Mirabilis jalapa*) and

moonflower (*Ipomoea alba*) depend upon scent to guide pollinators.

I have found in my garden that many plants with scented foliage seem immune to attack by slugs, insects, and other garden pests. My herb garden suffers very little damage from marauding critters, probably because insects find the scented foliage of many of the plants distasteful. I have noticed, too, that many scents that I find appealing are not attractive to others, and vice versa. Many people, for instance, enjoy the scent of marigolds, and others find it so objectionable that plant breeders have developed a scentless variety. Therefore, when gardeners select scents to enjoy in their gardens, it might be a good idea to select plants when they are in bloom to find out if the scent is an agreeable one.

Wise nurseries use the sense of smell to sell plants. Who can pass a hanging basket of petunias in full bloom and not be tempted to take it home? Why are fragrant roses at the entry of these establishments, and other shrubs and flowers moved to center front when their smell is most pleasing? They know that we are apt to take home something that smells good!

Some plants are fragrant only at certain times. Frequently scent is most pronounced in warm, moist air or at nightfall. Few people have really enjoyed the scent of orchids because the blooms have been refrigerated at the florist. Common snakeplant or mother-in-law's tongue (*Sansevieria*) puts out spikes of delicate white flowers about once a year. Many people have seen these flowers, but few know that they are fragrant. During the day they have no scent, but at night they are highly fragrant.

In my own yard and neighborhood, several scents of spring have kept me busy sniffing and photographing. One of my favorites, the banana shrub, has outdone itself this year. A member of the magnolia family, this shrub is aptly named because its scent is reminiscent of bananas. Actually this "shrub" may grow into a small tree. It naturally grows into an upright oval to rounded shrub up to 15 feet tall. Native to China, it was introduced in our country in 1789.

Small, creamy yellow, magnolia-like flowers edged with maroon bloom each spring and fall. Enjoying the blossoms on the tree is best, for when they are picked they fall to pieces very quickly. Usually evergreen in our climate, the handsome, glossy dark green foliage may freeze in severe winters. Banana shrub does best in sun or light shade in moist, fertile, well-drained, slightly acid soil. Once established, it needs very little care. Freedom from pests and slow growth rate make it a choice specimen plant for our area. Plant banana shrub for its upright, oval, positive form, fragrant flowers, and dense mass. The long-lived shrub will delight gardeners for years.

Sweet Olive, Tea Olive (*Osmanthus fragrans*) [30]

Sometimes in late winter or early spring when Amiable Spouse or I step out the back door, we detect a very pleasant fragrance wafting on the air. Amiable Spouse goes right to the source and breathes in heady drafts of the tantalizing scent. "If we could bottle this," he says, "we'd make a fortune." I, however, am content to enjoy the scent in the garden. The scent of such esteem comes from our sweet olive or fragrant tea olive. Native to Asia, this large shrub or small tree grows 30 feet tall or more and about eight feet wide. This shrub was one of Amiable Spouse's first requests when I began landscaping our yard, so I got it for him at Christmas several years ago. A large garden space can be filled with the fragrance of sweet olive. Even when tucked into back nooks and crannies, its impact can be significant. The strong fragrance can be smelled from several hundred feet away. Blossoms are visually insignificant. Tiny white flowers bloom in clusters along the stems. One might never notice them except for their enticing fragrance.

Sweet olive blooms during our cool season. Usually we expect it to bloom in late fall and again in early spring. I have noticed, however, that when winters are mild, it blooms most of the season. It is a long-lived shrub with few plant pests. Often it is found in old gardens of the South. Sometimes when old specimens have become too large as shrubs, they may be reclaimed as small evergreen trees by removing the lower branches.

Sweet olive does best in fertile, moist, well-drained, slightly acid soil. Full sun or partial shade suits it well. Propagation is by cuttings of half-ripened wood. Generally it is available at most local garden centers throughout the year. *O. fragrans* var. *aurantiacus* is a variety with striking yellowish orange flowers. It has larger, coarser-textured foliage than the regular sweet olive, and new growth is reddish bronze.

Our area is fortunate to have its own native sweet olive (*Osmanthus americanus*), commonly called devilwood or wild olive. It ranges from southeastern Louisiana eastward to Florida and north to Virginia. Normally it is associated with moist, fertile, acid soil but is tolerant of most conditions. Small, cream-colored flowers are not showy, but they are somewhat fragrant. Blooms are present in March and April. Dark blue berries about one-half inch in diameter ripen in September and provide food for birds and small mammals.

Devilwood is a neat, attractive, small evergreen tree that deserves wider use as an ornamental. It has a medium-slow growth rate and upright form with loosely spaced branches. Its smooth, silvery gray bark with coppery undertones is exceptionally attractive. Plant this native in light shade or full sun as it tends to get scraggly in heavy shade.

Devilwood gets its name from its extremely tough wood. A devil to work with for woodworkers and pruners alike, it is best situated where pruning will not be necessary. That is good, too, because it grows naturally into a beautiful shape without much help, and the strong wood stands up to gales and rough weather.

The native devilwood may prove difficult to locate, but sweet olive is readily available at most nurseries. Plant one in your garden for a special extra dimension of pleasure.

China Rose (Rosa chinensis)

Oh, it was a superb weekend—the stuff of which dreams are made. Amiable Spouse and I were at the river—Black Creek in Walton County, actually. The sun was high, the fish were biting, and the swamp roses (*Rosa palustris*) were in full bloom. We caught a good mess of fish, though not as many as we might have if the swamp roses had not been blooming. Amiable Spouse had to stop the boat quite frequently so that I could photograph them. All along the edges of the river, masses of showy, five-petaled, pink blossoms with bright yellow stamens cascaded from the banks. When the roses finish blooming, the petals fall into the water and are carried downstream on the current. *Rosa palustris* is native to flood plains, marshy or swampy shores, swamps, and wet thickets throughout the coastal South and into central Florida south to Polk County. Although it flowers only in spring, applelike fruits, called rose hips, extend the show for months and provide a feast for the birds.

It is humbling to see such a beautiful garden virtually untouched by human hands. No matter how hard we gardeners try, we can never achieve a garden of such grandeur and diversity. Yet we slave on in our feeble attempts. We may, on some very elemental plane, manage to arrange our small portion of the earth in a way that pleases us. Yet here for free is a garden whose dimensions and biological diversity are so great that our efforts seem of no consequence. Humbling, isn't it?

Though *R. palustris* is beautiful hanging above the river as it does, gardeners everywhere are better off to leave it in its native habitat. This shrub, which grows to six feet tall, spreads by underground runners. Along the riverbanks, competition is keen for every inch of growing space. If they thrive in this situation, just think what they might do in less restricted places like a home garden. Quite soon, I think, they would wear out their welcome.

Many of its cousins are more suitable subjects for the home landscape. In our hot, humid climate, however, it pays to be selective when choosing roses. Such diseases as black spot and powdery mildew thrive, and unless we have hours to devote to spraying and caring for these plants, we are better off choosing those that are naturally resistant to diseases and pests.

Some of the old China roses fit the bill for our climate. 'Old Blush', a beloved China rose, grows to five or six feet and is tolerant of salt air. Clusters of semidouble pink roses that darken with age bloom heavily in spring and fall with intermittent blooms throughout the summer. Fragrance is reminiscent of sweet peas. Though mildew or black spot may mar its foliage at times, it will not debilitate the plant.

Other China roses recommended for the coastal South include 'Louis Philippe', 'Ducher', 'Archduke Charles', 'Mrs. Dudley Cross', and 'Mutabilis'. Single flowers that open yellow and then change through pink to red as they age give 'Mutabilis' the appearance of a cluster of butterflies. All of the colors may be found on the bush at the same time. Also worth growing are 'Pink Pet', 'Hermosa', 'Belfield', and 'Cramoisi Superieur'.

Species roses such as Lady Banks (*Rosa banksiae*) [31] and

chestnut rose (*Rosa roxburghii*) also perform well. Lady Banks blooms only in the spring, but its cascades of light-yellow blooms on thornless canes are a memorable sight. Give it plenty of room, since it grows to about 20 feet tall and wide. A white-flowered variety is available and has a lovely violet scent.

As with any landscape plant, proper soil preparation and site selection are essential for success. At least six hours of sun and well-drained soil high in organic matter yield the best results. Although China roses survive with little fertilizer, an application of complete fertilizer every two to three months during the growing season will result in lush foliage and bountiful blooms.

If you have given up on roses, reconsider and try some of the old roses. I once heard it said that not every rose is right for every garden, but for every garden there are roses that are right. Why not give them a try?

Vines

Vines perform several tasks that few other plants can accomplish in the garden. A lovely backdrop for flower beds and borders can be made of vines, or they can separate garden areas by growing on a support or fence between them. They provide quick vertical elements where needed, and can soften the harsh lines of buildings, trellises, or arbors. Unsightly objects can be concealed, or a colorful vine can wind through trees and shrubs. Use of vertical space is maximized and minimum ground is required.

Vines, like some other groups of plants, may be perennial or annual. Choose a colorful annual vine to enjoy one season, and next year change the color scheme simply by planting a different seed. For a more permanent landscape element, a hardy perennial vine may be chosen.

Malabar Spinach (*Basella alba* 'Rubra')

One of my favorite vines is Malabar spinach. This fast-growing annual vine has big, heart-shaped green leaves that are as pretty as they are tasty. Frequently used as a spinach substitute, they are a flavorful ingredient for salads and sandwiches. My first seeds came from Aunt Gladys in Mississippi. The pretty vine crept along the ground and wove its way through other plants in her border. I gathered a few seeds and brought them home.

I planted mine at the base of a tall-canopied pine tree and gave it a sturdy wire trellis upon which to climb. It grew to the top of the six-foot support and cascaded back down gracefully. Small white blossoms followed by green berries that turn dark purple in fall decorate the vine. This abundance of berries assures that plants will volunteer next year. It is also a fitting addition to a wildlife garden since birds enjoy the berries.

If you are starting from scratch, wait until the ground is warm and settled in spring, and then plant directly where they are to grow. Plant in good garden soil and give the newly emerging vines plenty of water. You can start picking the leaves of Malabar spinach in about 12 weeks when they are three to four inches long. Add them to your salads, or grow the pretty vine strictly as an ornamental in your flower bed. You will be rewarded with a dependable show all summer.

Love-in-a-Puff (*Cardiospermum halicacabum*)

Ah, the pretty things that gardeners collect over the years! Every time I look at it I am smitten all over with love-in-a-puff. This annual vine has finely cut, attractive, two-inch lacy leaves. Dainty clusters of delicate white flowers remind one of lightly sifted snow. The tiny flowers are followed by papery, round, one-inch seed pods that are like small green balloons. The seed pods are as ornamental as the flowers. When they ripen and turn brown, a black seed about the size of a small pea is found inside the husk. The eye of this pealike structure is a perfectly shaped white heart.

Once you have love-in-a puff, you'll likely have it forever, for it reseeds prolifically. That proclivity does not make it invasive, however, for unwanted seedlings are easily removed. It seldom climbs more than four or five feet high, so controlling it is not difficult. In my yard it grows beside a pine tree where I have given it wire upon which to twine.

It's funny how I have become so attached to this little vine. I have never seen it in anyone else's yard except some of my friends', and they got it from me. No author that I have ever read has mentioned it. None of my books or magazines have articles about it. What's the deal?

I'm really glad that it has become a permanent part of my garden.

Carolina Jessamine, Yellow Jessamine
(Gelsemium sempervirens) [32]

"Wow!" remarked Amiable Spouse as he entered the house after fetching the morning paper. "Something really smells good out there!" He was speaking of the Carolina jessamine (often called Carolina jasmine) that blooms on the trellis outside our front door. Oddly enough, I threatened to cut it down this past summer. That was about the time I had to get a ladder and prune the writhing, tangled mass that grew higher and higher over the trellis and eventually leaned over and grasped the nearby limbs of the camellia. On and on it went until I clipped its grasping tendrils and halted its forward march.

Now I'm glad I kept it. The buttery yellow flowers brighten the early spring landscape and offer a delicate fragrance worth stopping to savor. Down the street, it blooms on a chain-link fence. Such placement brings the flowers down to eye level and allows it to be easily pruned. That should be a hint as to appropriate placement of this vigorous vine. It scrambles to the top of whatever support is available and blooms only on the top. The sides of my trellis are vacant except for the naked vines.

Look for Carolina jessamine as you travel along our highways. Throughout the South this native, South Carolina's state flower, shines from the tops of trees, shrubs, and fences like strings of Christmas lights in the spring. Beware, however, for it is one of our poisonous plants. Bees have been accused of making toxic honey, cows have been killed by eating the green vines, and children have been made ill by sipping nectar from its blossoms.

Armed with this knowledge, you may find a suitable place for Carolina jessamine in your landscape. Evergreen foliage, twining vines that can mask a chain-link fence or other structure, tolerance of our heat, humidity, salt spray, and poor soil are sound reasons why it is an excellent choice. Like sparklers flung across the landscape, the golden trumpets flash and twinkle as they usher in the glory of a brand-new spring.

Moon Vine, Moon Flower (*Ipomoea alba*)

"Hey, kids, come look at this," I call to my grandsons. In front of me a moon flower bud quivers. Max and Douglas run to watch. They are not disappointed. The tightly spiraled bud continues to loosen and unwind in tiny increments. Suddenly it gives one mighty heave and bursts open as if freed from the viselike clutches of some unseen hand. Before us glistens a six-inch flower of dazzling whiteness and purity. The children gasp and look at me in awed delight.

The moon vine is closely related to morning glory (*Ipomoea purpurea*). Just before dark, the flowers open to greet the evening, just as morning glory opens to greet each new day. Fragrance wafts on the soft, summer breezes, delighting our senses and attracting pollinating insects.

Although moon vine is perennial in its native tropics, north of Zone 9 it is an annual. Site it on a sturdy support where it can climb from 10 to 15 feet. Give it average soil and ample moisture. Feed with rose fertilizer or one with a high middle number. Too much nitrogen will result in more leaf than bloom. Mulch to even soil temperatures and discourage weeds. This treatment and a sunny place will yield many blossoms all summer.

Moon vines are easy to get started. Nick or chip the hard seed coats with a file or knife and soak the seeds in water overnight before planting. Plant in containers so that new plants are ready to set out when the weather is warm. I have better luck if they have begun vining and attained a bit of height before I transplant them to their permanent site. I have tried direct seeding them where they are to grow, but slugs relish the tiny sprouting plants. Getting the leaves above ground gives them a good start.

Be patient if seeds do not sprout as quickly as expected. Once I planted some in small pots and kept them watered for weeks. Finally, I gave up and emptied the potting soil into a large container for use at another time. All summer I was surprised to find moon flowers coming up in unexpected places.

Seeds may be collected and saved from year to year. People who grow moon flowers are usually happy to share with fellow gardeners. They are available at most mail-order seed sources or on seed racks at local outlets.

However you get your start, be sure to plant this lovely vine where you will see it often in the early evening. Place it near a porch or patio where you can enjoy the honeysuckle-like fragrance and pristine white blossoms.

Trumpet Honeysuckle, Coral Honeysuckle
(Lonicera sempervirens)

One of our most beautiful natives is trumpet honeysuckle. Some gardeners, upon hearing the very word "honeysuckle," immediately dismiss me as a complete fraud and forever after disbelieve every word that I utter. They have had experience with honeysuckle, and it was not a good one! These doubting Thomases do not distinguish one honeysuckle from another. Their experience was probably with the

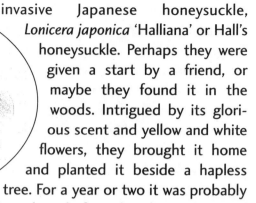

invasive Japanese honeysuckle, *Lonicera japonica* 'Halliana' or Hall's honeysuckle. Perhaps they were given a start by a friend, or maybe they found it in the woods. Intrigued by its glorious scent and yellow and white flowers, they brought it home and planted it beside a hapless tree. For a year or two it was probably fine, but then, before they learned its evil nature, it had consumed the tree. Now it was rampaging through the azaleas and sending up tendrils in search of its next victim, possibly the house.

Do not be snookered into believing that all honeysuckles are alike. Our native honeysuckle is a beautiful, well-mannered vine. Henry Mitchell, whose column "Earthman" was a weekly feature in the *Washington Post* for 20 years, called this vine one of our country's greatest treasures. Clusters of scarlet trumpets have no scent, but this unfortunate defect does not discourage hummingbirds who relish its nectar, nor the birds who feast on its berries.

Japanese honeysuckle is a dependable ornamental in northern states where cold weather keeps its evil character in check. In the South it is a good example of an exotic gone wild, and it is recognized by the Exotic Pest Council as a serious problem in 24 states. In the woods in Mississippi where I grew up, one can hardly walk because the honeysuckle is so thick. Its rampaging vines swallow up everything in its path and shade the sun from more desirable native plants. This causes the natives to decline and eventually die. It's another kudzu!

On the other hand, our native trumpet honeysuckle is a semi-evergreen vine that grows 10 to 20 feet tall, depending upon the height of its support. Slender, tubular, yellow to red flowers about two inches long bloom from April to May and sporadically into fall. Red, quarter-inch, berrylike fruits provide food for birds. Its range is from Connecticut to Florida and west to Nebraska and Texas.

Cultivars include 'Superba', which has larger flowers than the native variety, and 'Magnifica', which is a deeper reddish orange. 'Sulphurea' ('Flava') is a highly desirable cultivar that provides a literal shower of yellow flowers and bright green foliage in spring. 'Manifich' is light orange on the outside and clear yellow inside.

To establish trumpet honeysuckle in the landscape, plant it in moist, well-drained soil. It grows well in sun or shade, but flowers will be more numerous if considerable sun is provided. Some sort of support will be necessary such as a trellis, picket fence, or arbor. Prune after flowering to shape and control. If pruned in late winter, most of the flowers will be removed since it blooms mostly on old wood.

Trumpet honeysuckle can be propagated from seed if pulp is cleaned from them and they are given three months of cold, moist stratification. To stratify, place seed in a plastic bag in moist peat or sand and store in a refrigerator. After this treatment, plant the seeds in moist soil where they will germinate quickly. Cuttings also root easily if dipped in rooting hormone and placed in a growing medium.

For gardeners who are trying to incorporate more native plants into their landscape, trumpet honeysuckle is a good choice. Like many of our natives, it grows well in native soil, is drought tolerant, pest resistant, and performs well with minimum maintenance. It is a beautiful native plant that deserves greater use in our landscapes.

Mandevilla (*Mandevilla sanderi*)

Recently I was invited to give a program to a group of senior citizens in Crestview. They wanted to hear about flowers that do well in this area. That, as we all know, is a broad topic. For a 20-minute presentation, I knew that I would have to narrow my focus. So I gave the matter considerable thought. I figured that I would be talking to a group of people who might not choose to get out and do backbreaking labor in the yard. My thinking was on target, for I discovered a laid-back group of senior citizens who figured they had done their share of hard work. They were ready to play and enjoy life. If this meeting was any indication, they are well on their way. They certainly have earned the right, and I am in complete accord.

One of my suggestions was mandevilla (*Mandevilla sanderi*, formerly *Dipladenia sanderi*). In my neighborhood, this beautiful vine decorates many mailboxes and trellises. In Niceville, Florida, it has for several years been used extensively in front of the city offices and near the children's park. Such an eye-catching and high-performance plant is a good choice for attracting children's attention and for adorning large spaces.

Mandevilla comes in several colors and cultivars. One of the most popular is *M. sanderi* 'Red Riding Hood'. Blossoms are lipstick red accented by a vivid yellow throat. One of my favorites is the cultivar 'Alice du Pont' which sports bright pink flowers that open in characteristic pinwheel fashion. A light pink selection called 'Leah' with its dark pink throat is also striking in the landscape. Some people might prefer the beautiful white, yellow-throated *M. sanderi* var. *boliviensis*.

Whichever cultivar the gardener chooses is sure to please. Since its hardiness is limited to tropical areas, it most likely will not make it through our winters without protection. I have had it return from the roots in a well-mulched area, but I would not depend on it. Growing it in a container will increase the likelihood that it will last for more than one year. When winter comes it may be cut back and placed in a protected place such as a garage or greenhouse. Don't let it dry out completely, and do not fertilize during this period of slowed growth or dormancy. When warm weather returns, bring it out, water, and resume fertilizing.

Ideally mandevilla should be grown in a generously sized container with fertile, well-drained soil. Full sun is recommended, but I suspect that it, like most plants, would appreciate a bit of protection from our hot afternoon sun. It will perform best if it is fed regularly during the growing season with a balanced fertilizer.

Passion Flower, Passion Vine (*Passiflora incarnata*)

Long gone are my cotton-picking days. Just like yesterday, however, are my memories of those times. Like most other people born and raised in rural Mississippi in the forties and fifties, I was anxious to earn money any way I could. I remember being eager for the cotton

1 Summer Phlox *Phlox paniculata* 'Bright Eyes' (p.11)
2 Bat Face Cuphea *Cuphea llavea* 'Georgia Scarlet' (p. 4)
3 Butterfly Weed *Asclepias tuberosa* (p. 1)
4 Black-eyed Susan *Rudbeckia fulgida* 'Goldsturm' (p. 15)
5 Autumn Sage *Salvia greggii* (p. 17)
6 Gaura, Whirling Butterflies *Gaura lindheimeri* (p. 6)
7 *Salvia* 'Indigo Spires' (p. 17)

8 Forsythia Sage
   Salvia madrensis (p. 18)
9 Crinum Lily *Crinum asiaticum*
   (p. 33)
10 *Crinum* 'Louis Bosanquet' (p. 33)
11 Milk and Wine Lily
   Crinum x herbertii (p. 32)
12 Kahili Ginger
   Hedychium gardneranum (p. 47)
13 Louisiana Iris (*Iris* spp.) (p. 37)
14 White Butterfly Ginger
   Hedychium coronarium (p. 47)
15 Chinese Ground Orchid
   Bletilla striata (p. 28)

28 Lacecap Hydrangea
   Hydrangea macrophylla (p. 107)
29 Chinese Fringe, Fringe Flower
   Loropetalum chinensis (p. 113)
30 Sweet Olive, Tea Olive
   Osmanthus fragrans (p. 119)
31 Lady Banks Rose *Rosa banksiae* (p. 121)
32 Carolina Jessamine, Yellow Jasmine
   Gelsemium sempervirens (p. 125)
33 *Zinnia* 'Profusion White' (p. 189)
34 Blue Daze *Evolvulus glomeratus* (p. 191)

35 Fanflower *Scaevola aemula* (p. 191)
36 *Pentas lanceolata* with
   monarch butterfly (p. 180)
37 Coleus and ornamental potato 'Margarita'.
   The lime-green edging on the coleus leaves
   perfectly complements the lime green of the
   sweet potato. (p. 189)
38 Candytuft *Iberis* (p. 201)
39 Sweet Pea *Lathyrus odoratus* (p. 201)
40 Snapdragons *Antirrhinum majus* (p. 188)
41 Bromeliads are attractively displayed on
   cypress knee stumps near the author's entry.
   (p. 205)

42 The border in June.
43 A winter vegetable garden. Plants include multiplying onions, mustard, a variety of lettuces, kale, parsley, arugula, and mesclun mix. (p. 195)
44 *Melampodium* and *Salvia farinacea* combine to make a pleasing combination of colors. (p. 17)
45 This attractive mixed border includes various shrubs, perennials, and annuals. It is beautiful year-round.

46 The perennial border in October. Ginger lilies, salvias, firespike, and other plants fill the mature border with color.

47 Various textures and colors create an attractive landscape with nary a flower in sight. (p. 45)

48 Rain lilies (*Habranthus robusta*) bloom prolifically after spring's first major rain. (p. 211)

to mature and get ready for picking. To my brothers, sisters, and me it held the promise of new school clothes for the coming year. We were paid three or four cents for every pound of cotton we picked. Every night we poured over the pages of the Sears Roebuck catalog. Carefully we planned our prospective purchases and chose far more than our meager earnings would afford.

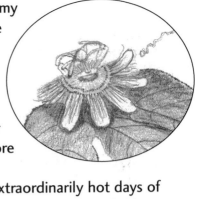

Not long removed in memory are the extraordinarily hot days of August and September when the whole family headed to the fields to gather the white fiber that was the substance of our immediate dreams. We dressed in long-sleeved shirts and pants with extra pads sewn into the knees that allowed us to crawl along the rows. With naked hands we picked handful after handful of fluffy white cotton from the prickly bolls and stuffed it into cotton sacks. Strapped over one shoulder and pulled along as we worked, these sacks became heavier and heavier. When they became so heavy that we could hardly pull them, it was time to weigh in.

Hands became bloody, knees blistered, and bodies acclimated to a numbness far beyond tiredness as we labored from dawn until dusk. New school clothes meant much to poor but proud Mississippi farm kids.

Now, what got me to thinking about all that was my recent infatuation with passion flowers. The native passion flower was a weed in the Mississippi cotton fields. Even then I admired its beautiful flowers, but the fruit was a refreshing treat that offered a short respite from the drudgery of the cotton row. I'd sit on my soft sack of cotton, peel the maypop, and fill my mouth full of the pulpy seeds. What a delicious treat this was as I sucked the juice from the seeds and then spit out the remains!

Some time ago I discussed this vigorous vine with Jack Wetherell, who was then the person most responsible for the Panhandle Butterfly House in Navarre, Florida. At that time I was considering eradicating the vigorous vine from my garden. During its first year, it was a source of delight. The second year, however, it began coming up in places far from its original position. I was becoming impatient with its aggressiveness.

Jack pointed out that it was a vine that we must grow if we were to continue our enjoyment of the Gulf and variegated fritillary butterflies. They depend upon it, for it is the host plant for their caterpillars. The Florida state butterfly, the zebra longwing (or zebra heliconian), also depends upon it, though I have never seen one of these in my garden. Jack was quite put out by the very suggestion that I might get rid of it.

The trick, then, is to find a place where the exuberant growth is an asset instead of a liability. I think I have found such a place. Bounded on two sides by the house, another by a concrete driveway, and another by the lawn, it manages to stay put. Though it comes up in the lawn, it never gets a foothold, for Amiable Spouse simply mows it down. Since it is not evergreen, it dies to the ground in winter and comes up the following spring. As long as I can keep it contained by the driveway, the house, and the lawn, I'll continue to grow it.

My efforts have paid off handsomely, for more fritillaries than I can count flutter around the vines laying their eggs. They pleasure me as they sip nectar from other flowers that bloom in my garden. Quite purposely the passion vines are in an area where they are not highly visible to human visitors. The butterflies, however, have no trouble finding them, and they become quite ragged from the munchings of the caterpillars.

Several types of passion vines may be grown. Some of them, however, are tropical species that will not survive our winter. Some, such as *P. jamesonii, P. coccinea, P. alatocaerulea,* and others may be grown in the tropical South. A recent addition to my garden is the cultivar *Passiflora caerulea* 'Constance Elliott'. This evergreen passion flower has stunning white flowers and is not as exuberant as our native. Time will determine if this beautiful vine will become a part of my permanent landscape. I can only hope so, for I am quite enamored with the unusual flowers.

The passion flower of the Mississippi cotton fields, however, is here to stay. No special care is needed for this native flower other than limiting its growth space. I continue to grow it for the butterflies and for the beautiful flowers and tasty fruits. Thank goodness I don't have to grow cotton and I no longer need school clothes.

Black-eyed Susan Vine (Thunbergia alata)

If I'd had a thousand black-eyed Susan vines for one of my garden club's plant sales, I could have sold every one of them. It was the star of the show. Every little sprig that I could find had been potted up, but it was not nearly enough to meet the demand. During the afternoon, I found myself digging up a few remaining wee specimens to share with some people who greatly admired it.

Climbing up concrete reinforcing wire attached to a pine tree at the head of the walk, it greeted visitors with hundreds of two-inch, bright yellow flowers with purple black throats. Held in perfect pose with each flower facing outward for maximum impact, these single, five-petaled beauties announced their presence with exuberance. Even at a distance, the posies radiated cheerfulness and shouted "Welcome!" to garden tour participants.

Black-eyed Susan vine is a perennial vine grown as a summer annual in our area. Some winters are so mild, however, that it survives. When spring arrives, it starts blooming. In severe winters it gets killed back to the ground. Much of the summer following a severe winter is spent growing to blooming size. Seeds from the previous year come up around the vine, and it is these small seedlings that I share with folks.

Flowers are available in orange, yellow, or white, and the vines grow to about ten feet tall. Though I had not noticed before, upon close inspection they seem to have a very light and delicate fragrance. My vines were started from seed that I ordered from a mail-order catalog. Since then I have seen it on seed racks at local outlets, so it is widely available. Most generally, it should be started from seed indoors and planted out in good soil in a sunny spot when the weather is warm. It can be used in hanging baskets, window boxes, or as a ground cover. It can also grow up a pine tree or other support as it does in my yard. Usually black-eyed Susan vines bloom all summer, but protection from the hottest afternoon sun will give it its best chance of prolonged bloom.

Black-eyed Susan vine is a member of the genus *Thunbergia*. *Thunbergia alata* is its scientific handle, and it is a close relative of the beautiful sky vines, *T. grandiflora* and *T. laurifolia*. My sky vine (*T. laurifolia*) finished its major bloom a couple of weeks ago. If the public had seen its magnificent clusters of tubular, flaring, sky-blue flowers with yellow throats, they would have wanted it, too. I had several pots to sell, but they were not in bloom and folks did not realize what they were passing up.

So goes life. Here today, gone tomorrow. Enjoy the beauty of the flowers, for beauty, like life, is fleeting. Smile back at the black-eyed Susan vine and remember the beauty of the sky vine if you saw it at all. Your days will be brighter and your life enriched if you are one of the lucky ones who responds to the beauty of a flower.

Confederate Jasmine (*Trachelospermum jasminoides*)

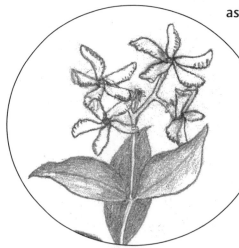

"What is that glorious scent?" my friend asked as she headed up my walkway.

"Why, that's one of the South's most memorable fragrances," I answered with conviction. The plant responsible for this heavenly aroma was Confederate jasmine. It scampers up a pine tree near my entry. Placed in this strategic position, guests enjoy its scent as they approach my door.

Scent, more than any of our other

senses, can transport us back to another time and place. With Confederate jasmine, that time is childhood, and the place is Grandmother's house. Grandmother called the plant star jasmine, and it scrambled over a barbed wire fence that surrounded the old home place. When I began choosing plants for my yard, Confederate jasmine was one of my must-haves. Still, when I smell it I am carried back to happy, carefree childhood days, pleasant memories, and warm feelings of my people and my roots. It's part of my heritage, and one sniff is all that is required.

Foliage of Confederate jasmine is evergreen, so it can perform in the landscape year-round. I might choose it for certain purposes even if it had no flowers. However, I'm genuinely delighted when the fragrant flowers appear from about mid-April until June. The waxy, white, pinwheel-shaped blooms lighten the spirits of all who come near. Its heady fragrance wafts on the warm, spring breezes and permeates the air for some distance. Fetching the paper each morning is a pleasurable experience. With a lawn chair, a cup of coffee, and the newspaper, I settle down near the jasmine. This must be pretty much what Heaven is like.

Confederate jasmine has several uses in the landscape. Since it readily twines around any support, it is a natural for covering trellises, pergolas, arches, or fences. It will also dress up a tree trunk or provide a screen to hide an unpleasant scene if planted on latticework or some other support. Sometimes it is used as a groundcover, but it needs to have shoots trimmed occasionally to keep it looking neat. This vigorous vine will eventually climb to the top of tall pines if left unpruned.

Evidently there are several cultivars or varieties of Confederate jasmine. One of my friends has it climbing up the supports of her front porch. Hers is white with a prominent yellow eye. Another friend has a yellow variety, and I saw a beautiful specimen with variegated leaves at one of my favorite restaurants.

To keep Confederate jasmine looking its best, plant it in part shade in well-drained soil to which organic matter has been added. Give it a deep drink about once a week if rainfall does not meet its moisture needs. Provide a good mulch around its roots, and fertilize when flowering is finished. Pruning is a necessary task if it is to be kept in bounds. It can be cut back hard when it has finished blooming, and wayward shoots may be nipped off anytime during the summer. Pests may include scale and whitefly, but mine has never been bothered enough to require spraying.

We who live in the coastal South are lucky, because Confederate jasmine is not fully hardy north of Zone 8. Here we plant it and take its beauty and charm for granted. We are truly blessed.

Other Reliable Vines

Name	Annual or Perennial
Five-leaf Akebia, Chocolate Vine *Akebia quinata*	P-Evergreen
Cross Vine *Anisostichus capreolata*	P-Evergreen
Dutchman's Pipe *Aristolochia* spp	P-Herbaceous
Climbing Aster *Aster carolinianus*	P-Herbaceous
Trumpet Creeper *Campsis grandiflora*	P-Deciduous
Trumpet Creeper *Campsis radicans*	P-Deciduous

for the Coastal South

Comments

Extremely vigorous, 1″ flower
  in spring, dark purple, fragrant

Extremely vigorous, native; in spring
  orange flowers with yellow throat

Conical, S-shaped flowers resembling
  a "Dutchman's pipe"

Native vine, covered with small lavender flowers in fall

Asian relative of native trumpet
  creeper; free flowering

Vigorous native, orange-flowered

continued on next page

Name	Annual or Perennial
'Madam Galen' Trumpet Vine *Campsis* x *tagliabuana*	P-Deciduous
Algerian Ivy *Hedera canariensis*	P-Evergreen
Nepal Ivy *Hedera nepalensis*	P-Evergreen
Persian Ivy *Hedera colchica*	P-Evergreen
Ornamental Sweet Potato *Ipomoea batatas*	P-Tender
Cardinal Climber *Ipomoea* x *multifida*	A
Morning-glory *Ipomoea purpurea*	A
Cypress Vine *Ipomoea quamoclit*	A
Sweet Pea *Lathyrus odoratus*	A Summer-blooming
Wisteria *Millettia reticulata*	P-Deciduous to semievergreen
Asiatic jasmine *Trachelospermum asiaticum*	P-Evergreen
Native Wisteria *Wisteria frutescens*	P-Deciduous
Japanese Wisteria *Wisteria floribunda*	P-Deciduous
Chinese wisteria *Wisteria sinensis*	P-Deciduous

Comments

Hybrid of native and Asian trumpet creeper; 3″ salmon-orange flowers

Groundcover or container plant

Climber; orange fruit

Large leaves; needs plenty of room

Dig tubers before frost; lime green, black, or tri-colored leaves

Deeply lobed leaves, 2″ crimson blossoms

Flowers open early in morning

Reseeds; red, star-shaped, 1″ flowers all summer

Plant in fall for early spring bloom; dislikes heat; fragrant

Not as vigorous as wisteria

Good choice for groundcover

More refined and delicate than Asian cousins; purple flowers in spring

Rampant

Rampant

Coastal Considerations

Salt-Tolerant Plants for Home Landscapes

Calls started piling up at the Extension office. Something was happening to landscape plants in many areas of town. A frantic call from a friend spurred me to action. "Marie," she lamented, "all my large azaleas are dying. Some of my plants look burned and are losing their leaves. My yard looks terrible! What's happening?"

Similar grievances were being voiced by residents across the coastal South. Prolonged recent droughts meant that irrigation systems were using more ground water than usual. Fresh, underground water was being depleted, so salt water from bays and the Gulf had moved in to take its place. Wells that had delivered good water for years began to spray salty water. Before homeowners became aware of the problems, many of their plants had begun to die.

Damage occurs when excessive concentrations of salts cause water to move out of plants through a process called exosmosis. Plants begin to wilt and literally die from lack of water. Of course, it's a Catch-22. The gardener waters the wilted plant. More saline water worsens the situation, and the poor plant is doomed.

My friend first noticed that some of her plants had leaves with burned margins or tips. In some cases, all leaves had fallen off and the plants were dead. Many large azaleas that she had treasured for years were history. Some recently installed plants languished in their planting beds, and the prognosis for their continued survival was grim.

By the same token, many of her plants were doing well. Several large live oaks, a hedge of wax myrtles, and some Southern magnolias continued to prosper. Ligustrum, yaupon, sago, shore juniper, pittosporum, and Indian hawthorn all flourished. They are the salt-tolerant plants that could withstand the salt water sprayed on them by her sprinkler system that had become a victim of salt-water intrusion.

These situations convinced me that much information is needed about salt-tolerant plants. After reading all the books I could find on the subject, searching the Internet, and reviewing years of magazine files and university documents, I came up with a list of salt-tolerant plants for the coastal South. Little did I know that I could have simply studied my neighborhood in order to make an accurate list. The objects of my study were close to home. A walk down Bayshore Drive in Valparaiso was an eye-opener. After a considerable time spent studying and researching salt-tolerant plants, I discovered that the proof of the pudding was right before my eyes.

Many salt-tolerant plants that thrive in my neighborhood are a part of the natural selection process. Some plants that my neighbors planted and tried were weeded out long ago by hurricanes, salt spray, and salty well water. They continue to be weeded out as droughts, storms, and other forces of nature test their limits. Those that have been here for many years are—obviously—salt tolerant! These salt-tolerant strong hearts can be expected to do well in almost any yard in the coastal South, from the beach to inland locations.

Salt-tolerant plants are adapted to the conditions of the seashore. Wind is a given, in the form of soft breezes, hard gales, or hurricanes. Winds may be intermittent or constant. They can strip away moisture, leaving brown, dehydrated leaves. Coastal air can quickly thicken into fogs that envelop plants in salt-laden moisture. Spray from the ocean deposits salt directly on plants. The sun along the beaches is more intense as it bounces off the white sand and water. Sandy, infertile soil is lacking in organic and nutrient matter. It dries out rapidly and is often alkaline, which locks up nutrients needed for plant growth.

Certain adaptations allow plants to tolerate these conditions. Gray-leaved plants reflect light, and many thick-leaved plants can prevent dehydration in these circumstances. Plants native to seacoasts are adapted to the wind and have deep, anchoring roots and sturdy stems and branches. Some ornamental grasses are well adapted because of their ability to sway in the breezes. The presence of a fence, a dune, a house, or a windbreak of shrubs, trees, or other barriers expands exponentially the list of plants that may be grown. Choosing shrubs for the landscape is an important process. If chosen wisely, they will do the job for which they were selected for many years. People who live near bodies of salt water will be wise to take into account the salt tolerance of plants they select to decorate their spaces.

In the lists that follow, plants have been grouped according to types and degree of salt tolerance. Those listed as very salt tolerant are highly resistant to salt drift and can be used in exposed environments very near bodies of salt water. Those labeled as moderately salt tolerant grow best when offered the protection of buildings, fences, or plantings of more salt-tolerant species. Slightly salt-tolerant plants should have considerable protection and be well back of exposed areas.

In my studies of this subject, I noticed that different sources offered different analyses of the salt-tolerant capacity of various plants. In these instances, I have simply included the plant in question in one or another of my lists. A bibliography of my sources is included at the end of the chapter for those interested in studying salt tolerance of plants in greater depth. Undoubtedly, it is a subject that bears further scrutiny.

Trees

Very Salt Tolerant

Chickasaw Plum (*Prunus angustifolia*) 15′–25′. Fruit is a 1/2″ diameter, rounded, lustrous red or yellow drupe. White flowers in spring.

Eastern Redcedar (*Juniperus virginiana*) 40′–50′. Pyramidal when young. Slightly pendulous in old age.

Japanese Black Pine (*Pinus thunbergiana*) 20′–80′ x 20′–40′. Several cultivars and sizes available. Shrub to tree.

Leyland Cypress (x *Cupressocyparis leylandii*) 60′–70′. Adaptable to extremes of soil. Withstands salt spray. Several cultivars. Short life, 10–20 yrs.

Live Oak (*Quercus virginiana*) 40′–80′ x 60′–100′. Magnificent shade and mansion tree. Sand Live Oak (*Q. geminata*) smaller in stature.

Sand Pine (*Pinus clausa*) Small- to medium-sized tree. Common near Atlantic and Gulf Coasts on hills and ridges of white sand.

Southern Magnolia (*Magnolia grandiflora*) 60′–80′ x 30′–50′. Many cultivars (100's). 'Little Gem' small. Useful wildlife tree. Prefers richer soil and some protection from hot sun.

Southern Redcedar (*Juniperus silicicola*) 40′–50′. For practical purposes *J. virginiana* with a coastal/Florida distribution. Literally grows on sand dunes, coastal marsh edges, sandy soils.

Southern Wax Myrtle (*Myrica cerifera*) 10'–15'. Large shrub or small tree. Attracts birds. Fragrant foliage.

Tamarix or Tamarisk (*Tamarix ramosissima*) 10'–15'. Zones 2 to 8. Fast growth rate. Fine, feathery appearance. Dirr observed plants growing in pure sand less than 100 yards from Atlantic. Salt and drought tolerant.

Yaupon (*Ilex vomitoria*) 15'–20'. Red drupe attracts birds. Many forms and cultivars. 'Nana' 3'–5'. 'Shillings/ Stokes' dwarf 3'–4' tall and wide, mounded evergreen plant. 'Pendula' weeping. Yellow fruited varieties, handsome bark.

Moderately Salt Tolerant

Black Tupelo, Black Gum, Sour Gum (*Nyssa sylvatica*) 30'–50'. Good fall color.

Chaste Tree (*Vitex agnus-castus*) 15'–20'. Flowers 3"–6" clusters; lilac or pale violet; fragrant. Also white and pink varieties.

Japanese Privet (*L. japonicum*) 6'–12' high. More of a dense evergreen shrub, but can be pruned into small tree. Several cultivars. Popular limbed up as small tree. NOTE: *L. sinense* is invasive.

Kousa Dogwood (*Cornus kousa*) 20'–30'. Large shrub or small tree. Blooms after *Cornus florida* and after leaves have emerged.

Laurel Oak (*Quercus hemisphaerica*) 40'–60'. Leaves persist through winter and drop in early spring.

Loquat, Japanese *(Eriobotrya japonica)* 15'–25'. Evergreen. White flowers. Yellow, edible fruits.

Redbay (*Persea borbonia*) 20'–30'. Small- to medium-sized evergreen tree or large shrub.

Red Maple (*Acer rubrum*) 40'–60'. Many cultivars.

Slash Pine (*Pinus elliottii*) 100'. Occurs naturally in wet flatwoods, branch-swamps, areas bordering shallow ponds, and along lagoons and bays near the coasts.

Waxleaf, Glossy, or Chinese privet (*Ligustrum lucidum*) 20'–25'.

Slightly Salt Tolerant

American Holly (*Ilex opaca*) 40'–50'. More than 1000 cultivars. Male and female required for berries.

American Hornbeam, Blue Beech, Ironwood, Musclewood, Water Beech (*Carpinus caroliniana*) 20'–30'. Withstands periodic flooding.

Bald Cypress (*Taxodium distichum*) 50'–70'. A stately tree, deciduous conifer. Sends up knees in shallow water but not under normal conditions in cultivation. Exceptionally wind firm.

Camphor Tree (*Cinnamomum camphora*) 40'–60' tall and wide. Evergreen. Blackish fruit messy. Shallow roots compete. Invasive.

Carolina Cherry Laurel (*Prunus caroliniana*) 20'–30'+. Large evergreen shrub or small tree. Withstands heavy pruning. White flowers, spring. Green fruits maturing to black are scattered by birds. Stray seedlings common.

Crape Myrtle (*Lagerstroemia indica*) Many sizes and cultivars.

Foster's Hybrid Hollies (*Ilex x attenuata* 'Fosteri') represents a group of interspecific hybrids between *Ilex cassine* x *I. opaca*. Includes 'East Palatka', Hume', 'Savannah'. Group includes some of our best landscape trees. Prefers loose, acid, well-drained soil. Avoid extremely dry, windy, unprotected places.

Jerusalem Thorn (*Parkinsonia aculeata*) 15'–30' tall and wide. Thorns. Sparse foliage. Yellow flowers. Picturesque form. Many tiny leaflets.

Silver Dollar Tree (*Eucalyptus cineria*) 20'–50'. Floral arranger's delight.

Spruce Pine (*Pinus glabra*) Longleaf Pine (*P. palustris*). Tall pines. Important for wildlife.

Sycamore (*Platanus occidentalis*) 70'–100' tall and wide. Huge tree. Large leaves, globose fruit, messy. Several diseases afflict. Dirr recommends that we might leave one growing if it already exists on the property, but does not recommend planting one.

Sweet Gum (*Liquidambar styraciflua*) 60'–75'. Colors well in fall. Gum balls messy but important to birds. 'Rotundiloba' sets no fruit, rounded leaf lobes. Several cultivars.

Willow (*Salix*) likes moist, wet places. Not good on dry beach but good in swampy, brackish water areas.

Shrubs   * Drought Tolerant

Very Salt Tolerant

Agave spp.* – Succulents. Mostly large with clumps of fleshy, strap-shaped leaves. Dies after flowering but sends up new suckers.

Common Lantana (*Lantana camara*)* Common lantana is invasive. Many named selections. Some hybrids between *L. camara* and *L. montevidensis* are reported to be sterile.

Coontie (*Zamia floridana*)* Native cycad develops no trunk. Makes low, rounded mass of evergreen, fernlike foliage.

Creeping Juniper (*Juniperus horizontalis*)* 1'–2' high by 4'–8' spread. Withstands hot dry situations and slightly alkaline soils. Native to sandy and rocky soils. Found on sea cliffs, gravelly slopes. Many cultivars; 'Bar Harbor', 'Procumbens', 'Emerald Isle', etc.(55 cultivars listed by Dirr).

Indian Hawthorn (*Raphiolepis indica*)* 4'–5' high. Several selections. Some larger, some smaller. *R.* 'Majestic Beauty' can reach 15'. Appreciates moist, organic soil but tolerant of sandy soils.

Laurustinus (*Viburnum tinus*)* 6'–12'. Fine upright-rounded evergreen. Pink budded 2"–4" flowers opening to white. Followed by ovoid metallic blue fruits that mature to black. Good for screening, hedging. Withstands salt spray. 'Eve Price' compact form. ' Compactum' 1/2 to 3/4 size of species.

Oleander (*Nerium oleander*)* 6'–12' high and wide. Flowers on new wood. Numerous cultivars available. Oleander caterpillar serious pest. Poisonous.

Pineapple Guava (*Feijoa sellowiana*)* 10'–15'. Evergreen shrub or small tree. Edible fruit. Tolerant of salt spray. Flowers delicate and spectacular.

Pittosporum (*Pittosporum tobira*)* 10'–12' high, up to twice as wide. Fragrant flowers in spring.'Variegata', variegated foliage. 'Wheeler's Dwarf' 3'–4' tall and wide.

Sandankwa viburnum (*Viburnum suspensum*)* 6'–12' high. Evergreen. Tolerates hot dry climate, sandy soils. White fragrant clusters of flowers.

Shore Juniper (*Juniperus conferta*)* 1–1½' x 6'–9'. Likes dry soil conditions. Cultivars 'Blue Pacific', 'Emerald Sea', others.

Silver Thorn (*Elaeagnus pungens*)* 10'–15' high and wide. Very fast growth. Needs frequent pruning. Attracts birds. Not for small property. Long shoots a favorite of floral designers.

Southern Wax Myrtle (*Myrica cerifera*)* 10'–15' high and wide. Can be pruned into small tree or rounded shrub. Attracts birds, fragrant foliage. Appreciates organic, moist, well-drained soil, but is very tolerant of dry soils.

Spanish Bayonet (*Yucca aliofolia*)* Adam's needle (*Y. filamentosa*)* Bear Grass (*Y. smalliana*)*

Yaupon (*Ilex vomitoria*)* 3'–4' tall and wide. 'Shillings'/ 'Stokes Dwarf' favorite landscape shrubs. Mounding shape, prunes well. 'Pendula' has weeping form. Several cultivars.

Moderately Salt Tolerant

Arborvitae (*Platycladus orientalis*) formerly (*Thuja orientalis*) 25' x 15'. Foliage in flattened sprays held vertically. Several compact cultivars. 'Bakeri' 5'–8'. 'Blue Cone' 8'. Others.

Bottle Brush (*Callistemon rigidus*)* 10'–15'. Red flower clusters at tips of branches like a bottle brush. Slow growing.

Chinese Holly (*Ilex cornuta*)* 'Burford' rounded 20'–25' tall. 'Dwarf Burford' rounded shrub 5'–6' +. 'Carissa' rounded 3'–4' high. 'Dazzler' 10' or more, 5-spined leaves. Many cultivars.

Chinese Juniper (*Juniperus chinensis*)* 67 cultivars listed by Dirr. 'Pfitzeriana' 10' high and 20'–25' wide. 'Hetzii' 15' x 15'. 'San Jose' creeping form 12"–18". 'Saybrook Gold' 2'–3' x 6' with bright gold foliage.

Chinese Podocarpus (*Podocarpus macrophyllus*)* 20'–35'. Evergreen shrub or tree. Needlelike leaves. Upright oval to columnar. Stiff, rigid. Tolerant of salt spray. Prefers well-drained, fertile soil.

Cleyera (*Cleyera japonica*) (sometimes listed as *Ternstroemia gymnanthera*) 8'–10' tall. Can be maintained 4'–6' feet indefinitely with proper pruning. Emerging leaves bronze/red. Best in shady situations. Prefers moist, well-drained soil, but is tolerant of less.

Common Fig (*Ficus carica*) 10'–15'. Coarse, broad rounded shrub.

Edible fruit. Favorite of many birds and people.

Coral Ardisia or Spice-Berry (*Ardisia crenata*) Small, slow growing; glossy, scalloped, dark green leaves. Clusters of crimson berries in winter. Shade loving. Moist, organic soil. Invasive.

Fatsia (*Fatsia japonica*) 6'–10' high but easily maintained lower. Large leaves, tropical in appearance. A plant for shady sites. Prefers moist, well-drained soil.

Glossy Abelia (*Abelia grandiflora*) to 8' tall. Evergreen to semievergreen. Several smaller growing cultivars: 'Edward Gloucher' 3'–5'. 'Francis Mason' 3'–4', pink flowers, yellow-variegated leaves. 'Prostrata' is low growing (1 ½'–2'). 'Sherwoodii' 3'–4'.

Japanese Barberry (*Berberis thunbergii*)* Many cultivars, sizes, colors. Thorns. Not as robust in our heat as farther north.

Ligustrum (*L. lucidum*)* (*L. japonica*)* See Salt tolerant trees. Can be pruned to shrub size.

Oregon Grapeholly (*Mahonia aquifolium*) 3'–6' or Leatherleaf Mahonia (*M. bealei*) 6'–9'. Very prickly leaves. Plant in shady location. Bright yellow flowers late winter. Bluish berries mature later and are relished by birds.

Sago Palm (*Cycas revoluta*)* 2'–3' tall in youth. Airy, lacy appearance of fern. Grows slowly to 10' and looks more like palm. (Cycad).

Satsuki azalea (*Rhododendron indicum*). Evergreen, spreading, dwarf azaleas. Large flowers in May. Several cultivars.

Saw Palmetto (*Serenoa repens*)* 4'. Usually underground stem. Palmlike appearance. Native.

Scarlet Firethorn (*Pyracantha coccinea*)* 6'–18' tall with similar spread. Evergreen. Red fruits ripening in September and persisting into winter. Very colorful. Thorns. Many cultivars, some with yellow fruits.

Sweet Viburnum (*Viburnum odoratissimum*) 10'–20'. Becomes tree-like. Clusters of lightly fragrant flowers in spring. Red fruit ripens to black. Good screen.

Turk's Cap (*Malvaviscus arboreus*) 6'+. Hummingbird attractant. Blooms in fall. Killed back to ground by frost.

Slightly Salt Tolerant

Althea, Rose of Sharon (*Hibiscus syriacus*)* 8'–12' shrub or small
   tree. Large, attractive 5-petaled flowers in summer. Many cultivars.

American Beautyberry (*Callicarpa americana*)* 3'–8'. Large shrub
   flowers on new wood. Cut back when overgrown. Does best
   with ample root moisture but is quite drought tolerant. Variety
   'Lactea' is white fruited. Good bird plant.

Banana Shrub (*Michelia figo*) 6'–8' possibly to 15'. Evergreen
   creamy yellow flowers. Powerful fruity fragrance like that of ripe
   bananas.

Bigleaf Hydrangea (*Hydrangea macrophylla*) 3'–6'. According to Dirr
   will withstand seashore conditions and actually flourish near
   the shore in full sun to partial shade. Many cultivars.
   Appreciates moist, well-drained soil.

Butterfly Bush (*Buddleia davidii*)* 5'–10'. Sometimes killed to
   ground in winter. Many cultivars and flower colors. Attracts butterflies.

Camellia (*Camellia japonica*) and (*C. sasanqua*). 6'–15'. Large evergreen shrubs. Flower in fall and winter. Shelter from strong, hot
   sun and drying winds.

Coral Bean, Cherokee Bean (*Erythrina herbacea*)* 6'. Native, deciduous. Thorns. Red flowers in spring. Good hummingbird plant.
   Red berries extremely poisonous.

Crape Myrtle (*Lagerstroemia indica*)* Small shrubs to large trees
   40'–45' in height. Many cultivars. Many new ones resistant to
   powdery mildew.

Gardenia (*Gardenia jasminoides*) 4'–6'. Evergreen shrub. Fragrant
   white flowers. Many cultivars.

Japanese Holly (*Ilex crenata*) Many cultivars, dwarf forms to 20'
   shrubs or trees. 'Helleri', 'Tiny Tim', 'Convexa'. Appreciates
   moist, well-drained soil, but tolerant of dry soil.

Kumquat (*Fortunella japonica*) 4'–8'. Can withstand down to 23°F
   for short periods. Responds well to good cultivation, moisture,
   etc.

Rice-paper plant (*Tetrapanax papyriferus*)* 10'–15'. Big, bold, long-stalked leaves are 1'–2' wide, deeply lobed. High winds tear leaves. Multiplies from suckers which may arise 20' from the mother plant.

Rose (*Rosa*) Many cultivars and species. Needs special care except for some species roses and old, or antique roses.

Sweet Olive, Tea Olive (*Osmanthus fragrans*) 10'. Glossy, evergreen leaves. Tiny, fragrant blooms in spring and early summer and again at beginning of winter.

Salt Tolerant Palms: Cabbage Palm (*Sabal palmetto*), European Fan Palm (*Chamaerops humilis*), Lady Palm (*Rhapis excelsa*), Pindo Palm (*Butia capitata*), Saw Palmetto (*Serenoa repens*), Washington Palm (*Washingtonia*), others.

Annuals

Very Salt Tolerant

Blanket Flower (*Gaillardia*)
Moss Rose (*Portulaca*)

Moderately Salt Tolerant

Ageratum, Floss Flower (*Ageratum houstonianum*)
Amaranthus spp.
Begonia (*Begonia* x *semperflorens-cultorum*)
Calliopsis (*Coreopsis* spp.)
Cornflower (*Centaurea cyanus*)
Cosmos (*Cosmos* spp.)
Drummond Phlox (*Phlox drummondii*)
Dusty Miller (*Senecio cineraria*)
Egyptian Star Flower (*Pentas lanceolata*)
Gazania Daisy (*Gazania rigens*)
Geranium (*Pelargonium* x *domesticum*)
Marigold (*Tagetes* spp.)
Ornamental Cabbage and Kale (*Brassica oleracea*)
Pot Marigold (*Calendula officinalis*)

Sunflower (*Helianthus annus*)
Sweet Alyssum (*Lobularia maritima*)
Verbena (*Verbena* spp.)
Vinca, Periwinkle (*Catharanthus roseus*)

Slightly Salt Tolerant

Candytuft (*Iberis*)
Catmint (*Nepeta*)
Coleus (*Solenostemon scuttellarioides*)
Impatiens spp.
Pansy and viola (*Viola* spp.)
Petunia hybrida
Pinks (*Dianthus*)
Sage (*Salvia* spp.)
Snapdragon (*Antirrhinum majus*)
Zinnia spp.

Perennials

Very Salt Tolerant

Beach Sunflower (*Helianthus debilis*)
Blanket Flower (*Gaillardia pulchella*)
Easter Lily (*Lilium longiflorum*)
Firecracker Bush (*Russelia equisetiformis*)
Lantana (*Lantana camara*)
Thyme (*Thymus* spp.)

Moderately Salt Tolerant

Amaryllis (*Hippeastrum*)
Butterfly Weed (*Asclepias tuberosa*)
Canna Lily (*Canna generalis*)
Cast Iron Plant (*Aspidistra elatior*)
Daylily (*Hemerocallis*)
Easter Lily (*Lilium longiflorum*)

Egyptian Star Flower (*Pentas lanceolata*) tender perennial
Fern-leaf Yarrow (*Achillea filipendulina*)
Firebush (*Hamelia patens*)
Gingers

 Butterfly Ginger (*Hedychium* spp.)
 Pinecone Ginger (*Zingiber* spp.)
 Shell Ginger (*Alpinia* spp.)
 Spiral Ginger (*Costus* spp.)
Gold Moss (*Sedum acre*)
Lavender Cotton (*Santolina chamaecyparissus*)
Lily of the Nile (*Agapanthus africanus*)
Milk and Wine Lily (*Crinum* spp.)
Persian Shield (*Strobilanthes dyeranus*)
Purple Heart (*Setcreasea pallida*)
Rosemary (*Rosmarinus officinalis*)
Sage (*Salvia* spp.)
Shrimp Plant (*Justicia brandegeana*)
Silver King Artemisia (*Artemisia ludoviciana albula* '
 Silver King')
Society Garlic (*Tulbaghia violacea*)
Stokes Aster (*Stokesia laevis*)
Verbena (*Verbena* spp.)

Slightly Salt Tolerant
Black-eyed Susan (*Rudbeckia*)
Blue Daze (*Evolvulus glomerata*)
Blue Plumbago (*Plumbago auriculata*)
Gerbera Daisy (*Gerbera jamesonii*)
Golden Dew Drop (*Duranta repens*)
Hardy Hibiscus (*Hibiscus moscheutos*)
Iris (*Iris* spp.)
Lamb's Ears (*Stachys byzantina*)
Lion's Ear (*Leonotis leonurus*)
Mexican Heather (*Cuphea hyssopifolia*)
Mexican Petunia (*Ruellia brittoniana*) Invasive
Princess Flower (*Tibouchina urvilleana*)

Tickseed (*Coreopsis* spp.)
Umbrella Plant (*Cyperus papyrus*)

Grasses

Very Salt Tolerant
Beach Panic Grass (*Panicum amarulam*)
Broom Sedge (*Andropogon scoparius*)
Dwarf Bamboo (*Bambusa multiplex*)
Giant Reed (*Arundo donax*)
Sea Oats (*Uniola paniculata*)

Moderately Salt Tolerant Grasses
Aztec Grass (*Ophiopogon* 'Aztec')
Black Mondo Grass (*Ophiopogon planiscapus* 'Nigrescens')
Mondo Grass (*Ophiopogon japonicus*)
Monkey Grass (*Liriope muscari*)
Pampas Grass (*Cortoderia selloana*)
Variegated Mondo Grass (*Ophiopogon planiscapus*
    'Variegata')

Vines and Groundcovers

Very Salt Tolerant
Algerian Ivy (*Hedera canariensis*)
Confederate Jasmine (*Trachelospermum jasminoides*)
Creeping Fig (*Ficus pumila*)
Cypress Vine (*Ipomoea quamoclit*)
Dichondra (*Dichondra carolinensis*)
English Ivy (*Hedera helix*)
Lily Turf, Mondo Grass (*Ophiopogon japonicus*)
Monkey Grass (*Liriope spicata*)
Railroad Vine or Beach Morning Glory (*Ipomoea
    pes-caprae*)
Shore Juniper (*Juniperus conferta*)

Virginia Creeper (*Parthenocissus quinquefolia*)
Weeping Lantana (*Lantana montevidensis*)
Winter Creeper (*Euonymous fortunei*)

Moderately Salt Tolerant
Bleeding Heart Vine (*Clerodendrum thomsoniae*)
Coral Vine (*Antigonon leptopus*)
Purple Heart (*Setcreasea pallida*)

Slightly Salt Tolerant
Grape(*Vitis* spp.)
Passion Vine (*Passiflora* spp.)
Wisteria spp.

Tropicals (Container Plants for Decks, Patios)

Very Salt Tolerant
Crown-of-Thorns (*Euphorbia milii*)
Night Blooming Cereus (*Hylocereus undatus*)

Moderately Salt Tolerant
Bougainvillea (*Bougainvillea* spp.)
Cape Honeysuckle (*Tecomaria capensis*)
Devil's Backbone (*Pedilanthus tithymaloides*)
Dracaena (*Dracaena marginata*)
Hoya (*Hoya carnosa*)
Ixora (*Ixora coccinea*)
Jade Plant (*Crassula argentea*)
Kalanchoe (*Kalanchoe* spp.)
Mandevilla (*Mandevilla splendens*)
Oyster plant (*Rhoea spathacea*)
Rubber Plant (*Ficus elastica*)
Snake plant, Mother-in-Law's Tongue (*Sansevieria* spp.)
Wandering Jew (*Zebrina pendula*)
Weeping Fig (*Ficus benjamina*)

Slightly Salt Tolerant
Allamanda (*Allamanda* spp.)

Chinese Hibiscus (*Hibiscus rosa-sinensis*)
Croton (*Codiaeum variegatum*)
Pencil Tree (*Euphorbia tirucalli*)
Schefflera (*Brassaia actinophylla*)
Star Jasmine (*Jasminum nitidum*) and other blooming jasmines

Bibliography

Bender, Steve. "Give Beach Plants a Chance." *Southern Living* (July 1999): 78, 79.

Black, R. J. "Salt Tolerant Plants for Florida." Florida Horticulture Department of Environmental Horticulture Fact Sheet ENH-26. University of Florida, Florida Cooperative Extension Service, Institute of Food and Agricultural Sciences, 1985.

Coyle, Gretchen. "Seaside and Seashore Gardening." *Flower and Garden* (June/July 2000): 24–27.

Craig, Robert M. *Plants for Coastal Dunes of the Gulf and South Atlantic Coasts and Puerto Rico.* U.S. Department of Agriculture. Agriculture Information Bulletin 460, 1991.

Dirr, Michael A. *Manual of Woody Landscape Plants.* Champaign, Illinois: Stipes Publishing Co., 1990 (revised).

Marshall, David W. *Tallahassee Gardening, Design and Care of the Southern Landscape.* Tallahassee: Tallahassee Democrat, Inc., 1994.

McSwain, Mary Jane. *Florida Gardening by the Sea.* Gainesville: University Press of Florida, 1997.

Perry, Mac. *Landscaping in Florida.* Sarasota, Florida: Pineapple Press, 1990.

Watkins, John V., and Herbert S. Wolfe. *Your Florida Garden.* Gainesville: University Press of Florida, 1968.

Shoreline Protection and Restoration: A Northwest Florida Homeowner's Guide. Northwest Florida Water Management District Public Information Bulletin 01-2.

Tenebaum, Frances, ed. *Taylor's Guide to Seashore Gardening.* New York: Houghton Mifflin, 1996.

Environmental Issues

Reasons for Concern

A presidential commission appointed to study our waterways has revealed some pressing problems. Not surprisingly, it reported that our oceans, rivers, coasts, and marine resources are in trouble. The commission found that ocean pollution, largely from farmland and urban runoff, is increasing so much near shorelines that proper coastal management is overwhelmed. "These are not problems that we can sweep aside," said James Watkins, who headed the commission.

We become concerned when reading reports from the U.S. Geological Survey (USGS), such as one published in 1999. After testing water and fish from sites around the country, it found at least one pesticide in almost every water and fish sample it collected. In some samples, as many as five different pesticides were found. According to the USGS, our lakes and rivers are similar to a low-grade toxic waste spill that extends to virtually every river and stream in the country.

Other concerns appear almost daily. The Nature Conservancy reports that scientists have determined that the world's average temperature has risen one degree Fahrenheit during the twentieth century. That, they say, is likely the fastest rise during the past 1,000 years. Their models predict surface temperatures rising on average three to ten degrees by the year 2100. Parching droughts, mightier hurricanes, and heavier downpours will likely become the norm. Recent droughts and population increases place greater demands on our already depleted water reserves. New condominiums and subdivisions go up at alarming rates. Where is it all to end?

I'll tell you what. I love our rivers, lakes, estuaries, and bays. The sight of dolphins cavorting just offshore, bait fish darkening the water, and mullet jumping thrills me in some elemental way. I want to keep them. I will do whatever I have to do to preserve our waterways and the beauty they add to my life. We simply must incorporate all the techniques at our disposal to make our landscapes and waterways as good as they can be without destroying them in the process. We have much to learn.

Other Dilemmas

My lawn is a constant source of struggles between right and wrong in earth stewardship. I love looking at a wide sweep of healthy, green lawn. It is a green cover for the ground that allows my grandsons free run of the place. I do not complain about balls bouncing over the lawn or little feet running across it. Amiable Spouse and I enjoy sitting in our chairs on the soft surface in the late evening and enjoying the coolest part of the day. Very few surfaces have so much to offer in comfort and use.

A fellow master gardener who lives on waterfront property in Fort Walton Beach depends upon his grass to hold soil near the water. "Don't talk to me of growing less grass in my yard!" he declares. "It is the only reason I still have property after Hurricane Opal swept through."

Lawns have long been a major feature of American yards. Once gasoline-powered lawn mowers became affordable for everyone, it seemed the way to go. No one paid any attention to the fact that lawn grasses are not native to the South. We didn't fuss that large amounts of water and fertilizer were necessary to keep them looking their best. We plied them with fertilizers, weed killers, and insecticides, and swelled with pride every time we looked at our perfectly shorn sea of green.

Many people move to the beautiful coastal South each year. Gardeners know that this population growth is affecting the availability and quality of water. As ever more homeowners pump water on their lawns with abandon, the aquifers become depleted. More septic tanks in rural communities increase the amount of fecal coliform bacteria and contribute to higher nitrate levels. Near coastal areas, salt water seeps into the fresh underground streams, and landscapes become victims of salt water intrusion. Water is in short supply, and gardeners everywhere face restrictions on the amount of it they can use on their landscapes.

We gardeners often have in our power the means to pollute our earth—perhaps more than any other group of hobbyists. In our efforts to grow beautiful plants and lawns, we spread chemicals willy-nilly with little thought of the consequences. We tear out indigenous plants that support native wildlife and replace them with high-maintenance imports. We clear land that adjoins the waterways so that we have greater visual and physical access to the water. Tons and tons of leaves and garden debris go to landfills each week. A drive down almost any street will expose piles of beneficial mulching materials headed for the dump.

"I'm only one person," we are apt to say. "What I do in my yard is less than a drop in the ocean." Perhaps this reasoning has some merit. However, if we all decided to make certain changes, we could make a significant cumulative difference.

How Can Gardeners Help?

Being a good environmental steward and having a beautiful garden sometimes seem opposing ideas. How can one grow beautiful flowers and shrubs that are not bug riddled and be in harmony with nature? How can we put away the sprayers and poisons that have been our first line of defense against marauding insect hordes? How can we wean ourselves from our dependence on chemical fertilizers that have kept our grassy swards emerald green for decades?

Gardeners want it both ways. We want our waterways and gardens, too. What we must do, then, is learn gardening strategies that will allow us to have both. In our landscapes we must choose plants that can survive on less water, and they must be heat and drought tolerant. They must be able to live with the pests and diseases that flourish here. Plants that can live in our yards with little or no additional fertilizer must be selected. We must carefully reconsider entrenched gardening practices that contribute to a diminished quality of life.

Attitudes toward having and maintaining large expanses of turf are changing. At one time, large, rolling lawns may have been appropriate. In today's crowded world where water is becoming increasingly scarce, they seem a foolish waste of resources. As we learn more, we become aware of other, wiser options. The cost of having large, attractive lawns may simply be too great.

The University of Florida has several suggestions. In its *Guide to Environmentally Friendly Landscaping*, several observations have come to the fore. The university notes that nature knows no property lines. Fertilizers and pesticides applied in one person's yard are washed to neighbors' yards and into the storm drains, ditches, streams, rivers, or ground water. A butterfly visiting in one yard may be poisoned in the next-door neighbor's yard. We are connected yard to yard, neighborhood to neighborhood, and ultimately to the water and other resources upon which life as we know it depends. More and more of us realize that the home landscape is part of larger natural systems. We believe that landscapes can be created that are an asset to nature instead of a liability. Also, we have learned that such an environmentally friendly yard can save time, energy, and money because intensive maintenance is not necessary.

How we use fertilizer in our landscapes has a significant impact on our environment. We must realize that streams and rivers carry nitrogen runoff from farms and lawns down to the Gulf where it creates algal blooms that consume oxygen and suffocate sea life. That's a big reason to examine our thinking about how green and big we want our lawns to be. Phosphorus, another element in fertilizer, is responsible for some algal blooms, and results are similar.

Recent studies have suggested that turf areas effectively remove many contaminants, so maybe the answer is not in doing away with lawns completely. The key is to use slow-release nitrogen fertilizers, to mow often, and leave grass clippings in place. We should be careful not to spread fertilizer on sidewalks and driveways, and to apply no more than is needed. Most lawns need no more than two fertilizations every year, once in spring and again in fall. No more than one to two pounds of actual nitrogen per 1,000 square feet of lawn is needed. Most ornamental trees and shrubs in the lawn area don't need any additional fertilizer.

Learning to use water efficiently is a necessary lesson that we must all learn. Trickle or drip irrigation can save more than 50 percent of water lost by overhead sprinkler irrigation. Early morning irrigation reduces water loss by evaporation since the predawn hours typically have higher humidity and lower temperatures. Likewise, irrigating during periods of light rain will make better use of water by preventing evaporation and allowing water to penetrate easily because the rain has broken the surface tension. Watering infrequently but deeply encourages plants to establish deep root systems that will be more tolerant of drought. Watering slowly allows water to soak into the ground and reduces runoff. Reducing the amount of water applied during late summer and fall is also a water-conserving practice. Plants are not actively growing at this time, and leaves and shoots have hardened off and lose much less water. They are therefore better able to withstand drought and water stress.

Many gardeners are embracing the tenets of Xeriscape. Simply put, these landscapes are designed for low water use. Plants are placed in the landscape so that those with similar water needs are grouped together. Generally, they are arranged into zones: natural, drought tolerant, and oasis. In the natural area, plants are selected that are adapted to the natural rainfall of the region. In the drought-tolerant zone, plants are used that can survive for long periods of time without supplemental irrigation. In the oasis zone, plants that have the greatest need for water are sited near the entry or in a highly visible place where will have greatest impact. Small water gardens may be incorporated into the landscape. The size of lawns is usually reduced, and drought-tolerant ground covers are used instead.

Mulch — An Idea Whose Time Has Come

What if, suddenly, homeowners decided not to place yard and garden debris on curbsides for the city crews to pick up and haul to the dump? What if, instead, there were laws that prohibited taking yard debris to the landfills and we had to use these materials in our own yards? Would our yards suddenly become junkyards? Could we live in such a place?

I have often been amazed by the piles of pine needles, leaves, and grass clippings placed on the curb for pickup in my own neighborhood. It is multiplied many times over by residents throughout the county. What's happening here? What is it that we are doing to our yards, not to mention to the earth as a whole?

When I look at the landscapes from which these riches come, I see that most of the time trees and shrubs have been raked under and around. The ground is left bare. The homeowner has worked all day and thinks he has done a good job contributing to the good looks of his yard and neighborhood. He's filled with satisfaction. Once again his yard is raked and clean. He can take it easy for another week.

Often the homeowner spent most of the day mowing his lawn. It is a perfect greensward. It has been fertilized, treated for insects, watered, and laid by for another week. The clippings are on the curb, and all's well in his corner of the world.

The yards may be clean looking, but my well-intentioned neighbors have not done themselves any favors. They have thrown away a treasure trove. Furthermore, they have denied birds and wildlife favorable places to search for bugs and worms, and they have thrown away the natural fertilizers that would have made their trees and shrubs healthier. They have increased their need for water and multiplied the intensity of their battle with the weeds.

I do not think for a moment that my neighbors and citizens of this county are intentionally creating problems for themselves and for society. Rather, I believe that they simply do not realize the consequences of their actions. They have not learned a better way.

What would happen if leaves, pine needles, and grass clippings that are thrown away were left on the lawn or under the trees and shrubs? Water would be conserved because the mulch holds in moisture. Fertilizer use would be reduced, because trees and shrubs maintained with a two- or three-inch layer of organic mulch do not usually need additional fertilizer. The mulch breaks down and enriches the soil naturally. Soil temperatures would be moderated, and competition from weeds would be diminished.

Furthermore, the area would be more attractive. A newly applied mulch does to a landscape what a new coat of paint does to a house. It's all spruced up. And it's a better way. It's better for gardens, for the earth, and for all its inhabitants. It's an idea whose time has come.

Managing Pests in the Landscape

If we are to have environmentally friendly gardens, we must take certain actions. Sound ecological choices and good gardening practices go hand in hand. For instance, we should carefully choose plants, provide the right conditions for them, check them regularly, and intervene when pest or disease damage reaches unacceptable levels.

Managing pests involves finding and using controls that are nontoxic or the least toxic rather than immediately reaching for a wide-spectrum insecticide. While such a product may kill the offending insect, it may also kill a bird or frog that feeds on a poisoned worm or insect. And it may also upset the balance of nature by killing natural predators and beneficial insects.

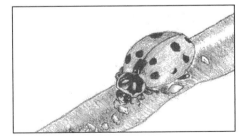

Tolerance of a few insect-chewed leaves is a key factor in creating a healthy garden environment. Expecting an insect-free yard is not practical. Such a situation would be more detrimental than beneficial. What would the birds, frogs, and lizards eat in such a place?

Another simple tactic is to select pest-resistant plants. If spraying is necessary to grow a particular plant, then consider how important that plant is to you. Many plants have been expelled from my garden because they were not worth the fight I had to wage against their pests.

Be sure to plant the right plant in the right place. No amount of care will make a sun-loving specimen do well in the shade or an azalea or camellia thrive in alkaline soil. Certain plants cannot tolerate heat, while others may not get the number of chilling hours required for bloom or fruit production. If plants in your yard are not doing well, chances are their cultural requirements are not being met. Replace them with plants better adapted to your site.

If we all used these easy-to-follow landscaping practices, we'd make a difference. I'm going to do it. If my neighbor does it, the results will be doubled, and so on and so on, ad infinitum!

Integrated Pest Management Offers Safer Pest Control Alternatives

Say what? IPM? Least toxic control? Beneficial insects?

Yes, yes, and yes again! These practices are our tickets to a cleaner environment. They are the answers to healthier living, a cleaner world, and foods that are free of insecticides and other poisons.

IPM stands for Integrated Pest Management. It includes all of the methods used to control pests. Strategies include repellents, traps, insect growth regulators, beneficial insects, barriers, insecticides, and many others. Simple principles and common sense practices are used to achieve gardens and home landscapes with acceptable levels of pests. The overriding goal is to use the least toxic control to keep pests in check.

Of course, the least toxic control is plain water. A strong spray from the garden hose will dislodge and drown pests, such as aphids, caterpillars, and spider mites. Be sure to spray the undersides of the leaves. Research at Texas A&M University found that spraying with simple water wands controlled 70 to 90 percent of aphids and mites.

Soap sprays will kill many insects if the spray hits the bugs directly. Most experts recommend commercial soap sprays because homemade sprays are more likely to burn the leaves of sensitive plants. However, if you wish to mix your own, add one tablespoon of dishwashing detergent to one half gallon of water. To be sure the solution will not harm your plant, spray a few leaves and wait 24 to 36 hours. Then check for leaf damage in the form of white spotting or yellowing, marginal leaf burn or leaf blisters, or leaf drop and tip dieback. If no damage is apparent, the spray is nontoxic to the plant. Insecticidal soaps have been proven effective for controlling aphids, scale crawlers, whiteflies, and thrips.

Oils have long been used to control scale on fruit trees. Oils kill many insects by clogging their pores and smothering them. Heavy oils may damage plants if the temperature is above 90°F. Some newer, lighter horticultural oils are recommended for use in summer. According to the University of Florida, organic horticultural oil sprays will control whiteflies even better than the most widely used chemical insecticide. Oil sprays also help control aphids, mites, leafhoppers, mealybugs, scales, plant lice, and mosquito larvae.

Insecticidal soaps are available at garden centers, and they can be mixed with light oil or other compounds to improve their effectiveness. A homemade soap-and-oil mixture can be made by mixing two tablespoons of liquid dish soap with an equal amount of cooking oil in a gallon of water.

Soaps and oils have several advantages over more poisonous insecticides. They are effective against a wide range of pests, and pests do not become resistant as they do to many insecticides. They are safe and easy to use and are less harmful to beneficials. Their cost is competitive, and they can be integrated with other tactics.

Try some of the least toxic controls to help in your battle against insect pests. Remember that all insects are not harmful, and that a garden with a few chewed leaves is a mark of an environmentally conscious gardener.

Enlisting the Aid of Beneficial Insects

Many homeowners have decided to use fewer poisons in their landscapes. This decision is necessarily accompanied by knowledge, for they are not choosing to be run out of house and home by hordes of insects. It is a commitment to use more environmentally friendly methods to control pests and to enlist the aid of beneficial insects that may already be present.

Beneficial insects should be conserved and promoted by selective pesticide use. First, of course, the gardener must learn which insects are beneficial. I well remember a time not long ago when I was visiting a friend and we were looking at the plants in her landscape. A recently installed oleander was covered with aphids and lady beetle larvae. We both recognized the aphids, but neither of us recognized the spiny, alligator-like ladybug larvae. She ran for the sprayer and its load of poison and hurried to rescue her new plant. Little did we know that the problem would have taken care of itself if we had let nature take its course. Many gardeners now plant flowers, ornamental grasses, perennials, herbs, and small shrubs in a no-spray area to encourage such beneficials as lizards, toads, spiders, and beneficial insects to settle there.

Besides knowing all stages of the lady beetle's life, every homeowner should take time and learn to identify other beneficials in the landscape. Such important predator insects as braconid wasps, damsel bugs, ground beetles, green lacewings, praying mantises, predaceous stinkbugs, robber flies, syrphid flies, tachinid flies, tiger beetles, and trichogramma wasps should be encouraged. Many gardeners plant pollen- or nectar-producing plants to attract and sustain them. Additionally, many of these beneficial insects can be bought and released into the garden when pest populations proliferate.

Homeowners should scout plants regularly and take appropriate actions. Often insect pests can be picked off plants by hand and

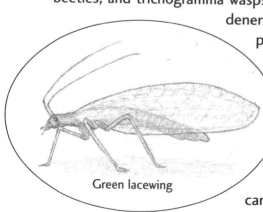

Green lacewing

squashed or drowned in a bucket of soapy water. Felder Rushing, horticulture agent for Hinds County, Mississippi, recommends taking three giant steps backward, removing one's glasses, and then looking at a plant to see if pest damage is apparent. If damage or pests can't be seen with this test, they do not need any treatment. Of course, his message is that homeowners should learn that some chewed leaves are acceptable. Remember that some pests are necessary to feed the beneficials.

If a decision is made to spray because pest populations have reached unacceptable levels, take the least toxic approach. Spray only the infested plants. Heavily infested or injured plants should be destroyed. If possible the pest should be controlled with soaps, oils, and biologicals that have minimal effect on the environment.

I will continue to work on my earth stewardship dilemma. Already I have reduced the size of my lawn. I have decreased fertilizer use, watered only when needed, and applied insecticides sparingly. Still, I grapple with the problem. There is much more that I could do.

Much can be done by all of us that will make our world a safer place for its inhabitants. Much can be done to insure that natural resources last for many more years. Much must be done if butterflies, birds, and other wildlife are to continue to enrich our lives. It bears some serious thinking. We need to learn a better way.

A Lesson Learned

For many years Amiable Spouse and I have shared our property with a beautiful little creature. Amiable Spouse calls it a glass lizard. We occasionally see the almost translucent creature slithering out of our way when we're out and about in the garden. We pay him no mind. He goes about his business and we go about ours. We live in harmony.

Not so with all of our garden tenants! The nemesis of steady gardeners like ourselves is the troublesome slug. I can always depend on a slimy trail of evidence, if not the vile creature himself, on the petals of newly opened flowers. A telltale hole is evidence of his destructive nature.

Getting ready for a plant sale is torment. I pot up hundreds of fragile plants only to have them riddled by the ruinous pest. Every time I lift a plant, there they are. Ornamental peppers are peppered with holes from the pillagers. Four o'clocks hardly resemble the sturdy plants that a generous gardener donated for the sale. Somehow I must find a control for Mr. Slug!

Long ago I learned that containers of beer lure hundreds of the odious pests to certain death. Amiable Spouse objects to such a use for perfectly good beer. Diatomaceous earth promises a miserable death to the creatures by cutting their soft bodies into shreds. Expensive! Copper strips propose to stop them in their tracks, but where am I to find enough to encircle my garden? Slug baits can be scattered around susceptible plants, but I worry about the birds and turtles who scratch in the mulch around the plants looking for their dinner. Of course, my gardening habits are partly to blame. I try to limit water use by mulching my plants. It's slug heaven!

One day I read about a trap that was sure to work. Birds couldn't get it, rain and the sprinkler system wouldn't dilute it, and it didn't pose a threat to wildlife. I had finally found an environmentally safe way to deal with the slugs. All right, I thought, I will fix the likes of the slimy creatures! I proceeded to cut the top four or five inches from a clear plastic soda bottle. Then I inverted the top and stapled it upside down into the bottle, added some slug bait, and placed the trap in a strategic location. The supposition was that Mr. Slug could get in, but he couldn't get out. To be perfectly honest, I did catch a few snails and slugs.

Then came a special day when many visitors were milling about

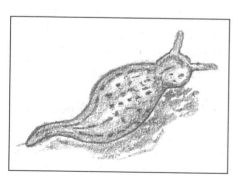

during a tour of gardens. Wouldn't you know—someone asked me how I controlled slugs. Confidently, I guided him to the dandy slug trap. I picked it up to show how clever I was. Inside the bottle was one of my beautiful glass lizards—dead, apparently for some time. I was devastated!

I've decided now that if Mr. Slug wants a plant, he can have it. Many ornamentals are impervious to his attacks, and I'll grow more of them. I only hope the glass lizard left some of his offspring to fascinate Amiable Spouse and me for years to come. Our world would be diminished without them.

Snail Killers

Two new products are on the market that kill slugs and snails and can safely be used around pets and wildlife. Both contain iron phosphate, which occurs naturally in the soil. Called Sluggo and Escar-Go, they are relatively nontoxic and even add small amounts of iron and phosphorus to the soil when dissolved. Slugs and snails stop feeding immediately after eating the bait and die within three to six days. Sounds like a dream come true!

What about Exotic Invasives?

Selecting plants appropriate for home landscapes is serious business. Should gardeners choose natives, exotics, or a mixture of both? Some homeowners insist on natives for their landscapes and object to exotics of any kind. Many of us appreciate natives, but also enjoy such exotics as hibiscus, camellia, pentas, and Japanese magnolia. Most of us enjoy some naturalized exotics that we encounter in wild places. None of us, however, would consider purposely planting an exotic invasive.

Exactly what is meant by these terms? According to the Florida Exotic Pest Plant Council (FEPPC), an exotic is a species introduced to Florida, purposefully or accidentally, from a natural range outside Florida. A native is a species whose natural range included Florida at the time of European contact (A.D. 1500). A naturalized exotic is one that sustains itself outside cultivation. An invasive exotic is an exotic gone wild. It has not only naturalized but is expanding on its own in Florida native plant communities.

Two categories of invasive exotics are defined by FEPPC. Category I includes plants that have caused documented ecological damage. This damage is caused when native plant communities are altered or changed in some way. Native plants may be displaced, or there may be changes in the structure or ecological function of the community, or hybridization of natives and exotics may occur. Category II includes species that have shown a potential to disrupt native plant communities and may at some time in the future be added to the Category I list. Presently, however, there is no documented evidence that they are disrupting native plant communities.

Some on the Category I list for north Florida are well documented. Most of us know to avoid and destroy such botanical pollutants as Japanese honeysuckle (*Lonicera japonica*), popcorn tree (*Sapium sebiferum*), water hyacinth (*Eichhornia crassipes*), and kudzu (*Pueraria montana*). Did you know, however, that the beautiful air potato (*Dioscorea bulbifera*) with its dark green, heart-shaped leaves is also on this list? The mimosa, or silk tree (*Albizia julibrissin*), coral ardisia (*Ardisia crenata*), elephant ear or wild taro (*Colocasia esculenta*), Chinaberry (*Melia azedarach*), camphor tree (*Cinnamomum camphora*), and shrub lantana (*Lantana camara*) are exotic invasives frequently sighted in my neighborhood.

Also frequently seen in area landscapes is nandina or heavenly bamboo (*Nandina domestica*). This landscape plant of long standing has become a thug. Beautiful red berries are attractive to birds, which spread the seeds into neighboring natural areas. One invasive that came as a surprise to me was the beautiful but ill-mannered Mexican petunia (*Ruellia brittoniana*). Until recently, I recommended this as a dependable perennial for our area. No more! Friends are still arguing about it. "It's one of my favorites!" they say. It still grows in my yard, but I will work to eradicate it now that its evil nature has become apparent.

Invasive plants vary from area to area. Some that are invasive in southern Florida are not invasive in the northern part of the state or in other regions of the coastal South. According to the Nature Conservancy, 126 invasive, nonnative plant species infest more than 1.5 million acres of natural areas in Florida. Up to 69 percent of these invasives were imported for ornamental use.

You can find the FEPPC List of Invasive Species on the Internet at http://fleppc.org/01list.htm. If you do not have access to the Internet, you can get a list by calling the extension office in your area. Ask for the Florida Exotic Pest Plant Council's List of Invasive Species.

Homeowners can help by removing these ill-mannered bullies from their property. Learn which plants are invasive in our area and avoid them like the plague. Gardeners must exclude known offenders, no matter how beautiful. We must become conscientious gardeners who plant locally but think globally.

Getting Back to Nature

The gurus, the visionaries, the farsighted leaders in the forefront of gardening are not the perennial plant experts, nor the woody ornamental pundits. They're not the folks who preach IPM (Integrated Pest Management) or ELM (Environmental Landscape Management) or least toxic pest control and Xeriscape principles.

No, the champions of today have seen disaster looming. What is happening to the world with today's landscape management practices is apparent to them. The decline in songbirds, butterflies, and wild creatures that add to the quality of life is obvious. The deterioration of lakes, streams, and other bodies of water is cause for alarm. Furthermore, they realize that how they manage their landscapes affects all this. They have resolved to make a positive difference.

These new heroes are imposing some tough sanctions in their own corners of the world. They have just said no to insecticides, poisonous chemicals, excessive water use, and harmful landscape practices. They insist upon plants adapted to the geography, hydrology, and climate of their yards. These idealists demand plants that can live with the insects, diseases, and critters that inhabit their spaces. Simply put, these forward-thinking gardeners are getting back to nature. They want native plants that evolved and grew in association with other native plants for thousands of years. They want plant communities that support a variety of wildlife species such as songbirds and butterflies and the flowers, bugs, mammals, and other organisms that weave an intricate system supportive of life.

A garden planted with native plants has a sense of place. A Louisiana landscape looks different from an Arizona scene. With a native landscape, gardeners can create for themselves a taste of the real and vanishing world that William Bartram described more than 200 years ago. After it is established, such a landscape will remain without much help from the gardener.

Environmentally savvy gardeners are getting rid of their gas-powered yard machines. They know that one gas-powered lawn mower emits eleven times the air pollution of a new car for each hour of operation. Gas-powered garden tools account for five percent of the nation's air pollution. Furthermore, closely mowed lawns are of little use to most wildlife.

Smart gardeners are implementing these more earth-friendly landscape practices so that an inhabitable world will to be here for their children. Planting native plants is a baby step in the right direction.

Wildlife

Gardening for the Birds

This morning I was enthralled by the antics of resident birds as I sat in my favorite chair with my morning cup of coffee. Ruby-throated hummingbirds sipped the offerings of the red pentas beside the window. House finches and cardinals vied for perches on the sunflower feeder. Nuthatches and tufted titmice scurried up and down and among branches of the mixed shrub border looking for their breakfast. Mourning doves glided in for a landing on the sand path. Brown thrashers feasted in the fig tree, and mockingbirds sang from the light pole while they waited their turn. Carolina wrens flitted in and out among the cypress knees that are home to my bromeliad collection. A woodpecker's drumming resonated through the morning air as it investigated a pine snag. Butterflies hovered and flew among the flowers. One basked on the sundial. Others sampled the offerings of a nearby mud hole. The world was alive with a cacophony of sound and flutterings of wings.

How did I get to be this lucky? What special things have I done to orchestrate this daily extravaganza? I remember the time when I didn't know a tufted titmouse from a chickadee. Birds were birds, and I took little notice of them. Somewhere along the way, my awareness increased and I began to buy books to identify them. My interest was piqued, and I began to learn more about their habits and requirements. Soon I found myself so intrigued that I began buying plants that I knew they'd like, installing bird feeders and baths, and constructing brush piles and dust holes. My efforts have been rewarded many times over. Gardening has always been a passion for me, but gardening for the birds has added a whole new dimension.

Birds, I have learned, require shelter from the elements, protection from predators, water and natural food, and nesting sites. At least some of these elements can be provided in almost every backyard. I began the venture in my garden by paying attention to the native plant species that already existed and making sure that they were retained. I was lucky, because I started with such native trees as mature Florida longleaf pines, large live oaks, laurel oaks, cherry laurels, magnolias, cedars, yaupon holly, and sparkleberry. Native shrubs included beautyberry and saw palmetto. To these I added a variety of shrubs that increased the availability of food and shelter. Not only did these shrubs help to meet the birds' needs, they also added shade, privacy, and color to my landscape. They act as a noise buffer between my property and the street, and many of them flower and attract pollinators. Because of the holly and other berried plants, I see flocks of cedar waxwings in spring. Among the shrubs I interspersed a variety of vines that clamber up trees and over fences. Trees add to the layers, beginning with understory trees such as dogwood and persimmon, and topping out among the lofty branches of pines, maples, and oaks. Annuals and perennials complete the smorgasbord.

Plants are not the only important feature in my yard that the birds like. I frequently see woodpeckers of various kinds debarking pine snags and dead limbs that are remnants from hurricane Opal. They're searching for insects that hide in the crevices or hollowing out nesting sites. Birds of various kinds use the dirt pathways for their dust baths and grit requirements. Brush piles provide hiding places for mice, garter snakes, lizards, toads, and many insects of immense interest to the wrens and other ground-feeding birds. Rocks are incorporated among my flower borders and are used as perches for the birds and hiding places for tasty ants and beetles. Natural mulch underneath the trees and shrubs is home for worms, roly-polies, millipedes, and other scrumptious morsels. Birdbaths are placed all around to meet water needs.

My National Wildlife Federation Backyard Wildlife Habitat is a home to a diverse group of plants and creatures. I have actively enlisted the help of this feathered pest control in my garden. Their list of gourmet treats closely resembles my list of most dreaded pests. My avian friends devour aphids, cutworms, caterpillars, grasshoppers, and other insects whose intent it is to dine on my ornamental plantings.

Since my love affair with the birds, I have become a more responsible environmental steward. I am much more tolerant of the insects that manage to damage some of my plants. I've decided, for instance, that if a plant needs poisons sprayed on it to survive in my yard, then that's a plant I can do without. Far too many desirable plants thrive and flourish in my garden setting without such harsh measures. I much prefer them.

Neither is my yard a mess of the jumblies as one might assume. It's not a wild garden, although it is attractive to wildlife. Its diversity offers seasonal change and color that is hard to come by in the coastal South. It's a place where Amiable Spouse and I enjoy sitting and becoming immersed in the sights and sounds of nature. Before we realize it, calmness and serenity seeps into our most inner spaces, and we are refreshed and our spirits renewed.

We Make a Butterfly Garden

Hours of work and planning are finally paying off. The open, sunny area behind the Valparaiso Community Library has become a garden. Members of the Valparaiso Garden Club, the junior gardeners, the Valparaiso Community Library, and the City of Valparaiso worked together to make it happen.

Originally the area was bordered by overgrown, diseased photinias and infested with a variety of weeds. The first step in its reclamation was removal of the diseased shrubs and weeds. City employees removed the overgrown shrubbery, and garden club members removed the grasses and weeds. A member brought his rototiller and turned over the soil. Other members sifted through the newly tilled soil and removed pesky weeds.

Several bags of organic matter and cow manure were tilled into the cleared soil. Mulch was spread to cover the whole area. Pine needles were scattered over the planting areas and pine bark mulch was used to cover the paths. Walkways were bordered with brick turned at an angle and partially buried. Railroad ties were positioned to attractively edge the perimeter of the garden. An arbor was added to hold vines for our expected winged visitors.

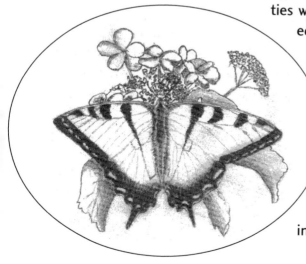

Each week the junior gardeners, with the help of garden club members, added plants to attract butterflies to this site. We made sure to include not only nectar sources for the butterflies, but plants for their larval stage as well.

First to be planted were fennel, parsley, and dill. These plants grow well in winter and spring. They will provide easy meals for Eastern black swallowtail larvae that are sure to hatch. To attract monarchs, plenty of milkweed has been planted. Passion flower vines will tempt gulf fritillaries. A pawpaw (*Asimina parviflora*) will attract zebra swallowtails, and Dutchman's pipe (*Aristolochia* spp.) may entice some pipevine swallowtails. *Cassia* can be expected to lure sulphurs to the area, and common buckeyes will appreciate the wild petunia (*Ruellia caroliniensis*).

These butterflies and others will be attracted by an abundance of some of their favorite nectar-bearing flowers. Annuals like zinnia, ageratum, pentas, and gomphrena wave their welcoming blossoms to the flying beauties. Perennials such as lantana, shrimp plant, firecracker plant, gaillardia, purple coneflower, plumbago, sage, and verbena will come back year after year. Shrubs include butterfly bush, firebush, and abelia.

Our sunny spot is filling in nicely. If we had a larger area we could include elms, hackberry, and mulberry trees for question marks; hickories and oaks for banded hairstreaks; pines for Eastern pine elfins; ash, plums, and yellow poplar for Eastern tiger swallowtails; red bay and sweet bay for laurel and palamedes swallowtails; and perhaps an apple, cherry, or willow for viceroys. Many of these native trees probably grow in nearby woods, and our nectar-producing flowers will bring the butterflies they attract into our garden.

Besides plants, we have included a damp area where butterflies can puddle. Damp areas may be made of a shallow area lined with plastic and filled with sand, or it could be a saucer or birdbath filled with pebbles, soil, or sand saturated with water. Basking areas have been provided by placing flat stones in a sunny place so butterflies can perch and warm their bodies. Fruit that is past its prime is placed in the garden to beckon other butterflies.

The welcome mat is out. Now we have only to sit on the beautiful garden bench and watch. With much excitement we anticipate their arrival! We built it; now they will surely come!

A Tale of Worms and Weeds

Members of the Valparaiso Garden Club had a special treat one fall. At our September meeting, each member was given a potted specimen of *Asclepias curassavica*, or butterfly weed. We took them home and planted them in the garden.

A few days later, I got a telephone call from a member. She had a monarch larva on her butterfly weed. She was pleased about this turn of events, but the brightly striped caterpillar had stripped her little plant to the bone. With no more butterfly weed, the poor caterpillar was starving to death. She tried to feed it parsley and dill. No luck. It wanted nothing but butterfly weed.

In desperation, she called me. "Help!" she wailed. "My monarch larva is starving!" At my urging, she brought the puny critter to my house in a jar. We picked some butterfly weed and tucked it in with the hungry creature. Within seconds, it was happily munching the fresh leaves. I sent my friend home with two butterfly weeds and instructions about raising the caterpillar in a jar.

To start your own butterfly nursery, select a large, clear jar. Poke holes in the lid. Fill it with milkweed leaves and put the caterpillar in. Remove droppings as they accumulate. Keep filled with fresh milkweed. In three to five days the caterpillar will climb to the lid at top of the jar. He will attach to the underside of the lid and form a chrysalis or pupa. Be very careful about handling the jar during this stage. In 10 to 14 days a beautiful monarch will emerge from its chrysalis.

Place the newly hatched monarch on a plant or underneath a tree. Be patient and wait for it to fly. Do not worry at this time if no milkweed is growing in the garden. The adult monarch sips nectar from many colorful flowers.

Sometime in October or early November when weather gets cold, the monarch will start its journey to one of 13 roosting sites west of Mexico City, Mexico, where it will overwinter. In spring it will fly back to our area and points farther north. It will find a partner and mate. Females will lay eggs on milkweed and the process will start again.

Butterfly weed is an excellent perennial for home gardens. For those who are unfamiliar with milkweed, a native species (*Asclepias tuberosa*) is found blooming alongside the road and in the woods during the summer. Look for bright orange patches of flowers. Chances are pretty good that a monarch caterpillar can be found feeding on this milkweed. The adult monarch searches out the plant and lays its eggs on it. How handy for the caterpillar! He hatches out to his favorite feast. Chances of larvae being eaten by a bird are very slim. Because the larva feeds on milkweed, birds find him very distasteful. Occasionally a larva may be eaten, but the birds soon learn a lesson. Some other butterflies mimic the monarch's coloration to keep from being eaten. Milkweed can be started from seed, or plants can be purchased from the nursery. Do not, however, attempt to remove plants from native stands. First, they are protected. Second, our native butterfly weed (*Asclepias tuberosa*) has a long, fragile tap root that is easily damaged. Most do not transplant successfully.

My friend called again in a few days. Her monarch had completed its metamorphosis successfully and was released to become a part of the wild population. She had played a part in this miraculous event, and she was overjoyed.

Happiness Is a Hummingbird in Your Face

Sometimes in summer I am privileged to see a hummingbird not two feet from my face. My heart skips a beat, and my coffee cup pauses in midair. I dare not even take a drink, for I am afraid that I will disrupt the show. Tiny ruby-throated hummingbirds regularly sample the pentas that bloom beside by window. Enchanted, I sit perfectly still,

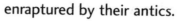

enraptured by their antics.

It is a frequent scene at my house since I have purposely added plants to my garden whose main purpose is to attract hummingbirds. *Pentas lanceolata* [36] is planted in several places throughout the landscape. Not only do the hummingbirds appreciate them, but the butterflies are frequent visitors, too. In my Zone 8b garden pentas are usually treated like annuals, though they are perennial further south. Those on the protected south side of the house come back reliably, but those less protected usually succumb to the cold of winter. They vary in size from plants eight to ten inches tall to large specimens four to five feet tall. Colors range from white to various shades of pink, purple, and red. Clusters of star-shaped blossoms bloom from spring until frost.

Another place where I frequently spy hummingbirds and butterflies is around the Turk's cap. Also called Turk's turban and Scotsman's purse, this shrubby perennial blooms from summer through fall. Each brilliant, red flower looks like an unopened hibiscus. I always know when my Turk's cap begins to bloom because the hummingbirds really start buzzing around. Butterfly weed does double duty as a butterfly and hummingbird attractant. Native over much of the country, this tough perennial is a handsome addition to the garden. Hummingbirds relish the nectar from the bright orange, yellow, or red flowers, and the red aphids that are often found on the leaves and blossoms of the plants provide additional nourishment. Near my back porch, firebush (*Hamelia patens*) is the setting for frequent hummingbird sightings. The South's native trumpet honeysuckle, (*Lonicera sempervirens*) is an irresistible temptress for the hummers.

Choices can be made from many hummingbird-attracting plants.

As I continued to watch my acrobatic visitor, he flew from the pentas to the border on the other side of the yard. There he sampled the hanging basket of 'Million Bells' petunias. He flew among the salvias, the hostas, the lantana, and the impatiens, tasting their offerings. At other times, I have seen hummingbirds careening around my tiger lilies, spider flower (*Lycoris radiata*), and four o'clocks (*Mirabilis jalapa*). Morning glory, scarlet runner bean (*Phaseolus coccineus*), and trumpet creeper (*Campsis radicans*) are some vines that have flowers relished by the hummers. Shrubs include butterfly bush (*Buddelia davidii*), hibiscus, and weigela (*Weigela florida*).

Besides flowers, special feeders can be used to attract hummingbirds to the garden. To make feeder solution, mix one part white, granulated sugar to four parts boiling water. Cool, fill the feeders, and hang in a shady place. Store extra solution in the refrigerator for up to a week, but freshen up outside feeders every three days. Clean feeders weekly with hot water, and use vinegar if a cleaning agent is needed since soap may leave a harmful residue. Feeders may be left up for as long as any hummingbirds are in the area.

According to the Hummer/Bird Study Group from Clay, Alabama, hummingbird feeders should be left up all winter. Contrary to popular opinion, ruby throats will not stay past their appointed time. Winter feeders attract hummingbirds that migrate to the Southeast from the Western states. According to hummingbird bander Fred Bassett, 188 birds of seven different species other than ruby throats were banded during one year. Most commonly seen during the winter is the rufous hummingbird. The second most common is the black-chinned. Also documented are Allen's, Anna's, calliope, green violet ear, magnificent, blue-throated, and white-eared hummingbirds.

Hummingbirds are not only entertaining creatures, they are beneficial as well. They serve as pollinators for the many flowers they visit, and because the nectar they drink does not meet all of their high energy needs, they must find some source of protein. That means that they gobble up many insects. Adults eat aphids, gnats, thrips, and tiny flies, and the baby hummer's diet is composed almost entirely of insects.

The first flowers that attracted hummers to my garden were planted simply because I love flowers—all kinds of flowers and the beauty they provide. A new vista opened, however, when I started noticing the hummingbirds. These winged creatures have given me another dimension of beauty. With wings that move so fast they're almost invisible, they hover over my flowers. No wonder John James Audubon called them "a glittering fragment of the rainbow," for that is a fitting description for this dainty creature.

The ruby-throated hummingbird is the kind that I am most likely to see in my Florida yard, for it is the most commonly seen hummingbird in the East, South, Midwest, and most of Canada. It is enough for me, though, for when yet another one streaks past my window, I marvel anew at yet another miracle of creation.

Conifers are Must-Haves for Bird-Friendly Backyards

Many trees and shrubs are used by birds, and habitats with their needs in mind contain an assortment of fruit- and nut-bearing trees and shrubs. However, no habitat for birds is complete without at least one conifer. Pines belong to this cone-bearing group and are among the most bird-friendly trees. Chickadees, nuthatches, jays, woodpeckers, brown thrashers, pine warblers, and many other species depend on pine seeds for part of their diet.

Large pines are preferred roosting sites for migrating robins. Mourning doves, purple finches, and others make nests in the trees. Scaly bark provides places for birds to stockpile seeds from feeders and other sources. Dead pine trunks make excellent snags. When storms have broken the tops out of our longleaf pines, Amiable Spouse and I have left the trunks standing when possible. According to Jeanne Lebow, a master naturalist from Mississippi, 43 birds use snags for nesting, perching, eating insects, or proclaiming territories. Cavity nesters such as pileated, red-bellied, red-headed, and red-cockaded woodpeckers rely on snags such as these.

In the coastal South, longleaf, loblolly, and slash pines are among the species that do well. All three grow into large trees. Which of these will do best on your property? It depends, as is usually the case. In my sandhill environment, demonstrated by their presence on the lot when Amiable Spouse first saw the site and claimed it for his own, longleaf pine (*Pinus palustris*) is probably the best choice. Occurring naturally on sand ridges in company with deciduous scrub oaks, it is a tall, stately tree sometimes called yellow or southern pine. The early grass stage lasts from one to three years. It is one of the most fire-resistant species and is quite resistant to diseases. Eventually, longleaf pines attain a height of up to 120 feet. Silvery white terminal buds decorate the tree in early spring, and large cones, five to ten inches long, provide seeds for resident squirrels and birds.

Slash pine (*Pinus elliottii*), often called swamp pine, grows to about 90 feet tall. With needles 5 to 11 inches long and cones 3 to 6 inches long, it occurs naturally in wet flatwoods, branch swamps, areas bordering shallow ponds, and lagoons and bays near the coasts. Loblolly (*Pinus taeda*), sometimes called old field pine, has shorter needles four to ten inches long and cones two to five inches long. Growing mostly in fertile upland sites such as old abandoned fields, it eventually reaches a height of about 100 feet.

Evaluate your site to see which pine will do best. If other species are growing naturally on your property, treasure them. By the same token, if no pines are on your property, plant one of the big three according to your site analysis. Slash pine is moderately salt tolerant, so if that is a factor, you might choose it. Florida longleaf is slightly salt tolerant. Those in my yard have withstood salt from the bay that has decimated metal windows and doors.

A word of caution might be in order, however. In hurricane winds such as those delivered by Opal, longleaf pines will snap at the top and come hurtling into the roof. None of ours blew over from the roots, but some tops did snap causing a great amount of anguish and expense. We have been replacing those lost from storms, but we're sure to site them some distance from the house.

Their value to my landscape, however, is considerable. Every needle that falls is used for mulching material. Shade provided by their high canopy is perfect for azaleas, camellias, and many plants that need some protection from the scorching summer sun. Their statuesque presence in the landscape can be achieved by few of their compatriots. They frame our two-story house in a way that few others could.

In short, I like these tough, native pines. In my yard, they're here to stay if the forces of nature permit. Birds, squirrels, other wildlife, and I will delight in their presence.

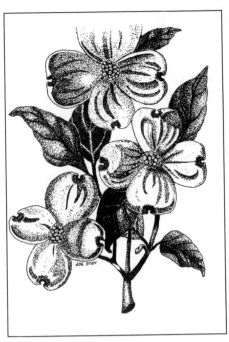

Seasonal Musings

Spring
It's the Loveliest Time of the Year

Spring is an exciting time for gardeners. Warmer days bring wave after wave of flowering plants. We watch the progression and revel in the beauty of each day. Sometimes we find ourselves trying to decide which week is the most beautiful. It's too great a task! As for me, I change my mind almost every week.

In the very early spring, Carolina jessamine, daffodils, and summer snowflakes tease us with promises of flowers yet to come. Late-blooming camellias decorate landscapes, and the buds of deciduous trees and shrubs swell and unfurl tiny leaves. Lawns green. Birds search for nest materials. The sun rises higher in the heavens.

Then come the azaleas! Southern gardens are awash with pinks, reds, whites, and purples. Magenta loropetalums add their color to

the medley. If colors were noise, surely the diverse hues are cymbals as they announce spring with their loudest clang. Then the amaryllises, irises, and roses begin to bloom. They equal or exceed the azalea show. Add to them the sights and scents of Confederate jasmine, sweet shrub, and banana shrub. Then picture yellow and blue annuals sparkling at the front of the border. Visualize the newly leafed trees in their spring green dresses. Add the songs of the birds and the blue of a sunny, spring sky!

Yet, as I look outside two weeks later, I see a completely different scene. Easter lilies have begun their show. Crinums are a pink bouquet in a sea of green as summer-blooming perennials finally begin to grow and fill their spaces. Autumn sage is in full bloom. Columbines are still lovely, and roses continue their show throughout the landscape. Leaves are nearly full grown on most trees and shrubs, and tiny figs, scuppernongs, and grapefruits promise a bountiful harvest.

Maybe now, I think to myself, is the most beautiful time of the year! I expect, though, that my fickle heart will change its mind again when the hydrangeas bloom, and later when the summer perennials steal the show. Such is the life of gardeners! We can't decisively and finally pick out the most beautiful time of year. Any time in a beloved and cared-for garden is a good time, and we live from day to day with the expectation that this beauty will continue to embellish our lives.

February and March in the Coastal South

Amiable Spouse was fussing at me again today. "Woman," he complains, "why do you want to slave outside from can to can't?" He struggles to understand why a person would choose to work until she's plumb tuckered out when one could just as easily be doing something fun like fishing, hunting, or shooting. What he doesn't understand is that, to dedicated gardeners, work in the garden *is* play. It is the necessary precursor of a brand-new season of growing things, new flowers to try, new combinations of old ones, new shrubs and trees, and a chance to right the wrongs of yesteryear. Just envisioning all the possibilities is an engaging occupation.

February and March are two of the gardener's busiest months. Hundreds of tasks wait to be done. Amiable Spouse says that we need a day stretcher. He's right, and God knows it, too. Soon He will begin lengthening the days a bit because He knows that we hortimaniacs need more daylight hours.

Pruning has kept me busy for several days. The fig tree has grown so large that I've had to curtail its exuberance before it overtakes the back quarter-acre. The scuppernong required a severe cutting back. Most summer- and fall-blooming shrubs have had their twigs clipped. One old ligustrum was cut back nearly to the ground. I have no doubt that it will come back with renewed energy when the weather warms and the sun shines higher in the sky. Now is the only time that broadleaf shrubs can be pruned so drastically and be expected to make a full recovery. Do not try this technique on needled evergreens, however, because they do not have latent buds beneath the old wood.

Roses should be pruned back to a few strong canes about knee high. Crape myrtle branches usually need thinning and possibly a little heading back to remove old seed heads. Do not, however, mangle them by chopping off their entire crowns. The beautiful form of the plant will be destroyed by this drastic procedure. If the crown of a crape myrtle must be chopped off to control its height, the wrong plant was chosen for the site.

Trees and shrubs may be fertilized in late February or early March. Make sure, however, that fertilizing practices are environmentally friendly. All plants do not need fertilizer. Most were growing quite well before we came along with our little sacks of fertilizer. Established trees and shrubs are examples of landscape plants that do well without fertilizer. Groundcovers can do just fine without fertilization because leaves, pine needles, and plant debris accumulate in these undisturbed areas of the landscape and provide nutrients. To fertilize in an environmentally friendly way, buy only those nutrients that will give the desired plant response, and apply no more fertilizer than the soil can hold until the plant takes it up. Avoid fertilizing surface waters and sidewalks, driveways, and nonvegetated areas, and use recycled organic wastes as sources of nutrients.

For those gardeners who aim for year-round color in the landscape, February workhorses include camellia, flowering apricot, Taiwan cherry, deciduous magnolia, redbud, red maple, Carolina jessamine, pear, native plum, crabapple, forsythia, flowering quince, and spirea. In early March, azalea, wisteria, fringe tree, silverbell, dogwood, banana shrub, and loropetalum provide bright spots in the landscape. Cool season annuals such as petunia, dianthus, snapdragon [40], pansy, and viola can be depended upon to enliven sunny beds until summer's heat shuts them down. In my yard, I'm looking forward to a show from nigella, stock, bachelor's button, poppy, candytuft, nasturtium, sweet pea, and chamomile because I planted seeds last fall. I'll add a bit of fertilizer now to keep them going strong.

Every night I go to bed exhausted from exploits in the yard. There are, however, visions of beauty in my head and jubilation in my heart as I give myself up to the regenerative sleep world. Tomorrow I will be up and at it again with renewed vigor. I am not really anxious to finish the job, however. Getting there is not important; the daily experience of such pleasant enterprise is the whole point.

The Glories of Another Gardening Season

The red maples are putting on their bright red blooms. Fields and woods are sporting new green blankets. Exuberant colors erupt in the woodlands as dogwoods, redbuds, and Carolina jessamine light the scene. Gardeners are in a high state of excitement. Spring is just around the corner!

Gardeners need no inspiration during these days of high spring. We are overcome with activity. Nature gives us impetus, and we go about at a feverish clip. There is much to be done. We spend hours putting seeds, bulbs, dry-looking sticks, and tiny plants in the ground. From these acts of faith we fully expect that our gardens will be more beautiful this year than ever before.

Already Amiable Spouse and I have prepared the beds. Peat moss and compost have been dug in. Slow-release fertilizer has been sprinkled on top of the soil. The beds lie in fertile readiness, anxious to receive their new wards. Every day I work toward filling them to the brim with colorful specimens.

We gardeners have it all fixed in our minds. We know just what we want, because we have worked it out in our heads all winter. I want a bed of dark-leaved sun coleus, such as 'Alabama Sunset' or 'Solar Flare', with chartreuse sweet potato (*Ipomoea batatas* 'Margarita') twining about its feet [37]. In front of my beautiful perennial plumbago I'm going to plant *Zinnia* 'Profusion Orange' [33]. These complementary colors will light up the area by the street with continuous summer bloom. I'm going to have a bed of blue *Salvia farinacea* 'Victoria' which has been a proven winner for me. In front of it will be variegated mondo grass, a low-growing grass that in combination with the salvia will provide a cooling counterpoint to other brightly colored areas.

Dead foliage around perennials can be removed any day now. Old foliage is removed before new growth begins but not before the last frost, for it provides a valuable blanket that helps protect ready-to-emerge sprouts. Such action really tidies up the garden, and on daily rounds my heart leaps as old friends spring forth. I give them a sprinkling of slow-release fertilizer or a shovel full of compost to get them off to a good start.

Summer's advance will bring less pleasant weather as temperatures soar. Right now, though, just being outside is delightful. The rewards of working in the fresh air of the garden among the company of such agreeable companions as flowers, butterflies, and other of God's critters is the glory that is another gardening season in the beautiful coastal South. My heart sings!

Summer
Bright Color for the Dog Days

Everybody keeps saying that the dog days of summer are here. What, exactly, does that mean? I know that it means that summer's hottest, most miserable, humidity-laden days have made their appearance. It's a time when folks need to be careful about working and being outside in the heat. Heatstrokes and other heat-related problems can befall unsuspecting people.

When I was young, the dog days were looked upon with disfavor. My parents taught me to be wary of dogs and wild animals that might carry mad dog disease (rabies) at this time of year. Terrible stories spread about people who got rabies. If a rabid animal was spotted in our rural community in Mississippi, the neighbors notified each other so that we could all be on the lookout. Mother would not let us swim in the rivers because she believed that we would get risings or boils because the water was poison at this time.

The dog days are the long, hot days that follow the summer solstice that happens around June 21. On that date, the most direct rays of the sun fall on the Tropic of Cancer, and that is the closest we get to direct sunlight. After that, the earth begins to tilt in the opposite direction, which sends the sun on its southern trek back past the Equator to points in the Southern Hemisphere so that we can have our fall and winter.

In July and August, Sirius, the dog star, rises just before the sun. The ancient Egyptians believed that this star intensified the rays of the sun. This is how the "dog days" got their name. Egyptians believed that the appearance of Sirius in the morning sky just before sunrise marked the beginning of the annual flooding of the Nile. It had religious significance for them. Their temples were oriented so that at the star's rising or setting the rays would reach the inner altar. Hippocrates taught the Greeks that this was the unhealthiest time of the year.

Understanding why Sirius has a negative connotation for many people is easy. However, there are other schools of thought regarding this star. The old man in Captain Ezra Harper's novel *Dogstar* believed that the spirit is a kind of energy. He thought that people and dogs had this spirit, and that when they died it went up to the stars. "I think their spirit goes up there, to Sirius, the Dog Star," he said when explaining to a child where dogs went when they died. "I can't imagine anything else that would keep it burning so bright and constant." There is even a website where people can memorialize their dearly departed canine friends by putting their pet's name by a glittering star on the monitor.

For gardeners, the dog days of summer are the days when outdoor activities are done in early morning or late afternoon. It is a time when some of our plants perish because they cannot stand the heat and humidity of our Southern summer. The dog days help us determine which plants are truly adapted to our climate. This is the time to look about and take notes. See what is blooming around the neighborhood, and make plans to get some of these plants this fall or next spring.

Observations in my garden reveal many plants that are blooming and doing well in spite of the heat. Many perennials bloom at this time. Black-eyed Susans and purple coneflowers are at their best. Summer phlox has just begun its summer show, and it will rebloom if blossoms are cut off as they diminish. Whirling butterflies are putting on a second flush of flowers after spent blooms were removed about two weeks ago. Fanflower (*Scaevola*) [35] is absolutely lovely with its purple, fan-shaped flowers. Butterfly weed, cigar plant, and purple shield (*Strobilanthes*) make a pleasing combination. Blue daze (*Evolvulus*) [34], blue plumbago, and society garlic lend their cool colors to the border. Brazilian verbena (*V. bonariensis*) and tiger lilies mingle their complementary colors to create a stunning display. *Salvia* 'Indigo Spires' rises behind a light-colored sun coleus and creates an interesting contrast in color and form.

Many annuals dress up the border in deep summer. Zinnia, Madagascar periwinkle, gomphrena, melampodium, celosia, pentas, begonia, ageratum, coleus, dusty miller, impatiens, and several others add lasting color. Shrubs such as crape myrtle, althea, and hibiscus add to the show.

As you know, if you are a gardener, and have probably guessed, if you're not, now is the time to look and enjoy the fruits of efforts that were expended this spring before the hot weather arrived. It is a challenge to keep the grass mowed and edged.

Do yourself a favor. Get a glass of lemonade and look at the flowers through the window. They may flourish during the dog days of summer, but most humans are more comfortable inside looking out. Play it cool. Stay inside!

Reflections on the Late Summer Garden

Ah, the dog days of summer are here! Amiable Spouse says that even the creeks back up under the bridge and sit there and hassle. Heat and humidity are oppressive, and most sane folks stay inside their air-conditioned havens until necessity drives them out. Gardeners, particularly hortimaniacs and floraholics like myself, however, have never been accused of being the most rational people on the face of the earth. We doggedly pursue our gardening passions and go about our business as if the heat were no big deal. We're addicted. We can't help it.

What I am most likely doing outside in the heat is dragging the hose around trying to save my languishing plants. Soon it is I who am withering, so the hose does a turnabout. The cooling stream provides an invigorating drink. Then as the water runs over my neck, arms, legs, and pulse points, I suck in my breath in startled exhilaration. I'm rescued, the plants are saved, and all is well.

It's not that I'm really working hard at this time. Mostly I just can't stay inside, especially in the early morning and late afternoon. I have to go outside to see what is happening. All the work of early spring and summer is over. Now I can sit back and enjoy the results of my labors. I walk around and deadhead the annuals and perennials as their flowers fade. They reward me with continued bloom. Their purpose in life is to bloom and set seed. If I delay this seed-setting process, they carry on in their attempts to produce progeny and I get to enjoy the results of their efforts.

I may stop to pull up a spent annual here and there. Whenever I do this, I dig in a shovelful of peat moss, compost, or manure to renew the spot. Fertilizer applied in spring has all been used, so flowers that are still blooming and growing appreciate a boost about now. I'll stop to pull a weed here and there because I do not want them to set seed and give me problems for years to come. I may squash a buggy pest or pull off a few diseased leaves as I see them. Generally I keep the garden groomed and looking its best.

Pentas lanceolata are in their prime now. They've been growing and blooming all summer, but now they are at their mature, most glorious best. Some varieties grow approximately four feet tall, while other, newer cultivars such as 'Butterfly Sparkles' are compact plants that grow only eight to ten inches tall. Available in pink, lavender, red, white, and many shades in between, they can be counted on for months of color.

Sweet autumn clematis (*Clematis virginiana*) is getting ready to fling its frothy sprays along the top of the chain-link fence that keeps my dogs confined to the backyard. This fragrant vine is an eagerly awaited event each August and September. Last fall after it bloomed, I cut it back to within inches of the ground. It continued to grow all winter and festooned the fence with beautiful green, silver-blotched leaves. All summer it continued its green show on the fence, providing a background for flowers that bloomed in front if it. Now it takes the spotlight with lacy sprays of creamy white flowers that perfume the backyard.

No particular care must be given this vigorous vine, but it needs plenty of room. During a year my vine covers about 20 feet of chain-link fence. The old vine sometimes dies underneath new growth, so cutting it back to the ground keeps it looking neat. Seedlings regularly appear beneath the mother vine, so sharing with friends is easy.

So much for the ravings of a hortimaniac. Get a glass of lemonade. Sit back. Behave like most sensible people and stay inside until the weather cools. I'll continue my hose dance and walk about the garden with a smile on my face and joy in my heart. It's what I do. I admit it. I'm hopeless!

Fall

Excerpt from the Diary of a Southern Gardener

More butterflies and hummingbirds than ever before are flitting around the yard. They hover around the zinnia, pentas, periwinkle,

buddleia, black-eyed Susan, celosia, salvia, and lantana. They linger around the ruellia's trumpets and the Turk's cap. The firebush that is blooming in the back yard is abuzz. I have arrived! Now I am really a gardener! The opalescent streak of the hummingbirds, the butterflies' aerial dance, the bees' persistent hum, the songs of the birds, and the barks of the squirrels are all evidence of my success.

Curbsides have become repositories for piles of pine needles ready to be picked up by city workers. I covet them; I want to gather them all. They're like brown gold. I use every one that falls in my yard and volunteer to rake my neighbors' yards. These needles form an intricate part of my landscape design. Their new cinnamon brown color beautifully carpets the natural areas. Shrubs are mulched and thus protected from drought, weeds, and lawn mower blight. Automatically they are provided with an acid, humus-rich soil in which they thrive. They're free, renewable, and native. The pine trees provide just the right light exposure for my much loved azaleas and camellias.

Days are beginning to shorten, and some mornings I detect a slightly cooler breeze coming from a somewhat northerly direction. Thoughts begin to turn toward my fall and winter garden. I begin thinking of all the splendid salad greens that I grew last winter and start getting yearnings and proddings to do a repeat performance. Seed displays and catalogs tempt me with many enticing varieties.

As the heat of August and early September begins to wane, the real gardening year starts in the coastal South. Perennials ordered from catalogs this summer begin arriving now, and this is the season to plant them. Contrary to popular belief, it is not winter's cold that kills so many of our hardy perennials. They are more likely to meet their end in summer's unrelenting heat and humidity. Fall planting gives them time to establish good root systems so they will be more able to endure the stresses of summer.

Crowded perennials such as Easter lilies, tiger lilies, and daylilies may be divided and replanted into newly enriched beds. African iris, crinum lilies, phlox, and other summer bloomers may also be divided at this time. The general rule of thumb is to divide spring bloomers in the fall and fall bloomers in the spring. That gives time for the plants to reestablish before bloom time.

Real gardeners will begin preparing soil for the fall and winter vegetable garden. For me, the highlight of the vegetable garden is my winter crop [43]. All winter long I harvest such delectables as spinach, kale, turnips, mustard, and cabbage plants, which make up the bulk of the garden. Beautifully colored and exotic-sounding salad greens add pizzazz. Some of them I have grown with a great deal of success, and some I'm anxious to try. Particularly successful have been arugula, California mesclun mix, and several varieties of loose-leaf and bibb lettuces. Along with the greens, I grow onions, radishes, carrots, and several herbs and flowers that add spice and color to my salads. These salads from my own garden have spoiled me, for all others pale in comparison. Store-bought salads are a thing of the past.

Annuals to plant now for winter and early spring color include sweet alyssum, calendula, California poppy, delphinium, dianthus, nasturtium, snapdragon, stock, viola, candytuft, and pansy. Bedding plants may be purchased at garden centers. The ever popular pansies and violas, however, will languish if the weather is still hot. It is better to wait until it has cooled down to set them out.

These welcome, cooler days draw neighbors out of their air-conditioned spaces. Leaves begin to show their colors. Birds and butterflies begin to gather and prepare for their annual migrations. Gardeners' thoughts turn to planting shrubs and perennials in fall's favorable weather. Exhibitors begin to plan their display for the county fair. The brave, bold hunters are getting restless. Fall is in the air.

A Fall Guide for the Southern Gardener

October and November bring some of our most beautiful days. Usually the terrible heat of summer is past, but we still have mild, pleasant days to spend outside. We will not admit to ourselves that a damaging freeze looms just over the horizon, or that a frost may send our tender tropicals to the ground in a matter of hours. We go about in a blissful state of denial, lollygagging about in the pleasant fall days. This is the time for long walks in the woods and road trips to see the fall colors in the countryside. It is a time to think of county fairs and flower shows.

So time passes. One day a chill in the air rouses us from our stupor. We realize that winter is coming, and thousands of things need to be done in the garden. Summer annuals must be pulled and composted or discarded. Winter- and spring-blooming annuals must be selected and planted. Container plants that have spent the summer outside must be brought in or placed in sheltered locations. Hardy herbs may be planted in the herb garden or in pots or borders. Spring- and summer-blooming perennials may be divided now, and it is the best time of year to plant new perennials, bulbs, trees, and shrubs. Many flower seeds may be planted now, and it is time to start the winter vegetable garden.

My vegetable garden is ready to be planted. Back around the middle of July, it got its yearly beefing up. Compost was spread about three inches thick over the entire surface along with whatever leaves and grass clippings I managed to collect. This organic matter was tilled into the soil. Then the area was watered thoroughly and covered with clear plastic for the rest of the summer. Now I am ready to uncover the plot, water it again, and sow my seeds.

Solarizing my vegetable garden plot each year is very important to the health and well-being of the vegetables that grow in it. By July most crops are finished for the year. I know that some people continue gardening throughout the summer. However, I have found vegetable gardening during the hottest part of the summer extremely challenging, to say the least. Bugs and diseases have had all spring and early summer to multiply to astronomical proportions, and mildews and fungi grow rampantly in the hot, humidity-laden air.

At some time of year the garden soil needs renewing. It needs to rest and get ready for another season. Why not July and August when plants struggle to survive? The hot sun is perfect for this job. Populations of insects, nematodes, weeds, and diseases are reduced by the solarization process. Organic matter decomposes in the heat, and millions of tiny microbes turn the soil additives into a form that fall and winter vegetables can use.

Full well I know that the chill of winter will soon be upon us. Little time remains for the season's last tasks in the garden to be accomplished. Oh, what a busy time is the fall!

Winter
Winter Approaches

On late fall mornings in October and November there's apt to be a bit of crispness in the air. It reminds me of all the tender plants I have collected all summer. They will need a place to spend the winter. It's a repeat performance of last year and several years preceding that! Every year I tell myself that I'm going to get rid of some container plants. I really mean it, too, but somehow it just never happens. Well-meaning friends share cuttings of their plants. I see something absolutely beautiful at the nursery—a "must-have" kind of thing. Wee snippets of this-es and thats grow into large pots of loveliness I hadn't counted on. The poor gardener usually has little choice in the matter.

A few years back Amiable Spouse built a greenhouse for my plants. It is a poor unsightly thing that was hastily thrown up one year when freezing weather threatened. He made a simple frame over which he stapled transparent, heavy duty plastic. It works well. If the weather is moderately cold, I burn a 100-watt bulb at night. In extreme circumstances, I have been known to use a small electric heater. I have lost very few horticultural treasures in my makeshift greenhouse due to cold weather.

Still, I'd like a proper greenhouse. A proper greenhouse would be so much more serviceable. If I had a fitting greenhouse, the squirrels would not have tried to bury an acorn in my flat of just-sprouted parsley and destroyed half of them. The wrens would not have built a nest in the newly planted hanging basket of walking iris and prevented me from watering it for weeks on end. The rain would not have poured in through the disintegrated plastic roof causing no end of misery and discontent.

I shouldn't whine. Already Amiable Spouse put new plastic over the roof. That prevented the rain from pouring in through the top. But now, the sides are beginning to fall to pieces. That's how the squirrel got in. It is time for new plastic to be stapled over the entire frame. I'm getting worried, but Spouse is unconcerned. "There's plenty of time!" he assures me. I am much put out by it. One day, by hook or crook, I'm going to have a real greenhouse!

Oh, well. The gardener must press on in spite of such vexations. By now, most of the annuals that provided color all summer have been pulled and relegated to the compost pile. Oh, I saved some of them. Gardeners cannot throw away seeds or plants that we or someone else might use later. Zinnia, marigold, love-in-a-puff, moonflower, and all manner of plants provided seeds that had to be saved. Cuttings of coleus and prized impatiens were rooted and placed in the greenhouse. Sprouts of pineapple sage, shrimp plant, and Cuban oregano are ready to be tucked in for safekeeping. The bromeliads have been removed from their cypress knee summer homes and placed in pots ready to slip into the greenhouse.

Just in time the garden centers are filling with annuals ready to be planted for winter color. Pansies and violas abound. Colorful ornamental cabbages and kales beckon. Dianthus and snapdragon line the shelves. Dusty miller, petunia, sweet alyssum, calendula, and stock promise colorful beds. Bulbs of narcissus, amaryllis, and hyacinths are ready to be purchased for winter forcing. Seed racks are full to bursting with delphinium, sweet pea, nasturtium, and candytuft.

There's still time to start a winter vegetable garden. If nothing else, an interesting combination of salad greens could be planted in a large container. A friend did that last year and ate salad all winter. Simply get a container such as a large wash tub or half whiskey barrel. Make sure that it has holes in the bottom and is well drained. Fill it with potting soil and mix in a bit of slow-release fertilizer. Sprinkle seeds of mesclun mix or assorted lettuces or salad fixings of your choice across the top. When they get a few inches tall, cut, wash, and toss into a salad. These "cut and come again" salad greens will make a believer out of you. Having a few fancy leaves to throw in with regular iceberg lettuce makes a big impact, both visually and to the palate. Toss in a few violas and petals of calendula. Sprinkle on a few chopped chives and dill, and you have a salad extraordinaire!

Winter Opportunities and Delights for the Dedicated Gardener

Opportunities abound for those of us who must garden in December and January. Most perennials can be moved or set out even if they are dormant. Hardwood cuttings of favorite trees and shrubs can be taken. Evergreens such as juniper, magnolia, and holly can be pruned and used for holiday decorations. Paperwhites, amaryllises, and hyacinths can be forced for bloom indoors. Tulips and daffodils can be planted for spring bloom.

Winter in the coastal South is ideal for planting trees and shrubs. Trees do much more than provide a natural ambience to our neighborhoods. Besides the seasonal joy of their flowers and fall colors, they give welcome shade in summer, help clean the air, cut energy costs for homeowners, protect homes from wind, and provide shelter and food for songbirds and other wildlife. On a hot day, neighborhoods with trees enjoy temperatures as much as 12 degrees cooler than community areas without trees. Of course, trees produce life-giving oxygen and remove air pollution.

Birds offer welcome splashes of color on the wing. Frequently sighted birds on the winter feeder include the tufted titmouse, house finch, cardinal, blue jay, nuthatch, Carolina chickadee, various woodpeckers, and goldfinch. I usually see the first goldfinches of the season toward the end of December. This is the only time of year that I put out thistle seed (Niger). The goldfinches eat it eagerly, but at other seasons of the year it is wasted. Scratching about in the litter underneath the feeders are mockingbirds, Carolina wrens, mourning doves, and brown thrashers. We may be thrilled by brief glimpses and rare sightings of migrants passing through.

Winter is a good time to add plants that will attract more of these colorful winged creatures to the yard. Be sure to include plants that provide multiple layers of vegetation. Such trees as blackgum, magnolia, oak, pine, sweetgum, tulip poplar, maple, and Eastern red cedar provide a top layer or canopy. A suitable understory might be made up of such native shrubs and small trees as American beautyberry, grancy gray-beard, oakleaf hydrangea, red buckeye (*Aesculus pavia*), sparkleberry (*Vaccinium arboreum*), and wax myrtle (*Myrica cerifera*). The lower level could be made of such perennials as rudbeckia, salvia, and various ornamental grasses that provide seeds attractive to birds. Differing levels of vegetation and diverse plants make a varied habitat that will attract many different birds to your landscape.

If days are too raw to be outside, the gardening catalogs that come in the winter force hard decisions and moments of disconsolate pleasure. Disconsolate because I cannot have all the glorious offerings; but pleasurable, nonetheless, because I can have some of them, and the very sight of them makes my heart leap. How glad I am that I'm a gardener and so many simple things offer such joy!

Plant Seeds of Hardy Annuals

I've been all a-dither lately, rushing about like a mad woman trying to get everything done in the garden. A killing frost surely is approaching, and many cuttings must be taken before that time. I'm making tip cuttings of plants that get killed to the ground in winter. Confederate rose, Turk's cap, and angel's trumpet root easily in water. If I wait until cold cuts them down, however, it is too late. Once the roots begin, I pot them up and place them in a protected location until spring.

Also, I'm pulling out the spent summer annuals, digging in soil amendments, and planting seeds like crazy so that I will have spring bloomers that can be had no other way. So far I have planted bachelor's buttons, sweet peas, candytuft, nigella, sweet alyssum, stock, nasturtium, calendula, and several herby things that will add to the winter and spring garden.

Bachelor's buttons (*Centaurea cyanus*) are an old-fashioned favorite. Last year they lasted through June and delighted me with hundreds of blue, lavender, and pink blossoms over a long period. Their silvery foliage was an added bonus. Around a birdbath, they were a focal point in the mixed border. Summer perennials were not yet blooming and early spring bloomers had faded, so they were especially welcome.

Sweet peas (*Lathyrus odoratus*) [39] bring back memories of Granny's garden. Nothing in memory matches their fragrance. I always dig in some cow manure and peat moss in an area and then install a concrete reinforcing wire cage. Then I plant the sweet peas and sprinkle a slow-release fertilizer over the surface of the bed. They climb up the cage and bloom in early spring. How welcome they are in my garden!

Then, there's old-fashioned stock (*Matthiola incana*). Starting plants by seeds is really the only way to get the greatest benefit from these fragrant flowers. I have in past years bought transplants ready for setting out in spring. They never match plants started from seed in vigor and flower power.

Candytuft (*Iberis*) [38] seeds are saved from year to year. This fall after I dug the caladiums, I replenished the soil and shredded some of last spring's dried flower heads over the area. They are up now and promise another beautiful show this spring.

Love-in-a-Mist (*Nigella damascena*) is coming up from last spring's flowers. I will shred a few of the seed heads collected last spring over the area to insure a plentiful crop of blue blossoms. Ferny foliage and attractive seed heads guarantee their space in my garden.

Pot marigold (*Calendula officinalis*) is always a crop in my winter herb garden. Pretty orange or yellow petals are snipped over many a salad to add welcome color.

Sweet alyssum (*Lobularia maritima*) has been planted in its usual place at the front of the border. It took a while for me to learn that these tiny seeds require light to germinate. This year I sprinkled them where I wanted them to grow and left them uncovered. Keeping the bed moist enabled them to germinate. I will enjoy their delicate, fragrant blossoms all winter and through much of the following summer.

These pretty flowers will decorate my winter and early spring garden. Joining them will be dill, parsley, ornamental cabbages and kales, lettuces of various colors and textures, mesclun mix with ferny salad greens and purple mustard, corn salad, and pretty 'Bright Lights' Swiss chard.

Hardy annual seeds must be planted in fall to garner some of nature's most beautiful gifts. Plant now while there's still time.

A Meal Fit for Royalty

Frequently in the wintertime Amiable Spouse and I have a special meal. I cook up a mess of mustard greens and cornbread. We eat it along with onions, radishes, and some tender raw mustard leaves. It is a banquet fit for a king. After the heavy meals of the holiday season, it is like a tonic. Of course, the mustard greens are special. I pick them from the garden while they are young and tender. I pinch leaves off and leave the plants in place. They will continue to produce all winter. A little plot about eight feet square provides all that Amiable Spouse and I can eat for the season.

When I'm ready for a mess, I take a big brown grocery bag out to the garden and fill it with mustard leaves. Then I bring them in and wash them in the kitchen sink. A little water is put into the pot and then it is stuffed as full of mustard greens as possible. I bring them to a boil, add a bit of ham and salt, and cook until they are tender. With a knife I cut them into pieces, and they are ready to dish up.

Amiable Spouse likes to start his meal with pot liquor and corn bread. He crumbles corn bread into a bowl and spoons liquid from the mustard greens over the cornbread until it is a soupy mixture. He then pours some pepper sauce on it made from the summer peppers, sprinkles on a little black pepper, and begins to eat. I can tell when he particularly likes something. He takes a bite and grunts. Now and then the grunt is repeated.

The cornbread must be just right. First, preheat the oven to 450° F. Pour a couple of tablespoons of oil into a black iron skillet. While it is heating on top of the stove, mix the cornbread. It must be medium or coarse stone-ground meal to which no leavening agents have been added. Mix cornmeal and a little salt. Add water until it is all wet and pour into the sizzling skillet. Press it down with your fingertips. Bake in the hot oven until brown. My goodness! It turns out like a crisp corn chip. It must be a Southern thing. Spouse was raised in Alabama and I in Mississippi. It's the kind of cornbread we both ate as children, and it's the kind I always make unless I'm making cornbread dressing. Then I must have real buttermilk cornbread.

After Amiable Spouse finishes the pot liquor and cornbread, he returns to the bowl for a big helping of greens. He fills his plate, adds pepper sauce and black pepper, and places a teaspoon or so of may-onnaise on the side of his plate. He then peels off a layer of onion, dips it into the mayonnaise and takes a bite along with his first mouthful of greens. He grunts again. That mayonnaise ritual must be an Alabama thing, because no Mississippian from my neck of the woods ever did that. I fix mine the same way he does, but I don't eat mayonnaise with my greens. He thinks I'm missing the best part.

The pepper sauce is special, too. Each summer I pick the hot peppers, wash them, and remove the stems. Then I dry them and pack them into jars. I boil plain white vinegar and pour it over the peppers. The pepper of choice for this concoction is cayenne, but I also like to add a few mild banana peppers to my sauce. The greens are just not right without this sauce.

These kingly meals took some advance planning. In early fall I prepared the plot for my winter garden by digging in generous amounts of compost. I let the soil cure for a couple of weeks, and then I broadcast mustard seeds over the ground. Soon little plants were coming up. I thinned them according to package directions and spread slow-release fertilizer in the bed. Now they are ready to eat. Amiable Spouse and I are just beside ourselves.

Protect Tender Plants from the Cold

Amiable Spouse finally managed to get my greenhouse covered for the winter. Already this year he has had to cover it twice. Made of a frame over which he staples heavyweight plastic, it lasts for only a few months. The relentless rays of the summer sun disintegrate it and it literally crumbles to pieces. Pine cones fall through the roof and tear large holes. Rain pours in, and squirrels get in and dig in my plants. It's all quite frustrating.

This year Amiable Spouse purchased some plastic with built-in ultraviolet shield. It was quite expensive, but it is heavier than the plastic he had been using. A three-year guarantee against sun dam-age promises a longer life, but it is not guaranteed against falling pine cones. We agreed that this would be the last time that he covered the frame with plastic. Next time, he's going to build me a real greenhouse. He thinks he has a three-year reprieve, but I doubt it!

We will see how this story ends, because Amiable Spouse has much hunting, fishing, and shooting to do. His priorities have been out of order lately. Flower shows, butterfly gardens, and greenhouses have been claiming too much of his time and attention. I want him to stay amiable, so I'm going to send him off to the hunting camp soon.

The greenhouse is very important to me. In it are hundreds of plants that would not survive outside during our winter. Hanging baskets removed from the swings and arbors hang from the rafters. Underneath benches are ferns, begonias, and many other plants that are not winter hardy. The greenhouse is groaning at the seams, and many plants remain outside that cannot be placed inside its protective walls. Some things can be done, however, to protect the remaining plants from winter damage.

Some marginally hardy plants will be placed under a tree canopy that will reduce cold injury. Some will be placed near the house and a blanket thrown over them during freezes. Many spend the winter under a covered patio. Blankets protect them during the most frigid nights.

Another trick has enabled me to leave many of my ferns and marginally hardy plants outside under the covered entry. They are decorated with Christmas lights for the holidays. I leave the lights on the plants all winter. After the holidays they are not turned on except during freezing weather. With the addition of a light blanket or sheet, they are adequately protected.

I do not use plastic to cover my plants. The protection it offers is minimal, and if it is left over the plants the next day, the sun is apt to cause the plant to overheat and literally burn to death.

Mulch is tucked carefully around the roots of plants in the landscape. Low growing ground covers have a blanket of pine needles on freezing nights. Before a freeze is expected, the landscape is watered thoroughly. Well-watered plants suffer less damage than those suffering from drought.

For those of us who have large collections of plants, these strategies are necessary. Plants are too expensive to replace each year, so these measures are an important part of our yearly gardening activities. It's time to "make haste," as Mother would say, for old man winter is nipping at the heels of autumn.

Overwintering Plants Calls for Creative Solutions

I just counted, and the results are not surprising. The Florida room is the winter home of some 75 plants. About half of them spend the entire year here; the African violets and Chinese evergreens, for example, are permanent residents. Added to the collection now, however, is an odd assortment of thises and thats that were just too pretty to relegate to the greenhouse where they are rarely seen. Little treasures that bring back memories of friends who shared with me or events that I enjoyed during the summer line the window sills.

Included in this mélange are several bromeliads. Particularly attractive now are the flaming swords of *Vriesia ensiformis*. Bright, red-orange spikes are emerging and will last for months. *Neoregelia spectabilis* features green leaves with pink-tipped ends reminiscent of painted fingernails. *Aechmea fulgens discolor* is a beautiful vase plant with leaves that are green on top and reddish purple underneath. Next spring a purple flower spike will appear, followed by coral berries that will last for many months. Rounding out the bromeliad display is an assortment of *Tillandsias*, some medium sized and some diminutive so that several make a small dish garden. Various earth stars (*Cryptanthus*) and assorted queen's tears (*Billbergias*) complete the show.

If you have never grown bromeliads, you have missed some of the most interesting jewels in the plant kingdom. More than 2,000 species exist. Some are grown for foliage alone, while others are grown mainly for their flowers. Many are suitable for indoor culture. In summer most of mine reside outside on cypress knee stumps, but they must be moved to protected positions in winter. [41]

Included in this Florida room conglomeration are small snippets of one thing and another that bear close watching. Cuttings of this and that acquired from here and there are part of what makes plant collecting fun.

The heart-shaped leaves of my recently acquired lemon-lime philodendron (*Philodendron scandens* 'Lemon-Lime') are stunning in their yellow container. I happened upon this plant at a plant swap in Pensacola last summer. Since I was one of the last ones to choose a plant, pickings were slim. Most people had passed by this pale philodendron, thinking that it was sadly lacking in nutrients. It was just a snippet—a small, partly wilted sprout. I was lucky enough to have seen the parent of this scrawny plant in a recent flower show where it received several horticultural awards. It came home with me and is in the process of growing up to rival its parent in horticultural merit. How glad I am that no one else recognized this rare treasure!

Two hanging baskets have been brought inside. One is a sambac jasmine (*Jasminum sambac* 'Maid of Orleans'). This cultivar of one of the oldest jasmine species is intensely fragrant. One or two blooms perfume the room, and it has been blooming all winter. The other hanging basket is a speckled hoya (*Hoya carnosa*) that was given to me by a fellow horticulturist whom I greatly admire.

Then, of course, there is the single leaf cutting of a beautiful little cut-leaf philodendron given by a flower show school instructor to each student. It promises to be highly useful in floral design as well as beautiful in the container. It has a long way to go. The tiny prayer plant (*Maranta leuconeura*) rescued from my ruthless sister-in-law's compost pile is expressing a very floriferous gratitude. How lucky I am to have such a room for plants during the winter! They keep me from being so starved for greenery and flowers during a time when so few are blooming outside. They refresh my outlook and lift my spirits.

Gardening for the Love of It

The Call of High Spring

Oh, it's high spring. The outside beckons. I prune, plant, and dig. Time slows. Birds sing and search for nest materials. The sun's rays warm my back, and pleasant but mindless tasks give my thoughts free rein. Stillness enters the center of my consciousness. I lose something of myself and seem to expand and break up to become a part of the larger universe. The self-imposed walls and fences that bind me to the earth disintegrate, and peace surrounds me. All problems and stresses of daily life fade into the distance. Happiness and contentment are my companions, and I want them to stay forever.

I think this is a feeling that only gardeners can know, and perhaps fishermen and a few other lucky people whose hobbies allow them to be quiet and tune in to the world around them. I am reminded of the words of an old hymn that I sang in church as a child. "I come to the garden alone, while the dew is still on the roses . . . and the joy we share as we tarry there, none other has ever known." The joy is as real as the words to this old hymn.

Hunger or thirst finally drives me inside. The peacefulness, however, stays with me for some time. Times like this let me know that the garden is a healing place. I am strengthened because of my relationship with it. My burdens are lighter; my yoke is easier.

Oh, well, I guess I sound a little crazy when I go on like this, but other gardeners understand. They know well the familiar call of the garden. Meanwhile, I'm giving myself up to the peaceful plant world and the birds and bees that will be my company. Later this afternoon I'll float in, and after a while my feet will light on solid ground.

Gardeners Reap Many Benefits

I'm a gardener. I must have been born that way. Though I try, I cannot remember a time when gardening was not important to me. It has always been my hobby. Lately it has become more like an obsession. I can't fathom why this is so. Maybe it's just the first time that I don't have to work for a living. Now for the first time ever, I have the luxury of living my dreams and doing mostly as I please—within the budgetary restrictions of a retired schoolteacher, that is.

It's hard to say exactly when I crossed the line between hobby and obsession. I know that I have, because tearing myself away from the garden for even a short trip is hard. Amiable Spouse would be content to spend the summer in the Rockies. I can't tear myself away from the garden that long. I'm afraid I'll miss the amaryllises or the tiger lilies.

I need my piece of ground. The daily encounter with the garden touches some deep, inner space and stills the nagging beasts of everyday torments that snap and snarl about my edges. It's like a fire in the darkness that keeps the wolves at bay. When I am in my garden, the creatures of the shadows keep their distance.

Indeed, the monsters don't stand a chance! I'm shielded by mighty armaments. The flowers, trees, and shrubs are conservators of my peace. Sounds and sights of birds, butterflies, and other creatures that share my space strengthen me. In the garden I am impervious to hostile influences that threaten my inner sanctum.

Those who share my passion know that a garden is not a thing; it is an experience. We not only garden; we study about it. We want books about it and all the tools of the trade. We want to visit other gardens and attend seminars and classes to learn more. We swap plants and buy all that our budgets permit.

I guess that's the way it is with many hobbies. Amiable Spouse knows how I feel—not because he gardens, but because he is an avid sportsman. He's as devoted to his hobby as I am to mine. He match-es me, want for want, gadget for gadget, and trip for trip. He needs a gun for target shooting, one for pheasant hunting, one for deer hunting, and a few to look at. He needs a boat and a place at the river, and he needs to go places in pursuit of his game. We encourage each other because we understand so well!

Studies show that the mere presence of plants and gardens reduces stress. Indications are that plants and gardens may curb van-dalism, domestic violence, and other forms of crime. We know, too, that gardening is a very healthy activity. It ranks number two after weight lifting in helping women to prevent osteoporosis. It combines exercise, love of nature, and the joys of creating, discovering, and nurturing beauty.

For me, gardening is a necessity. Tending my garden is para-mount to caring for my mind, body, and soul. It's the place where I feel most alive. Gardening is a spiritually grounding activity. It is exer-cise and fresh air and reconnecting to nature. It's a place where I've found solace during life's curve balls.

When I taught school and became exhausted from the daily chal-lenges of dealing with sixth graders, I took a day off once in a while to spend in the garden. I chose the day carefully. I wanted it to be a full day with nothing to do except garden. I told my principals that I was sick, and indeed, I was. From sunrise until sunset I pursued my restora-tive tasks. Finally, when the day was done, I was physically exhausted but emotionally and spiritually refreshed. The next day in the classroom was pure magic. I had a whole different perspective, for tolerance and patience was restored. The children were angels once again.

That's the way it is with gardeners. We plant flowers, herbs, and vegetables. We cultivate and till the soil, but we harvest so much more. Peace and tranquility are in our storehouses ready to nourish us when we need sustenance.

The Show Goes On

It's funny how things happen in the garden. This spring Louisiana Iris bloomed with exuberance right in the middle of the border. Colorful red, blue, and white blossoms provided a show quite early. Behind Iris, Agastache 'Honey Bee Blue' began her upward climb. In front of it, Tibouchina started peeking from the ground.

As summer progressed, Iris finished blooming and her foliage started looking quite ratty. Behind it, Agastache continued reaching for the sky. Spiky blue flowers became the star of the show. In front of it, Tibouchina commenced to grow. Iris could not be seen between Agastache and Tibouchina.

The march of summer advanced into fall. Agastache's spikes turned brown. I pruned the fading blossoms, and her position of prominence was diminished. Iris continues to hide, but if I search, I can see green sprouts pushing up through the earth. Tibouchina is now the star of the show. Pretty, round, five-petaled purple princess flowers cover the five-foot-tall, shrublike plants. The show goes on!

That's the way it is. A garden in which all plants look good in all seasons is not nature's design. Gertrude Jekyll, the eminent English plantswoman who greatly influenced garden design, believed that certain areas of the garden should be devoted to certain times of year. Within these seasonal gardens, pleasing color combinations could be achieved using plants that bloomed during that season. She had an early spring border, a middle spring border, a late spring border, and so on. Her woodland garden alone contained ten acres, which she considered a small area for such a garden. Not only did she have acres to play with; she was also rich and had a team of gardeners at her beck and call.

That's not the way it is for most of us. On my reasonably sized suburban lot, I must make the best of every square inch. In my perennial border, I have plants that bloom at different seasons, and I believe that it looks quite good almost anytime. Some progressions resulted from a happy accident, such as the progression of Iris, Agastache, and Tibouchina described above. Other combinations have been painstakingly planned. Some of these have turned out well, and some have been dismal failures. The thing that I try to remember is that nothing in the garden is permanent. Displeasing associations can be fixed next year.

It helps to remember that many plants are appreciated not just for their flowers, but for their foliage as well. Many perennials such as *Phlox divaricata*, *Phlox subulata*, and *Sedum acre* have evergreen foliage. Though they provide a stunning show in early spring, their foliage serves as a backdrop for flowers at other seasons.

Many plants are grown primarily for their foliage. [47] Consider colorful caladiums, coleuses, and Persian shields that decorate our summer borders. Variegated shrubs and grasses fill spaces with their contrasting colors and forms. Green itself ranges from the bright, chartreuse of *Ipomoea batatas* 'Margarita' and *Sedum acre* to the blues of many hostas and grays of lavender cotton (*Santolina chamaecyparissus*) and artemisia. Then, there are the purple to black foliages of black sweet potato (*Ipomoea batatas* 'Blackie'), black mondo grass (*Ophiopogon planiscapus* 'Nigrescens'), and purple fountain grass (*Pennisetum alopecuroides*). Some foliage looks white in the landscape, such as Aztec grass (*Ophiopogon jaburan*) and Japanese silver grass (*Miscanthus sinensis* 'Variegatus'). Having a garden whose color is achieved with foliage alone would be fun.

Textural contrasts, such as spiky African iris foliage behind low growing arborvitae fern creates interest even when no flowers are present. Large leaves beside small leaves, spikes against low-growing masses, soft leaves and shiny leaves side by side, and arching forms reaching out beyond the round forms nearby all add to the allure of the garden.

Many things make up the whole of the garden. When I look at mine, I can usually find something of beauty, even if no flowers are blooming. Beauty, folks say, is in the eye of the beholder. Maybe I see beauty because I love it so, and that, most people say, is blind.

A Well-Designed Backyard

I just love my back yard these days. It is a good example of excellence in landscape design.

In the far right corner a native oak leaf hydrangea unfurls its signature leaves and white blossoms. Next to it, a green Japanese maple puts on a new green dress for all to admire. The Japanese magnolia was dazzling earlier, but now its large, somewhat furry leaves are maturing to their dark, summer green. English dogwood has largely finished its show, and thunbergia on one corner of the fence has been beautiful with its downward-hanging, but upward-facing, lavender blossoms.

The tulip poplar was a little late leafing out this spring, but I expect it to blossom soon. Last year was the first time it bloomed, so I expect another show this year if I am observant. The river birch has new, lime-green leaves on weeping branches that quiver in the slightest breeze. At the corner of the house the red Japanese maple is resplendent growing above the azaleas that hover about its feet.

Ornamental grasses that were cut back last month are putting out new blades and promising another year of beauty. Among them are such favorites as Japanese silver grass (*Miscanthus sinensis*) and variegated Japanese sedge (*Carex morrowii aurea*). Black mondo grass (*Ophiopogon planiscapus* 'Nigrescens'), Aztec grass, and several cultivars of liriope round out the display. Shades of purple, red, green, and nearly black are evident in their new growth. Later the ornamental sweet potato 'Margarita' will curl its yellow green vines among the dark grasses and light them up like a neon sign.

Mexican bush sage (*Salvia leucantha*) is blooming, and daylilies are in heavy bud. Holly fern, Persian shield, and double impatiens decorate the ground beneath the river birch. Sharing this bed are container plants such as angel wing begonia, a tall, yellow walking iris, and several specimens from the greenhouse that spend the summer outdoors.

A blueberry given to me by a friend blooms and bears fruit every year. I never get any of it, because the birds watch it unceasingly and pounce on it just as the first bit of blue shows on the berries. Quite surprising me with its landscape attributes, the blueberry is attractive almost year-round. In late fall and early winter the leaves are brilliant red, and in spring, pretty bell-like flowers bloom.

On the fence, native trumpet honeysuckle flings out its clusters of small red trumpets. Hummingbirds zoom by as they visit it and the salvia. Squirrels tease my dogs by climbing down the trees just beyond their reach and chattering and flicking their tails. Birds of various kinds perch in the crape myrtle tree awaiting their turn at the feeder. Doves cruise in for a landing, and a noisy wren searches for spiders and bugs on the fence and driftwood.

The backyard is a place that Amiable Spouse and I have made that suits our purposes and need for privacy. Our grill is on the back porch. We cook, sit and read, or just admire the scenery. We unwind here. The backyard is home to Stardust and Sunshine, our two miniature pinschers. It holds my unsightly but functional greenhouse and our storage shed. I don't mind them because they serve such a necessary purpose.

That is what I mean when I say that it is a good example of excellence in landscape design. Outdoor space is organized to meet the needs of the people who use it. This is our private area and our storage area, screened from the eyes of the public. It meets our needs, and in the process, it delights us. That's what landscape design is all about.

The Sensual Garden

The spring garden is a virtual repository of scents. Each trip outside brings wave after wave of tantalizing smells. Just outside my front door Confederate jasmine favors me with its clovey spiciness. Beside the driveway sweet shrub yields a whiff of its fruity scent. Down the sidewalk the fragrance of crinum lilies fills the air. By the mailbox, an old-fashioned rose shares its dizzying perfume. Sweet peas on a nearby trellis remind me of Grandmother's garden. The redolence of petunias, pinks, sweet alyssum, stock, and nasturtiums causes one to slow and bask in the splendor of it all. The fig tree has its own signature aroma, and the curry plant in the herb garden announces its presence as one rounds the corner. The grapefruit tree in bloom is fragrant beyond belief, and in the backyard, the banana shrub is reminiscent of the fruit that bears its name.

In the herb garden one cannot resist running a hand over the scented geraniums and rosemary. Without a doubt, the herb garden is more rewarding to me because of its scents than for any culinary benefits. Amiable Spouse had high hopes when I first began collecting herbs. He had visions of culinary masterpieces prepared with snippets of this and that. Little did he know that I mostly just enjoyed smelling them. Dividing mints, lemon balm, and lemongrass is a pleasurable repast. Lavender and artemisias vie for their share of attention. The licorice smell of Mexican mint marigold, fennel, and licorice plant makes their spots secure. Pineapple sage and *Salvia officinalis*, or common sage, and thymes of various flavors add their allure.

In summer the oriental lilies exude their sweet perfume. Butterfly bush and golden dewdrop attract pollinators with their fragrance. Evening brings the musky scent of moonflowers, angel's trumpets, four-o'clocks, and gingers of various kinds. Soft, humid Southern air is perfect for holding the scents of the garden in place for hours.

What could outdo the splendor of night-blooming cereus? Here's a good reason to stay up late. This tropical cactus opens its flowers after ten o'clock in the evening. That's past an early-rising gardener's bedtime—unless the night-blooming cereus is in full bud. Then the scent and sight of this infrequent spectacle offer the best excuse I can think of to stay up that late. By morning the limply hanging blossoms offer little hint of its nighttime magnificence.

Late winter brings the delicate scent of daffodils, wisteria, and sweet olive. A bit later, magnolia blossoms add their lemony fragrance to the air. Gardenias announce their presence from all vantage points. The soft, delicate essence of Hyperion daylilies beside the front walk greets visitors and pleasures me each time I walk by.

Most people select plants for the beauty of their flowers. For them, fragrance is often an unexpected bonus. Amiable Spouse thinks that a plant has little use if you can neither eat it nor smell it. Though I am sometimes held captive simply by the beauty of a flower, fragrance adds another dimension of pleasure. Those who remember Grandmother's flowers often select plants for the power of their fragrance, and the beauty of the flower plays second fiddle. The fragrant garden pleases more than just the eyes. The nose and our precious memories get involved when we stop to smell the flowers.

Are You a Floraholic or Hortimaniac?

This morning the heat was sweltering and the humidity oppressive, but I was outside anyway trying to accomplish a little more of my mission in the yard. After all, time waits for no woman. I was able to handle the torrid mugginess of the Southern summer morning until about midmorning.

As I entered the house, my patient, tolerant Amiable Spouse laughed and shook his head in hopeless resignation. I looked a mess. I'd dug a large clump of crinums—well, I started digging them. My shovel is new, so I knew better than to use it for prying them from their tenacious earth-hold. (Yesterday I broke the handle of the old one trying to wrest these crinums from the ground.) Today I resorted to a strong pipe. Finally the clump was muscled from the ground. Then I used the water hose to wash soil from their roots and the separation process began. There I was, on my hands and knees, tugging and splashing, prying and pulling. At last the roots became disentangled, and before me were nine large crinum bulbs. Five of them were planted in a new bed I had prepared earlier. The other four were planted in containers to be given away or donated to plant sales.

Sound familiar? I had on my old clothes, of course, which have been subjected to this treatment many times. When my task was finished, I was glistening profusely. (All enlightened persons know that Southern ladies don't sweat.) I was a muddy mess, so I turned the hose on myself. What ecstasy! The cooling stream provided a much needed drink. Finally, after repeated passes of the hose, I had rid my body of most of the mud. It was at this time that I decided to give it up for the morning and came walking into the house.

"What would your garden club members say if they could see you now?" asked Amiable Spouse.

Good question. My garden club friends think the real me is that freshly showered, impeccably groomed person with the creased shorts and pressed tee shirt that reads, "Trowel, do I love thee!" They don't see me on the front line and in the trenches doing battle with a stubborn crinum. They see me in the grocery store and at club meetings. Little do they know my dirty secret!

Sometimes I wonder how many more gardeners there are who are as addicted and obsessed as I am. I know and recognize a few of these people. We hang out in the same places. I see them at the nursery and in the garden section of the bookstore. They are members of my garden club or master gardeners' association. Their gardens, like mine, are peopled places; peopled with memories of persons who gave them this rose or that lily. They visit my garden and I theirs. We swap plants and speak the same language. They're my chums.

There are, I believe (besides the above), several signs or indicators that may serve as addiction warnings. Ask yourself these questions to see if you verge on becoming a horticultural and floral junkie.

Are you disappointed if the day's mail does not include a gardening magazine or catalog? When you get one of these, do you rush inside and read it from cover to cover before you finish preparing dinner for your family? Do you sometimes make out orders for plants you can't afford? Worse yet, do you sometimes order them anyway?

Have you investigated every nursery within a 50-mile radius and exhausted their offerings for plants suitable for your yard? Is your idea of a good vacation a visit to a famous garden or arboretum? When you're away on a particularly satisfying trip, do you worry about whether the sprinkler system is working properly? When someone asks what you want for your birthday, do you know immediately about a gardening book you're dying to have? Would you rather go to the nursery or garden center than to the mall?

If you answered yes to any of the above questions, you are definitely at risk of becoming a floraholic or hortimaniac. You may find yourself hallucinating about this flower or that one. The rose you left at your previous home may be causing unwanted flashbacks. You may find yourself craving just one more flower and promising yourself that it will be the last one for a while. Or you may succumb to temptation and come home with a carload of new plants and wonder where in the heck you're going to put them.

We know that gardening is a healthy activity. Schools, prisons, nursing homes, sheltered workshops, and hospitals increasingly employ horticultural therapists. Many hospitals and wellness centers have therapeutic gardens.

The American Horticultural Therapy Association claims that about 600 horticultural therapists practice this profession. They are armed with results of studies that show that gardening offers such benefits as lower blood pressure, increased self-esteem, increased upper body strength, and improved mental attitude.

In addition, it provides sensory stimulation and a sense of accomplishment. Gardening as a microcosm of nature echoes the human experience of setbacks and failures. If we can triumph over disasters caused by weather, insects, or circumstances beyond our control, then we can succeed in other areas of life as well. Of course, we floraholics know these benefits. They've been evident to us from the very beginning. Gardening to us is essential; everything else in life is only desirable.

Those who are about to join our ranks are in for the ride of their lives. They are about to develop a passion they will pursue in one way or another for the rest of their lives. They are about to become enmeshed in the ever-recurring miracles of creation and, like us, will be ensnared.

Every day we gardeners greet the new day with eagerness and go to bed with a feeling of satisfaction. We live with almost certain knowledge that our efforts have made the world a more beautiful place. We know beyond a doubt that our gardens are treasured gems entrusted to our keeping for a time. We are the luckiest people on the face of the earth!

Kindred Spirits

My garden is a peopled place. Within its boundaries are reminders of folks who have enriched my life in a real and tangible way. How dear is the rose that blooms beside the garage that is a cutting from my mother's garden! Such treasures as Texas blue star, eyelash begonia, and bromeliads of several varieties are legacies from Aunt Gladys.

Inez, my son-in-law's grandmother from Pensacola, is the source of blue plumbago. Passionflower and 'Margarita' sweet potato are gifts from Master Gardener buddies, and members of my garden club have contributed various horticultural treasures.

We gardeners find each other, somehow. No other interest that I know exceeds gardening as a source of lifelong friendships. We meet at organizations where we gather because of common interests. Some of my best friends belong to garden clubs, plant societies, flower arrangers' guilds, and other organizations where those of us with floraholic tendencies are wont to gather. Telephone calls from people who read my articles and neighbors who walk by my yard and stop to chat are constant proof of the garden's ability to weave a web of relationships between people and the almost limitless world of plants.

Recently Katie Moody, a dedicated garden enthusiast of long standing, called me. She had read an article I wrote about old roses, and she wanted to share hers with me. She gave me a cutting from a rose that her family brought from DeFuniak Springs more than 80 years ago. It has been blooming in Niceville since then. Regrettably, she does not know the name of this old rose, but that will not diminish my enjoyment of it if I can get it rooted and established in my yard.

I was privileged to a tour of Katie's garden, and what a treat that was! A natural stream meanders from one side of her yard to the other. In it are bream and catfish that she feeds with bread crumbs. Bridges and walkways allow passage over the stream in several areas. Near a gurgling waterfall is a strategically placed bench. Katie says that peace lives there, and it is her favorite place for meditating. In shady places along the stream are ferns and native groundcovers, gingers, shrubs, and flowers of many varieties. Though the temperature that day soared into the high 90s, under the trees along the stream the air was considerably cooler than elsewhere. Poisons do not have a place in Katie's garden. She told me that she feels good when she walks into her garden because she believes that it is a clean, unspoiled place. A few weeds and chewed leaves do not bother her. I share her sentiments.

Another of my favorite gardeners and a treasured friend is Norma Eastman. Norma flatly states that old age has not crept upon her; it has leaped. Yet, she loves the garden and flowers more than anyone else I know. It is apparent when she comes home from a shopping trip with her car loaded with plants. Can she plant them in her yard? No, certainly not. Her strength is too diminished, and yet, she has high hopes.

This year Normie bought a rototiller. I guess she thought that this wonderful machine would be the answer to her dilemmas. Amiable Spouse assembled the device for her and gave her lessons on how to crank it. Unfortunately, she did not have the strength to pull the string starter hard enough to start the engine. One day shortly after she bought the apparatus, I drove by her house. She was sitting on her front steps with the tiller in front of her. Her head was cocked sideways, and she was staring at it in a perplexed way. I could tell that it had beaten her. Since then, I have not seen the machine. It is hidden in one of her storage buildings, I suspect.

Yet she continues to gather plants from a variety of sources. What interminable spirit! We humans do not give up easily. Norma is Finnish, and that ancestry, I suspect, has made her as stubborn as a mule. Gardeners are like that. Hope springs eternal. Beautiful flowers and plants beckon to Norma more strongly than her will to resist. Recently Normie had a truckful of soil dumped in a pile in her front yard. Here she happily plants her new acquisitions.

In Katie and Norma I have found kindred spirits. We understand each other because of our mutual gardening passions. I am reminded of them daily as I walk in my garden and see the plants that they have shared with me. They are a part of the familiar faces and generous souls who people my garden.

Garden for the Health of It

Like much of nature, I awaken in spring. The greening of the earth and warming of the air are my wake-up calls. Every morning I can hardly wait to check out the garden. I take my coffee cup outside and sip and look. I want to see what has pushed up from its winter bed. It's an adventure, for every day I find something that was not there yesterday.

As I walk, I notice that the emerging tibouchina foliage is not as green as it should be. I set the coffee cup down, get out my trusty old wheelbarrow, and load it full of compost. Other things will benefit from a shovelful of the good stuff. Aphids cover the new shoots of the daylilies, so I head to the kitchen to mix a batch of soapy water for them. The Easter lilies are far too crowded. I dig and pot a few for plant sales.

Slug damage is apparent around the morning glories. I head to the storage shed for Sluggo. It's obvious that the pentas and hibiscus are not going to recover from winter freezes, so I dig them and prepare the soil for new ones. One thing leads to another, and before I know it, the day is half gone and I have forgotten why I first went outside.

Are there benefits to be had in the pursuit of my hobby that are less obvious than a pretty yard? Could digging, planting, and tending the garden be good for me? Are there some rewards that I have not even thought about, such as emotional well being and mental health?

The physical benefits of exercise are well documented. Most of us know that people who exercise regularly have a lower rate of cardiovascular disease. When my doctor asks what I do for exercise, I tell him that I garden. He seems happy with that answer.

From time to time I become convinced that I need to walk a couple of miles every other day or so. For a month or two I stick with the regimen, but then, for one reason or another my good intentions fall by the wayside.

Not so with gardening. Never has there been a time when I had to make myself go outside and work in the garden regularly. It is something that I love doing. Perhaps that is the main test of a good exercise program. It has to be an activity that works for each individual.

Then, too, many people are goal oriented. We need to see the results of our efforts. Mowing the lawn, planting flowers, and growing vegetables have very real and tangible rewards. One has only to look to see positive results. The feedback is almost immediate.

Before retiring from teaching, I dragged in from the schoolhouse almost every afternoon completely spent. After shedding my dress-up clothes and donning my old gardening outfit, I rushed out to the garden. There I gained strength and comfort as I went about my simple gardening activities. Cares that had seemed so heavy at the schoolhouse melted away. I became refreshed and rejuvenated.

Maybe some tiredness remained, but it was a different kind of fatigue than the mental exhaustion that came home with me.

These feelings point out the stress-relieving aspects of gardening. Studies at the University of Florida suggest that simply walking in botanic gardens lowers people's perception of their stress level. Health insurance companies are quick to agree. Results of a recent national survey of American Medicare beneficiaries conducted by researchers at the University of North Carolina are not surprising to me. They found that the average monthly health care expenditures of regular gardeners were 17.2 percent lower than those of nongardeners over the 12-month period studied.

Those of us who love gardening and do it regularly know these benefits well. We want to share the good news. The message is as plain as the nose on your face. Take care of your garden and yourself at the same time. Get digging!

The Perennial Quest of Steady Gardeners

The arrival of new garden catalogs each year is an eagerly awaited event for steadfast gardeners. Like notes from one sixth grader to another, they are pored over and studied until they become dog-eared. All the new flowers are included in a glorious array of dazzling photographs and tempting descriptions. Many agonizingly delightful hours are spent researching and deciding which of them to order. If I did not suffer certain monetary constraints, I might order the whole shebang. Unfortunately, however, I must discipline myself quite severely in these matters. Choices must be made; I simply cannot have them all.

New perennials to add to the border are often the objects of my quest. Almost everything I have ever read recommended planting in drifts of three, five, or more. With this in mind, I finally settle on three each of Agastache 'Honey Bee Blue', Origanum 'Herrenhausen', and Coreopsis 'Flying Saucers'.

About the first of October the tiny plants arrive, and I plant them promptly in soil improved with generous amounts of compost. Then I watch them throughout the winter and spring. Will they pass muster in my perennial border? Trying new plants is always an exciting learning experience. Sometimes I just don't like what I learn.

The one that delighted me most from this order was *Agastache* 'Honey Bee Blue'. These three plants grew to about five feet tall and were covered with blue, spiky flowers. Bumblebees hovered around them until their legs became so laden with pollen they seemed to have difficulty flying from flower to flower.

Other varieties of *Agastache* are available, too. I have *A.* 'Meadow Queen', but it suffers in comparison to the 'Honey Bee Blue'. Growing 12 to 16 inches tall, its spikes of pink flowers flop around a bit. Maybe if it had more sun it would perform better. It was shaded out quite early by its larger cousin.

The other plants that arrived in that same order have not fared so well. The *Coreopsis* 'Flying Saucers' did not withstand repeated slug attacks. Possibly I could have saved the tiny plants if I had been more diligent and put out saucers of beer or scattered slug bait around them each evening. I hate to get into that habit, though, because I would have to do it all again next year. My tendency is to let the bugs have a plant if they insist. Poisons kill the good bugs along with the bad, and I worry about the birds and bees, not to mention my dogs, Stardust and Sunshine, who go among the plants daily on their regular cat patrol.

Besides, too many plants do well and seem immune to slugs and other pests. At the very least, they are strong enough to fend for themselves if given good soil and adequate moisture. These are the ones I want for my garden.

I can just hear my friends who are wildflower fanatics. "But, Marie," they'll say, "coreopsis is our state wildflower. We even have a license plate to commemorate it. It should have thrived in your garden!"

Maybe. I know that it thrives on roadsides and in sandy, sunny meadows where the *Master* Master Gardener supervises things. However, in my heavily mulched, amended, and frequently watered soil, some wildflowers sulk, and slugs proliferate at the speed of light. The coreopsis simply did not make it. I was disappointed because the University of Georgia recommended it highly. They said that 'Flying Saucers' did not burn out during the heat of our summer like some

other coreopsis.

Origanum 'Herrenhausen', according to the catalog, grows two to three feet tall and 20 inches wide and is beloved for its beautiful clusters of purplish pink flowers that appear from July until frost. Mine possibly spread like it was supposed to, but it hugged the ground at two to three inches, not feet, and it did not thrill me with the promised beautiful clusters of flowers. I think the catalog people confused their feet and inches.

'Honey Bee Blue' *Agastache* bedecked my garden that first spring. However, it did not turn out to be perennial. It does reseed, so each year I am blessed with more of the blue spiky flowers. Oh, well. Nothing ventured, nothing gained, as they say. We live and learn. And the world turns. Soon the catalogs will tempt me again.

Remembering the Basics

I've done it again. Overloaded my you-know-what. So many worthwhile projects beckon! There's just no way on God's green earth that I can ever do all the things I want to do.

I continue to raise my hand. "I'll do it!" I say. And I really want to! Until, one day, there are no days left on the calendar. They're all filled. My time is taken up. All accounted for. All gone.

And I get tireder and tireder. Shingles strikes! Misery! "Slow down!" the doctor says. I start reevaluating, trying to decide which of my activities to retain, which to let go.

"What are the really important things?" I ask myself. Of course, Amiable Spouse wins that test. He's first. Then there are the children and grandchildren. The value of time spent with them is incalculable.

After I think this through, I begin the culling process. Here I am, retired, at liberty to choose my activities and do exactly as I please. Amiable Spouse tells me that I gave up a perfectly good paying job to do all this!

Soon reality sets in. I remember. Central to all my activities is the simple act of gardening. Being outdoors. Digging. Planting. Growing. Watching the butterflies, the bees, the birds, and all the other critters that are part of the interactions of nature.

I had forgotten all this. I needed a break. I skipped the Master Gardener meeting today. Instead, I dressed in my grubbies and headed for the yard.

The bromeliads, you understand, were in danger of being frost nipped. Removing them from their cypress knee summer homes and getting them ready for winter occupied my morning. One after another they came down; old mother plants were discarded, the pups potted up, the best among them groomed for the fair, and the others cleaned up for the Florida room.

Then, of course, there were the spent caladiums with their leaves flopping about, all faded, and just a shadow of their former selves. I dug them up and placed them in flats in the garage where they will be safe from winter's cold. Next summer they'll shine again.

How wonderful was my morning! A bit cool, perhaps, but what a relief from the oppressive heat and humidity of summer! Busy in the garden. Heart singing. Engrossed. No other thoughts. Cares behind me. Wet and muddy from head to toe. Happy! Carefree! I was in my element once again. I was gardening.

In the end, none of my activities were deleted. The race continued unabated the very next day. After all, these projects were of my own choosing. Master gardening. Garden clubbing. Floral designing. Flower show judging. Then there are the junior gardeners. Prime Time. Programs. District meetings. State board meetings. Newspaper and magazine articles. Books.

I want them all. In the future I may have to give up some of my undertakings. I just need to remember the basics from time to time. After all, I'm a gardener. How could I forget?

Index

Note: Illustrations are indicated by **boldface** type.
Color pictures are indicated by **boldface** and *italic* type.

About the Author

Marie Harrison was born and raised in rural Mississippi at a time when our country was just pulling out of the Great Depression. Each of the nine members of the family worked hard for life's necessities. They milked cows, raised chickens and gathered eggs, grew large vegetable gardens, and were largely self-sufficient. Even so, in the Bullock family it was understood from a very early age that the children would go to college. It was always "when," not "if," you go to college. Both education and hard work were held in high esteem.

Marie earned a B.S. Degree in Music Education from Mississippi State University and then went on to earn her M.A. from the University of South Alabama. She taught school in Mississippi and Florida for thirty years and retired in 1997. Loss of a spouse, remarriage, and a move brought her to her present home in Valparaiso, Florida. Here she shares life with her husband, John Harrison, whom she affectionately calls "Amiable Spouse" in her writing. Marie and John share five children and four grandchildren.

Immediately following retirement, Marie began making up for lost time in pursuit of her lifetime gardening passion. She joined the Valparaiso Garden Club in September of 1997 and served as president from 1999–2001. From 2001–2003 she served as Director of District I of the Florida Federation of Garden Clubs. Through the FFGC she earned credentials as an Accredited Flower Show Judge and a Floral Design Instructor. She continues to be very active in this organization.

In 1998 Marie fulfilled a longtime ambition when she earned the status of Florida Master Gardener. She served on its board of Directors and continues to participate actively in the Okaloosa County Master Gardener program. In 2001 she was awarded the Florida Master Gardener Award of Excellence for her work in Educational Materials Development. She developed educational programs complete with slides and literature on such topics as perennials, salt-tolerant plants, flowering shrubs and vines, plants for the floral designer's landscape, gardening for wildlife, native plants for home landscapes, and others.

Marie is a charter member of the Choctaw Chapter of the North American Butterfly Association (NABA). She also holds memberships in the National Audubon Society, National Wildlife Federation, National Arbor Day Society, American Horticultural Society, the Hummer/Bird Study Group from Clay, Alabama, and various flower show judges' councils and flower arrangers' groups.

After retirement, she began writing a weekly gardening column for local newspapers, the *Beacon Express*, the *Destin Log*, the *Walton Log*, and the *Crestview News Bulletin*. She is a contributing writer for *Florida Gardening* and feature writer for *Pensacola Today.*

Marie's gardening interests are broad in scope. She maintains a large perennial border and a not-so-measly group of flowering trees and shrubs. Herbs and vegetables, fruits, container plants, and many others are scattered throughout the landscape. Her garden contains plants for floral designs, and she incorporates plants to attract butterflies, birds, and other wildlife. Her garden is a National Wildlife Federation Backyard Wildlife Habitat and is frequently included on community tours of gardens.

Marie teaches gardening classes at Okaloosa/Walton Community College in their Prime Time Classes, a part of the National Elderhostel Institute Network. She is a frequent lecturer at seminars, garden clubs, and other civic groups. Marie continues to be a force in horticulture education in her community and in Florida. Through this book she hopes to help gardeners throughout the coastal South learn to garden more effectively and with keener insight into the impact they make on the environment.

Notes

Notes

Notes

Notes

Notes

Notes

Notes

Here are some other books from Pineapple Press on related topics. For a complete catalog, write to Pineapple Press, P.O. Box 3889, Sarasota, Florida 34230, or call (800) 746-3275. Or visit our website at www.pineapplepress.com.

The Art of South Florida Gardening by Harold Songdahl and Coralee Leon. Gardening advice specifically written for the unique conditions of south Florida. A practical, comprehensive guide written with humor and know-how.

Exploring Wild South Florida by Susan Jewell, *Exploring Wild North Florida* and *Exploring Wild Northwest Florida* by Gil Nelson. A series of field guides with information on all the parks, preserves, and natural areas, including wildlife to look for and best time of year to visit.

Flowering Trees of Florida by Mark Stebbins. Full-color guide to 74 outstanding tropical flowering trees.

Growing Family Fruit and Nut Trees and *Exotic Foods: A Kitchen and Garden Guide* by Marian Van Atta. How to enjoy all phases of growing and preparing your own delicious fruits, nuts, vegetables, herbs, and wild edibles.

Guide to the Gardens of Florida, Guide to the Gardens of Georgia, Guide to the Gardens of South Carolina by Lilly Pinkas. Guide to the featured species and facilities offered by public gardens. Color photos and line drawings.

Poisonous Plants and Animals of Florida and the Caribbean by David W. Nellis. An illustrated guide to the characteristics, symptoms, and treatments for more than 300 species of poisonous plants and toxic animals.

Seashore Plants of South Florida and the Caribbean by David W. Nellis. A full-color guide to the flora of nearshore environments, including complete characteristics of each plant as well as ornamental, medicinal, ecological, and other aspects. Suitable for backyard gardeners and serious naturalists.

The Shrubs and Woody Vines of Florida, The Trees of Florida, and *The Ferns of Florida* by Gil Nelson. Comprehensive guides to Florida's amazing variety of trees, shrubs, vines, and ferns. Useful to the naturalist, professional botanist, landscape architect, and weekend gardener. Color photos.

Key West Gardens and Their Stories by Janis Frawley-Holler. Fascinating guide to the lush gardens of the southernmost city. 173 large color photos.